RUNNING THE TABLE

RUNNING THE TABLE

The Legend of Kid Delicious,
the Last Great American
Pool Hustler

L. Jon Wertheim

Houghton Mifflin Company

BOSTON   NEW YORK

2007

For information about permission to reproduce
selections from this book, write to Permissions,
Houghton Mifflin Company, 215 Park Avenue South,
New York, New York 10003.

Visit our Web site: www.houghtonmifflinbooks.com.

Library of Congress Cataloging-in-Publication Data
Wertheim, L. Jon.
Running the table : the legend of Kid Delicious, the last
great American pool hustler / L. Jon Wertheim.
p. cm.
Includes index.
ISBN-13: 978-0-618-66474-0
ISBN-10: 0-618-66474-2
1. Basavich, Danny. 2. Billiard players—United
States—Biography. 3. Billiards—United States—
Biography. I. Title.
GV892.2.B37W47 2007
794.72092—dc22 [B] 2007009423

Book design by Melissa Lotfy

Printed in the United States of America

MP 10 9 8 7 6 5 4 3 2 1

Lines from "I've Been Everywhere," words and music by Geoff
Mack, © 1962 (renewed) Rightsong Music, Inc. All rights ad-
ministered by Unichappell Music, Inc. All rights reserved. Used
by permission of Alfred Publishing Co., Inc.

For Ellie, my road partner

*And for Benjamin Barnes and Allegra Fay,
our kids delicious*

I've been to:
Reno, Chicago, Fargo, Minnesota,
Buffalo, Toronto, Winslow, Sarasota,
Wichita, Tulsa, Ottawa, Oklahoma,
Tampa, Panama, Mattawa, La Paloma,
Bangor, Baltimore, Salvador, Amarillo,
Tocapillo, Barranquilla, and Padilla

. . .

See what I mean?
I've been everywhere, man
I've been everywhere, man
Crossed the deserts bare, man
I've breathed the mountain air, man
Travel—I've had my share, man
I've been everywhere

— Geoff Mack, "I've Been Everywhere"

CONTENTS

PROLOGUE

Jeez, that fat man, look at the way he moves. Like a
dancer. And those fingers, them chubby fingers. That
stroke, it's like he's playing the violin or something.

—Fast Eddie Felson (Paul Newman), marveling at
Minnesota Fats (Jackie Gleason) in *The Hustler*

THE BIG FELLA waddled down the hallway of the hotel, grinning
and nodding graciously. The pool tribalists called out his name
or patted him on the back. When you're five feet nine inches and
tip the scales at 320 pounds or so, it's not easy to walk without
breaking stride. But Danny Basavich had no choice. He'd over-
slept on this listless morning in January 2006 and now was
minutes from forfeiting a match in the Derby City Classic, a
twelve-day gambling marathon masquerading as an annual pool
tournament.

His personality as generously proportioned as his physique,
Basavich tried to acknowledge everyone at the Derby City venue
—the Executive West Hotel, a shopworn hostelry hard by the
Louisville Airport, designed by someone with a deep appreciation for the 1970s. As he shuffled down the hall, Basavich smiled
his infectious smile, quickly pressing his stubby right hand into
his admirer's, a handshake that effectively conveyed the message
"Luv-ya-but-I-gotta-run."

In a disarming voice that recalled Wolfman Jack with a New
Joisey accent — *e*'s screeching like old train brakes, *p*'s and *t*'s pop-

ping like fireworks — he shouted out a stream of "Catch me when I'm done playing, Chris" and "You got my cell number, right, Petey?" and "Let's grab a drink later, Alex." Without exception, everyone was called by his first name, a Dale Carnegie lesson he'd learned years before.

He arrived at table 17 just in time. With his girlfriend, Danielle, a clutch of friends, and dozens of railbirds looking on from aluminum bleachers, Basavich unsheathed a custom-made Pechauer cue. His opponent in this early-round Derby City match was José Parica, one of the brighter stars in the pool cosmos. A slightly built Filipino who looks to be in his mid-fifties, Parica performed with an even disposition, neither surly nor affable; just focused and impassive, his body language betraying nothing.

Minnesota Fats famously wore a carnation in the lapel of his bespoke suit. Though comparably built, Basavich didn't go quite so far with his fashion. Still, he looked resplendent in drooping black trousers, black loafers, and a herringbone jacket that did its moaning best to cover his girth. His thatch of straw-colored hair had been generously gelled and his goatee neatly trimmed. Like many hefty men, he'd tried to drown his insecurities in an ocean of cologne. He somehow looked both older and younger than his twenty-seven years. His boyish, contagious smile was, as ever, in full bloom. At the same time, his swollen belly and arthritic movements suggested a man well into middle age. His green eyes sparkled and swiveled from side to side as he stared at the configuration of balls on the table.

The best American pool players were once irrepressible, wild and woolly figures straight out of Damon Runyon, all trash talk and color and bluster. But once they started getting beaten by Asians and Europeans — who, the conventional wisdom went, weren't better players but simply possessed superior powers of concentration — the Americans grew stoic and emotionally frozen. In this sense, Basavich was a pure throwback. Above the crack of the balls on the surrounding tables and the echoes of clinking beer bottles, Basavich directed an ongoing monologue to the folks on the rail, to his cue, to himself. After one particularly dazzling piece of shotmaking, a smile stole across his face as he said, to no one and everyone, "Didn't think a big guy like me could pull that off, did ya?" It's always "big" with Basavich. Never "fat."

Derby City had already crowned champions in bank pool and one-pocket, and now the tournament culminated with the nine-ball championship. A form of rotation pool, nine-ball requires players to rack only the first nine balls in a diamond formation. A player wins by pocketing the yolk-colored nine ball, but on every shot he must hit the lowest ball on the table first. Usually the player devises a pattern of shots through the rack, or what remains of it, that has him pocketing the one, the two, the three, and so on, until he's taking aim at the nine ball to win the game. At Derby City, the first player to win the race to seven games wins the set and advances to the next round.

In the movies, pool is played at warp speed. The balls invariably collide violently on impact. The pace is rapid-fire. The players attempt high-risk, high-reward shots. It's all pyrotechnics. Real pool, at least at the highest level, is much more clicking than clacking; it's a sport of ellipses, not exclamation points. The balls don't often rocket into the pocket. They tend to enter casually, as if they're slipping out and quietly leaving the party, landing with a gentle *ka-tonk*. The players discharge their duties at a leisurely pace, especially Basavich, whose excruciatingly slow playing is as much his hallmark as his overstuffed physique and bottomlessly charismatic personality. Sizing up shots like Tiger Woods studying a putt, he takes his time, rocking back and forth in the manner of a man who has to pee.

In professional pool, you can go for hours without seeing a holy-shit-you-gotta-be-kidding-me shot. It's all about positioning and control. Because of the way they expertly maneuvered the cue ball, Parica and Basavich went entire games without having to hit a single shot that would give a decent recreational player trouble. Of course, it's where the cue ball ends up *after* hitting the object ball that makes it all possible. That's where the genius resides. It's position play that separates the pros from the ball-bangers.

There's something both absurdly simple and impossibly complex about the way Basavich plays. His backswing, not unlike his body, is short and compact. His break is more about control than force. Little about his style could be described as exciting. But there is an undeniable artistry and dignity — a majesty, you could even call it — to his game. He has that highly developed pool cortex that enables him to think four or five shots ahead. Often he even sees the whole rack unfolding right after the break. He is steady and balanced and supremely confident. With the equilibrium of a Zen archer, he plays as though the mere prospect of misfiring hasn't crossed his mind. Then, just when his game takes on a mesmeric quality, he plays a dazzling shot that defies the conventional laws of physics.

Tied with Parica at six games apiece, Basavich sized up a three-rail kick shot on the six ball. After determining that it was merely geometrically improbable — not impossible — he took aim. He inhaled, exhaled, and pulled off the shot. The railbirds clapped and whistled. Parica shook his head in a sort of gracious resignation, a rare show of emotion. Impervious to any pressure, Basavich ran out the remaining balls to take the set. Basavich seven, Parica six. After shaking his opponent's hand, Basavich playfully pumped his pudgy fist for an imaginary television camera. Then he kissed his girl.

There was a time, not long ago, when this kind of performance at the table would have earned Basavich $5,000 or $10,000 or, if everything really broke right, twenty-five large. He would have celebrated with a trip to the local diner or watering hole, lavishing on himself three or four cheeseburgers, washing them down with a tankard's worth of Coors Light. Maybe later that night, for good measure, he'd have fired up a joint or sprinkled his cash at a strip club. As the old pool joke goes, he would spend his money on booze and women and gambling, and he'd simply fritter away the rest of it.

But that was when he was a road hustler, crisscrossing the lower forty-eight on unending ribbons of asphalt, slinking from town to town, busting the locals, prospecting for that next big score.

Pool hustling is a dying art. In recent years, road action has been "knocked" by everything from the poker boom to the proliferation of casinos (which seduce the same species of young, hypercompetitive, incurable gambling men who once frequented pool halls) to three-bucks-a-gallon fuel prices to Internet forums that expose the identity of even the stealthiest of hustlers. But as recently as 2003, no one was plundering the pool halls of North America with more success than Basavich. Back then he was anonymous; only his bloated belly — not his reputation — preceded him when he walked into a room. Eventually he took on a quality that spells doom for a hustling career: he became notorious. Athletes in other sports gorge themselves on the nectar of fame. But for any pool hustler worth his chalk, even demimonde celebrity is a professional death sentence. By the winter of 2006, Danny Basavich was no longer a hustler; he was a pro pool player.

After beating Parica, Basavich unscrewed his cue, carefully placed it back in its leather holster, and walked through the Executive West lobby. He headed for the room on the fourth floor that he and Danielle were sharing with another player, Chris Bartram, to defray the $69-a-night tariff. He picked at some leftover Thai food in a container on a desk next to a pile of dirty socks and a well-worn road map. He then cocooned himself in his blanket, trying to get some sleep for the first time in two days. He had another match later that night. If he could win that, he'd be assured of finishing in the money. Which meant he'd be eligible for a whopping $160 jackpot.

Throughout the Derby City Classic, large placards hang high over some of the pool tables, adorned with the words "No Gambling." Or so it appears, anyway. If you look closely, it really says "No No Gambling." "In other words, you must gamble," Greg Sullivan, the event's organizer and a leading billiards supplier, says with a glint in his eye. "A double negative. You follow?"

The signs are as good a metaphor as any for the sport. And let's be clear before we proceed any further: it is a sport. Pool is all angles and perspective and spin. It's illusion and guile. It's subterfuge and artifice. And the self-contained culture of the Derby City Classic is contemporary pool distilled to its flavorful essence. The event is like a giant magnet, drawing thousands of hustlers, hucksters, backers, and assorted grifters for an around-the-clock gambling marathon. "Derby City," as everyone calls it, is a top-flight event on the pro pool circuit. But the tournament play can often seem about as relevant to Derby City as religious observance is to Mardi Gras.

It's about the no no gambling.

At any hour of the day, most of the fifty-one tables throughout the hotel are being used for money games, designated as such by the stack of bills held in escrow atop the fluorescent lights above the tables. The stakes range from a dinner tab to "serious timber"— one backer called in advance to ascertain whether there was a vault that could hold his $250,000 in cash. The cleanup crew that washes the balls and tends to the table felt every morning has strict instructions to work around games in progress. Gambling and pool have always been intertwined. Even the sport's name derives from gambling: "pool" refers to pooling money to determine odds. The repeated efforts to divorce the two and sanitize pool, to "class it up" with smoke-free rooms and sterile, franchised halls with bistro menus and wine lists, have, predictably, failed. Like it or not, the chance to beat the other guy out of his cash is ultimately the lifeblood of the sport.

As Basavich played Parica in a sanctioned match, Cliff Joyner, a portly Atlantan with caramel-colored skin, battled with Cincinnati's Eric Durbin, an intense, slightly haunted-looking pool sorcerer who claimed he was a few weeks removed from a ten-month drug-related sentence in an Ohio prison. The game was one-pocket— as much a mental as a physical exercise, it requires players to sink eight balls into a single designated pocket— and the stakes were considerable. Both Joyner and Durbin had arrived in Louisville accompanied by backers. When Joyner offered Durbin a two-ball handicap and the right to break in a "four-ahead set" (the first player to seize a four-game lead would win), the backers put up $5,000 apiece. Once word of the handicap passed through the crowd at the hotel, the set generated exponentially more side action, as railbirds scrambled like Wall Street traders to throw money on "the break" (Durbin) or "the rack" (Joyner).

Joyner and Durbin had started their duel at six the previous evening, and as momentum swayed back and forth like a pendulum, the "birds on the rail" who had wagered a small fortune grew more animated. Never mind Basavich versus Parica in the sanctioned match; they were tangential. This was *action.* As night turned into day, the two players kept at it, taking only brief breaks to drag on cigarettes, mainline Red Bull, or hit the rest room.

Finally, around 6 A.M., Joyner came up with a brilliant flourish of shotmaking and, to the delight of half the room, closed out the set. "That's my motherfucker!" screamed one of Joyner's backers, now several thousand dollars wealthier, patting the player on his Atlanta Braves cap. For a guy who had just finished twelve straight hours of playing and lost a lot of people a lot of money, Durbin was hardly the picture of despondency. "I'll win it back, no problem," he said with a thousand-yard stare. "Just gotta get back in action."

Almost by definition, pool players are gamblers. Most would put money on a cockroach race if you laid the right odds. The action at Derby City was hardly restricted to the tables. The halls were lined with gin rummy games. Texas hold 'em games were as easy to come by as male pattern baldness. Players flipped coins and pitched quarters and bet with each other on card tricks. Thanks to the wonders of WiFi, one backer played online poker on his laptop as he watched a nine-ball game. There were reports of headbutting contests, spitting contests in the parking lot, high-stakes coin flips, and clubless golf matches, in which players sneaked onto a nearby course and threw their golf balls for eighteen holes. The previous year, Charlie "the Hillbilly" Bryant, a well-known pro player, had memorably broken another player's ulna during a $500 arm-wrestling match in the Executive West bar.

With all the testosterone coursing through the hotel, it was not surprising that word got around of a high-stakes bet over genital endowment. (The loser allegedly glimpsed his adversary's manhood and forked over his money without enduring further humiliation.) A more resourceful grifter reportedly made bets that "I have a cock that hangs below my knee." When skeptics put up the money, the man rolled up his pant leg to expose a tattoo on his calf: a rooster with its neck in a noose. "See?" he said, smiling. "A cock. Hanging. Below my knee." He revealed to one player that he wins around $1,000 a year with the trick, but it has also occasioned a few broken bones. "So," he was said to have explained philosophically, "it's a win-some-lose-some kind of deal."

For those old enough to remember it, Derby City recalls Johnston City, a month-long rackhanalia held in the smoky poolroom of a small Illinois town and nicknamed "the Hustlers' Jamboree." Run by the infamous Jansco brothers, Johnston City featured such intense gambling that when one player dropped dead of a massive coronary the hustlers at the adjacent table continued their game, repositioning themselves, until the police arrived and took away the corpse.

Johnston City thrived for years. ABC's *Wide World of Sports* even filmed the annual event six times, and the show's director, Chet Forte, a notorious whale of a gambler, allegedly tried to hustle big action in between shifts. But in early 1972, Johnston City was raided by the FBI and the IRS. The feds shut the hall down, padlocking the doors and confiscating the players' cash and Cadillacs. "The soul of Johnston City lives on here in Louisville," says "Toupee" Jay Helfert, a bald-pated veteran roadman, nicknamed for his trick of beating suckers out of their money and then returning a few weeks later disguised in a hairpiece to win again.

The pool world has a vocabulary all its own. Fans are "sweaters" and "railbirds," financial backers are "stakehorses," punks and quitters are "nits," double-crossers are "dump artists," and money is "cheese," "bones," "cake," "cabbage," "timber," or "dimes." The Inuit have nineteen different words for snow; the pool world has at least as many for money. It has its own circadian rhythm and internal clock, one that is about twelve hours different from the rest of civilized society. It has its own customs, leather-and-denim-based dress code, even its own cholesterol-laden cuisine. Pool has its particular values and social mores, as folks come and go, appear and disappear — intense friendships and alliances form and then dissolve — with unusual speed.

And it's a culture that keeps to itself. Rich and rambunctious as the Derby City Classic scene is, you suspect that the vast majority of Louisvillians have no idea it takes place every year. It certainly isn't covered in the newspapers or on local sports-radio shows. You wonder how many people drive by the Executive West, see the jammed parking lot, and just assume the Shriners or the Fuller Brush salesmen are holed up inside.

Danny Basavich used to be at the gravitational center of the pool phylum, hustling suckers and getting big action. But now —like most pros, sufficiently well known that they're no longer able to play incognito—he's been displaced to the margins. At three or so one morning, he figured he'd spotted one mark he could take down for a few grand, a cocky-looking local kid named Dale, wearing a Louisville Cardinals cap backwards, a brown leather bomber jacket, and a pair of sweatpants. As he'd done countless times before, Basavich would pose as the slovenly fat guy, ask the kid if he wanted to hit a little nine-ball for money, and let prejudice take over. *No way can that fatass beat me.*

Basavich was on the verge of getting his first money game of the week when the kid's stakehorse, a lanky Asian slickster in a rugby shirt, intervened.

"Dude, you can't play him," the stakehorse said, pulling his boy aside and pointing to Basavich. "I ain't backing you against him. He'll annihilate you."

"What are you talking about?" Dale pleaded. "You know how good I play."

"Fuck, man. Are you fuckin' kidding? You know who that is?"

"Nah, who?" said Dale.

"Shit, man. That's Kid Delicious." The stakehorse then stated what so many others knew, that Kid Delicious guy—that obese, hail-fellow-well-met with the ice-breaking personality and paint-peeling voice—may well have divorced more pool players from their money than anyone else under the roof.

RUNNING THE TABLE

1

THE OPENING BREAK

CREDIT THE HUNGARIAN. Credit ol' Andy Nozsaly, or Nozaly, or maybe Sozaly. Something like that. He's no longer with us, and no one seems quite sure what the hell his exact name was anyway. But credit him for the opening break, as it were, in Danny Basavich's narrative.

During an oppressively hot summer in central New Jersey, when Danny was fourteen, he found a job working for Nozsaly's furniture restoration business. Doris and Dave Basavich were all for it. Their son was a heavyset kid, not exactly teeming with ambition, and this menial job would get him out of the house, fire him with some sense of responsibility, and even put a little money in his wallet.

So every weekend, in air as sticky as cotton candy, Danny would get on his bike and head to the Englishtown Auction, a flea market in Manalapan, New Jersey, to help out the old man. Sweating enthusiastically through his T-shirt, the kid would lug mahogany tables, apply coats of varnish to desks, and restring wicker chairs. At the end of the day, after he'd loaded everything into Andy's truck, he'd open his palm. The old man would do the math—"eleffen hours at vor dollars an hour, carry ze vun . . ."

— and put forty or fifty hard-earned dollars in the kid's pudgy hands. Danny would blow his cash on video games and ice cream and other fleeting teenage pleasures. Then he would be back the next Saturday morning to repeat the drill.

Midway through that brutal summer, Danny spent a lunch break trolling the flea market for bargains. He stumbled on the baseball card concession and made a breathtaking discovery. That year, the Upper Deck brand scattered bonus cards in certain packs, which made them slightly thicker than the regular packs. Using the micrometer he had in his pocket, Danny could, without opening the pack, figure out which ones contained the valuable bonus cards. He would buy only those packs, then promptly resell the valuable cards at a huge markup.

And he realized something else: the Topps brand always put cards into packs in the same sequence. So if, say, Ken Griffey Jr. followed Carlos Baerga once, he followed him every time. By opening the wrapper the slightest bit and peeking at the last card, Danny could determine the contents of the entire pack. He would purchase choice packs for $1 and sell the contents for ten times that. Pretty soon, Danny had little use for Andy's sweatshop. Four bucks an hour to lug furniture? Hell, he could make a few hundred bucks a week buying and selling the right packs of baseball cards.

As Danny's spending habits grew more extravagant, Doris and Dave grew suspicious. He reassured them that, no, he wasn't selling drugs, stealing, or doing anything illegal. Beyond the money, the scheme filled him with an intoxicating rush. Using wile and guile, he was outsmarting the rest of the world. His conduct resided somewhere in an ethical gray area. He wasn't technically earning the money, but neither was he outright stealing it. A con. A grift. A hustle. A smudging of the line between right and wrong. Whatever, it came with a spike in adrenaline, and it felt good.

Doris and Dave Basavich owned a women's clothing shop in the Sheepshead Bay section of Brooklyn, and for the first twelve years of Danny's life the family lived near the store. When the neighborhood started to slide, they decamped for New Jersey, seeking the trappings of suburban life. They kept the store, and for Doris and Dave, the hour-long commute from Jersey to Brooklyn was a small sacrifice to make in exchange for safer, more comfortable surroundings. But it meant that Danny and his younger sister, Kimberly, were frequently on their own. With his parents working late hours at the shop, Danny was free to eat as he pleased, and as any unsupervised teenager would, he made Big Macs, Klondike bars, and gobstoppers the cornerstone of his diet. He wasn't just growing up quickly, he was growing *out* quickly too.

If teen obesity is now a hot-button topic, affecting a staggering one in three adolescents, Danny was ahead of the trend. By the time he reached bar mitzvah age in the early 1990s, his weight was north of two hundred pounds. He wasn't just fat; he was shaped a bit like a brandy snifter, with normal-sized legs suddenly sprouting into a bulge of an abdomen. Before Danny's freshman year of high school, Doris and Dave sent him to Camp Shane, a weight-loss camp in upstate New York. ("Lighten up at Camp Shane!" gushes the familiar weekly ad in the back of the *New York Times Magazine*.)

Danny has two enduring memories from that summer. He made a fortune selling contraband candy bars to other plump campers with little will power. And not only was he agile and athletic enough to win the camp tennis tournament; he also beat the best player from the "thin kids' camp" across the lake. He recalls it as "a scene from a movie," all those heavyset kids cheering him on against the skinny, preppy kid from the monied camp. He doubts he was ever more popular than he was that day.

Danny lost thirty pounds that summer, but when he returned to New Jersey, he promptly gained the weight back. Not that it bothered him much. Like a lot of overweight kids, he cultivated both a thick skin and a finely calibrated defense mechanism, poking fun at his physique before anyone else could. He was an outgoing, modestly popular kid who didn't give his parents much trouble. He did well in school. He had friends. He was prone to "low periods," days of pitch darkness when he could scarcely haul himself out of bed. But what teenager doesn't have moody spells? Doris and Dave chalked it up to adolescence.

In the fall of 1992, Danny entered his freshman year at Manalapan High School. A massive public school in the belly of New Jersey, MHS could have been plucked from a Bruce Springsteen video. The suburban school had a rigid caste system, one that didn't much accommodate freshmen, particularly ones with squawky voices who looked as though they had swallowed a blast furnace.

Danny didn't fit in, but neither was he invisible. If Manalapan High had the usual tribes — jocks, geeks, Goths, stoners — Danny was a grifter. He was the kid who would buy candy and Rice Krispies Treats in bulk and surreptitiously hawk them at a steep markup between classes. He ran the poker game during study hall and the football pool on Fridays. School was less a place of learning than a place of business, his peers not so much classmates as suckers. Relishing the same rush he got fleecing the other guys by selling them prize baseball cards, Danny was making $500 a week just by going to school. He was always looking for an edge, an angle, looking for what he would later call "the nuts."

Early in his sophomore year, Danny got busted for running the football pool. The principal demanded names. Reluctantly, Danny ratted out some of his classmates, and, overnight, it wasn't only clothes that he had trouble fitting into. The bullies shoved him against lockers, hid his jacket, knocked books out of his arms. Danny and his parents met with a "child study team" at the high school: a school psychologist, a guidance counselor, and two teachers who vowed to help kids solve their problems. Nothing much came of it. Their attitude was: *You're fat, you deserve to be picked on.*

Danny once watched another target of the bullies try to fight back. The kid was hogtied to a motorcycle and dragged down the street. He woke up in the hospital. Danny decided that taking the abuse beat the alternative. As is usually the case with bullies, for all their punches in the gut and slaps on the neck, the real beatings Danny took were emotional ones. As a matter of ritual, he was being humiliated in front of his friends, and, worse, in front of the girls. He was the object of an unending stream of fat jokes. He grew paranoid and thought his classmates were making fun of him even when they weren't. Danny realized that he was being so careful about what he said and did — sifting every comment, every move, to try to ensure it wouldn't trigger a taunt — he stopped being himself.

Eventually the bullies broke him. After a particularly brutal tormenting session, he ran out of class in the middle of the day and took refuge in the woods behind the school. He was asleep when the police found him. He vowed that he had spent his last day at Manalapan High.

An old saying has it that proficiency at pool is a sure sign of a misspent youth. In Danny's case, pool may well have saved his life. A high school dropout at the age of fifteen, Danny entered a period of unrelenting malaise. He would sleep for entire days and, when he finally woke, eat unholy quantities of food. He had always endured stretches — "full-moon phases," his parents called them — when his energy lagged, when he cried though he couldn't explain why, when he was consumed by feelings of worthlessness and sometimes worse. But now the full-moon phase was showing no sign of letting up.

He was suffering from what was obviously deep depression. Save eating, he lost interest in every activity that once gave him pleasure. His weight climbed steadily. He gave his prize possessions — bowling balls, tennis rackets, trophies — to his father and told his parents not to feel guilty if anything bad happened to him. That's when Dave Basavich got scared. *My gosh*, he thought, *my kid doesn't want to live anymore.* He and Doris took Danny to a child psychologist, who quickly made the diagnosis of bipolar disorder.

Danny already knew that his body was unsound; he didn't want to hear that his mind wasn't working right either — not realizing, of course, that his weight and his depression were inextricably linked. He tried his best to ignore the diagnosis and never returned for a second therapy session. The shrink prescribed antidepressants, but Danny claimed that they made him "feel like I'm not myself," and threw them away. So he suffered.

Meanwhile, the New Jersey child-welfare authorities, alarmed by the disappearance of the chunky sophomore, went after Doris and Dave. Danny would have to attend school until he turned sixteen or else he would be removed from home. Dave and Doris begged for their son to be transferred to the high school in nearby Freehold or Marlboro. The authorities said no: the semester had already started, and besides, what kind of message would that be sending the kid? He needed to confront his problems, not run away from them. Dave suggested home-schooling, but that request, too, was denied. "Look," Dave told the investigator on a home visit, "if he's forced to go back to school, he's going to kill himself." The investigator was unmoved.

Though Dave Basavich was Jewish and Doris was Protestant, they enrolled Danny in a private Catholic school. Doris and Dave dropped off their son on his first day. He felt ridiculous dressed in an ill-fitting white shirt, black pants, and clunky dress shoes that squeaked when he walked. But he made it through the first week without incident. Then, on the bus ride home, a thug friendly with the bullies at Manalapan High recognized Fat Danny and threatened to beat him up. That was Danny's last day at Catholic school.

Next Danny was enrolled in Old Bridge Adult High School, a nearby alternative school filled mostly with young mothers who had dropped out of high school when they'd become pregnant. He had to attend classes for only an hour a day, three days a week. The rest of the class work he could do at home. The only male in his class, Danny finished six semesters' worth of high school courses in less than six months. It was awesome, he says. He wasn't even sixteen, and already he had a high school diploma. Another fleece, another corner successfully cut.

He quickly realized, though, that when you're fifteen and through with school, when you have no girlfriend and no driver's license, and when you live in suburbia (before the dawn of the Internet and 200-channel satellite TV), there are a finite number of ways to spend your days. On a typical lazy afternoon not long after his graduation, Danny tried to thwart boredom by riding his bike down Route 9 to Elite Billiards, a pool hall in Marlboro. He'd been in Elite a few times and figured there were worse places to wile away some hours. Hospitable in its way, the hall had twenty-eight well-kept mahogany tables and a few seven-foot co-op seven-by-seven barboxes, the seven-foot tables. There was a genial owner, a full bar, and a cast of regulars who, like crazy uncles, were more endearingly quirky than dangerous. As pool halls went, Elite could almost pass for upscale.

Danny had always liked pool, though he played only casually. His introduction to the sport had come early: his maternal grandfather, John Schust, was an accomplished shark who claimed to have won a car by hustling back in the 1930s, and he taught his grandson basic technique. A Sears barbox table took up space in the Basaviches' basement, and though it was mainly used to fold laundry, Danny played sporadically and even won twenty bucks from time to time in money games against his friends. The act of thrusting a stick into a ball—sometimes violently, sometimes as delicately as swaddling a baby in a blanket—had come easily to him. And, odd for someone so restless in a school classroom, at the table Danny displayed exceptional patience and powers of concentration.

That afternoon at Elite Billiards, as he hit balls alone in the dim light, shafts of sun bouncing off the table, Danny was, for the first time, truly mesmerized. By the mix of simplicity and complexity. By the limitless possibilities every table presented. By the angles. By the peculiar rhythm. By the way you could lace a cue ball with just the right amount of spin and turn it into a guided missile. By the way time dilated when you played. Soon he lost himself in what serious pool players call "the green felt ocean." He'd break the balls and begin a game of solitaire, and when he next looked at the clock, hours had elapsed.

He'd rack the balls and walk to the other end of the table. Imitating the pros he'd occasionally seen on television, he'd chalk his cue a few times, survey the table, take a few practice strokes. Then he'd break the balls, an act he likened to cracking an egg, the contents splattering in different directions. Working his way around the table, he'd take aim at the balls in ascending numerical order. Each time one fell into a pocket, it provided Danny a small but unmistakable euphoric jolt. Soon he set challenges for himself. There were fifteen balls on the table. If he gave himself, say, twenty-four attempts, could he make all fifteen disappear? Okay. Now, could he clear the table in twenty-three tries?

He was back at Elite the next day, and the day after that. When he was with his parents and sister on the weekends, he could only think about returning to the pool hall and trying a new spin or a different pattern of balls. Fortunately, Jay, the kindly owner, had taken a liking to Danny and charged him a flat rate of $10 a day in table time.

His crying fits had subsided, and he was no longer waking up eighteen hours after he fell asleep. His parents and sister joked that Danny's sullen alter ego — the guy who moped and cried and ate and then went back to sleep — "had gone back into hibernation." Pool was in fact Danny's therapy, his sanctuary. Screw the bullies at Manalapan High. Screw the fat jokes. Screw the girls who didn't give him the time of day. Screw the unsympathetic teachers who blamed him and his physique for his troubles. The maple pool cue felt like a pistol in his hands, instilling in him power and self-confidence. The feelings of worthlessness and the suicidal thoughts were retreating. Relieved that their son's mental health had seemed to stabilize, Doris and Dave Basavich once asked Danny to explain: why pool? Danny stuttered and mumbled and then replied, "It makes me feel *alive*."

Already equipped with general technique, Danny soon picked up pool's nuances. Standing before the table, he could manipulate balls any way he wanted, finding angles and vectors that seemed to violate geometric axioms and the laws of motion. He could hit the cue ball just right and it would perform like a dog that had successfully completed obedience school. He noticed that other players were watching him, whistling in admiration when he drilled a cut shot or worked his way out of a cluster.

It was reciprocal romance. For the first time in his life, he was good — scarily good — at something. While Danny wasn't going to win the hundred-yard dash or dunk a basketball or break open-field tackles in football, he discovered that he was a world-class athlete of a different kind: his hand-eye coordination, his manual dexterity, his feel were one in a million. As for his bloated belly and his nonexistent physical fitness, well, they didn't much matter. Sure, a few minutes into a practice session he would be basted in perspiration, streams of sweat opening on his brow, under his arms, around his belly. Sure, lacking in flexibility, he might need to use a bridge (that implement that looks like a branding iron, used to reach distant balls) more often than other players. But he could still execute all the shots, and fueled, perhaps, by adrenaline, he hardly ever grew fatigued at the table.

He wasn't merely good at pool; he was a natural. Unlike the piano and tennis and other activities he'd tried as a kid, he didn't need an instructor. Everything about pool seemed to make such inherent sense. *Of course you need to angle the cue ball to the left when aiming at a ball across the table. Of course you need to adjust your stick for more steeply angled shots.* Anything else would have felt unnatural, illogical.

And Danny quickly grasped the cardinal rule for improvement: practice your weaknesses. He had mastered cut shots and tricky caroms and three-rail kicks and long shots. He knew how to apply the right amount of draw, or backspin, so the cue ball hits the object ball and retreats, as though it had suddenly thought better of moving forward. So instead Danny devoted his time to improving his break, his spin, his ability to break up a cluster. Before long, he had advanced from a C player to a B player.

Happy that *something* was finally igniting their son's pilot light, Doris and Dave said nothing when Danny spent upward of sixteen hours a day at Elite. They figured it was a phase, and the same way he outgrew his *Star Wars* action figures and baseball cards, this intense interest in pool eventually would abate too. When it did, they'd help him find a job or apply to college. But in a matter of weeks, Danny's high run of balls went from ten to twenty to thirty. Like so many serious players, he likened it all to an addiction. He woke up thinking about pool. All he wanted during the day was a dose of pool. And when he got it, he was euphoric. Then he went to bed anticipating his next fix.

If the sport itself held him in thrall, so did the ambiance at Elite. He loved the confluence of chalk and stale beer and the subtle undertones of secondhand smoke that lingered in the air. He loved the classic rock — Jethro Tull and Bad Company and Led Zeppelin and Bachman-Turner Overdrive — that served as a sort of auditory wallpaper. He loved the faintly menacing hustlers, the shortstops (good local players), the railbirds, and the other "men of the cloth," with names like Blood, the Claw, Neptune Joe, Gypsy Bob, the Exterminator, Mark the Shark, and the Peruvian Prince. They were twice Danny's age and seemed to have no obvious source of income or gainful employment. (Except for the Exterminator, who, as Danny came to understand it, really did slay vermin during the day.) But they took him under their collective wing and happily shared their tricks. He cracked them up with his jokes, awed them with his skill, and treated them with a reverence that suggested he felt lucky to be in their presence.

One afternoon, Mark the Shark bet Danny five bucks he couldn't make a particularly difficult cut shot. When Danny did, Mark reached for his wallet. "You can keep your money," Danny said, "if you look me in the eye and say at the top of your lungs, 'Danny Basavich is the future of pool.'"

Mark started to speak when Danny stopped him. "I'm just playin' around. I don't want no one to overhear you and think I'm cocky."

Danny may have been an outcast in the halls of his generic suburban high school or in the typical New Jersey mall. But in the pool hall, among this most motley of crews, he found kindred spirits. At Elite Billiards, the misfits fit in.

Self-taught at first, Danny leaned on the regulars for advice and tips. Instead of taking formal lessons, he spent incalculable hours "sweating" the top players and then unleashing a barrage of questions. When Neptune Joe Frady or Al Lapena, a refugee from the Philippines who hustled countless sops by pretending that he didn't speak English, would finish a game, Danny would be waiting. *Why didn't you go for the nine combo when the seven was hugging the rail? What were you thinking when you played that safety? Why did you go for the cut shot and not the double bank?* He made them all feel important, validating what they did and indulging them with a postgame interview, much the way athletes in other sports are besieged by reporters after hitting the winning jump shot or slamming the walk-off home run. Everybody benefited. They got their egos stroked; he got a wealth of free advice.

At one point, Neptune Joe offered Danny pool's version of a Zen riddle: "What is the difference between a very good player and a great player?" The answer: "A very good player will practice a shot until he gets it right; a great player will practice it until he never gets it wrong." Danny internalized the message.

The next step entailed taking on the superior players and getting "match play," even if it came at a price. Neptune Joe, the best player in New Jersey at the time, would spot Danny the five-and-out — Danny needed only to sink the five ball to win — and still beat him badly. For two years straight, Danny reckons he made a weekly habit of enriching Frady by $25 or $50. Donating, they call it. He figured that playing against stiff competition was the best way to improve his stick and rationalized it as a cheap private lesson. Plus, he was making plenty of money the other six days of the week by thrashing the weaker players. Before long, he was riding his ten-speed to Elite and often winning enough money to take a taxi home with the bike in the trunk. He'd pull up in a cab, give the driver a $20 tip, put some money in his parents' vault, and go to sleep feeling as if he were the biggest of the big shots.

He was an honest kid who stayed out of trouble and had no problem differentiating between right and wrong. But somehow the choreography of the bamboozle — the laying of the trap, the play-acting, the assumption of other identities — was almost as much fun as the game itself. As rapidly as Danny picked up the nuances of the table, he was also a quick study of the thermodynamics of the hustle. And the first rule of hustling — just get the other guy to the damn table; the stakes will escalate on their own — played to his core strength of making everyone in his orbit feel comfortable.

An early hustle entailed riding his bike to a nearby college campus — Kean, Rutgers, once Princeton. His first stop was the campus bookshop. If they had his size, he would buy a sweatshirt. Then he would finagle his way into the dining hall, grab a piece of chocolate cake, repair to a toilet stall, and smear some cake on his sweatshirt and face. He would then walk into the campus pool hall, provoking taunts and giggles, and purposely fumble a stash of hundreds as he tried to buy a Coke in the vending machine.

Invariably, he'd be asked to put $20 on a game. The college kid would win and then call his friends. *Come down here quick! I got this clumsy, fatass freshman ready to gamble away a stack of hundreds!* Eventually, when the stakes had reached sufficiently large proportions, Danny would run rack after rack, busting the frat boys — sweet payback for all those times he'd been teased about his weight.

Every Wednesday night, Elite was the site of a tournament that drew the best hustlers from New Jersey, New York, and Pennsylvania. Everyone ponied up $50, and by the time fifty or sixty players had entered, a nice payday hung in the balance. Based on the honor system — always a dodgy proposition when pool hustlers were involved — the players handicapped their own games and were spotted balls accordingly. The pros were fifteens, the B players sevens and eights. Though Danny was a ten or eleven, he sandbagged down to a seven. Few knew how well he really played, and he sure didn't look like a pool shark. So when he played pros the likes of Neptune Joe Frady or Frankie Hernandez, Danny would get the five, six, seven, eight, and nine. Soon he was winning the $3,000 pot.

That's when he first started showing a streak of confidence that had eluded him in every other part of his life. He'd tell opponents that they shouldn't feel bad about losing because he was going to be a pro one day. "They're going to talk about me after I'm dead." Perhaps because he said it with a smile, perhaps because he had the sort of body that resisted serious treatment, no one paid him much mind.

At seventeen, he had a novel experience: he met a girl who liked him. Danielle Graziano wasn't just attractive, she was also unbothered by Danny's rolls of fat. "Who wants to snuggle up with a twig?" she told him. They'd met at the pool hall, and though they lived a few towns apart, they connived ways to meet at a mall or a park. Danny liked her plenty, but after a few weeks he had to cut her loose. "You're a great girl, but you're taking away from my pool playing," he told her. Here he was, a seventeen-year-old virgin, desperate for a steady, cute girlfriend. He finally wins the lottery and then rips up the ticket. That's how much pool meant to him.

Like mobsters and boxers, pool players don't truly come into their own until they assume a nickname. So it is that the Republic of Pool is populated with a Scorpion (Johnny Archer) and a Black Widow (Jeanette Lee), a Gunslinger (Dave Matlock) and a Rifleman (Buddy Hall), a Freezer (Scott Frost) as well as an Ice Man (Mika Immonen). Not unlike acquiring a tattoo, taking on a handle is a rite of selfhood, a means of expressing a personal totem. Nicknames run the spectrum from the menacing ("the Lion," "the Cobra") to the geographic ("Spanish Mike," who is in fact Puerto Rican) to the euphonious ("Scott the Shot," "Shannon the Cannon," "Earl the Pearl"). Some are clever. "Weenie Beanie" Bill Staton, who once appeared on *The Tonight Show* with Johnny Carson, was so nicknamed because he made his real money from the hot dog stands he owned. Others are quirky. Take the New York–based player George SanSouci, who goes by the moniker "Ginky," the first "word" he spoke as a baby. Apart from conferring a sense of status, nicknames also serve a practical purpose in the pool world. For a player who dreams of one day marketing himself to the mainstream, "Minnesota Fats" is a hell of a lot catchier than his given name, Rudolph Wanderone. (For that matter, as a player Willie Mosconi was far superior to Minnesota Fats but far less notorious, largely because he lacked the showbiz instincts, including a killer handle.)

As a teenager, Basavich was, inevitably, known as "Fat Danny." For obvious reasons, he hoped for a nickname that was a little more flattering. But, much like his clothes, nothing quite seemed to fit—not "Handsome Dan," not "the Jewish Jester," not "the Boss," an homage to Bruce Springsteen, the bard of New Jersey, who lived a few towns over. He was still Danny Basavich d/b/a "Danny Basavich" when, at age seventeen, he drove to Chelsea Billiards in Manhattan on a Saturday night.

Though it has since been reincarnated as a trendy, upscale hall that sells ahi tuna entrees and premium champagne at the bar, in its heyday Chelsea Billiards was a spacious, down-and-dirty "players' room" in the heart of New York City which in Danny's eyes took on the dimensions of an urban castle.

The place drew an evening crowd of casual players, bored college kids, and couples — gay and straight — on an inexpensive date. But as the night progressed and the last baseball and basketball games played out on the big-screen televisions, Chelsea morphed into a hustlers' paradise with lots of action. The best players on the East Coast showed up and brought their backers. The rail was a kaleidoscope of square jaws, flinty eyes, satin jackets, polyester pants, gold chains, and bad comb-overs. It wasn't unusual for players to get a game for a few hundred a set and then wager four or five (or ten) times that by betting on the side.

At the time, a slender, flashy, up-and-coming player, Eddie Hubler, was the beau prince among the railbirds. Nicknamed "Kid Vicious," Hubler was winning big and had a legion of backers. Danny hadn't smeared cake on his sweatshirt or poured beer in his hair, but when he walked in, he looked as slovenly as ever. He had been to Chelsea once before, several months back, and got hustled for a few hundred bucks. On this night, forty-two hundred-dollar bills were tucked in various pockets of his baggy pants. He took a table and warmed up alone without drawing much notice from the railbirds. At two in the morning, he asked one of them, "Who's the best player here?" When the bird answered "Kid Vicious," Danny nodded and said, "Think he'll play me even?"

Taking Danny for a fat slob, drunk on either Jack Daniel's or self-delusion, the railbirds quickly brokered a game. Danny and Vicious would play a set for $1,400. Danny then bet the remaining $2,800 in his bankroll with the railbirds. That $4,200 was all he had to his name. Had he lost, he would've had to drive back to New Jersey on local roads, to avoid turnpike tolls. But his thinking at the time was blissfully simple: there was no way he was going to lose. It was just not in the realm of possibility. So why not try to bet as much as he could?

The concept of mental strength takes on a curious dimension for a player given to pitched battles with depression and regular crying fits. But from the time he began playing competitively,

Danny possessed an uncanny ability to shoo away distractions and conjure his best pool at critical moments. It wasn't so much that, like all the best athletes, he elevated his game when the pressure was ratcheted highest. It was more that he didn't perceive the situation as particularly stressful. "Why would I get nervous?" he wondered. "I'm doing what I love and I have a chance to win money. Why would anyone be nervous about that? I'm nervous when I'm depressed. The whole reason I play pool in the first place is because it doesn't make me nervous."

To the dismay and stunned amusement of the railbirds, the heavy, unshaven kid with the gravelly voice was a peerless player. His early lead took the noise right out of the place, and he polished off Kid Vicious with a flourish of shotmaking. Doing his best to conceal a smile, he took his $4,200. Suddenly his wallet was swollen like it had never been before. As he unscrewed his stick and prepared to leave Chelsea, an embittered railbird whistled and then cracked, "Kid Vicious just got hustled by Kid Delicious."

Everyone laughed. Danny figured it was yet another fat joke. But here he was, $4,200 richer than when he'd walked in. He had just played jam-up pool to pull off a score. It was going to take a hell of a lot more to dampen his mood. On his way out, he said it to himself: *Kid Delicious. Kid Delicious.* Damn if it didn't have a nice ring to it. Thus was born one of the catchier *noms de pool* the sport has ever known.

He had yet to turn eighteen, and already Kid Delicious was running out of honest competition around New Jersey, and hustling near home had a limited shelf life. Sure, he could always head to a college campus and swindle a frat boy out of a few hundred bucks. But any local player worth busting for real money was getting the wire on that fat kid with the unforgettable nickname. Banging balls at Elite one night, Kid Delicious discussed his fate with the regulars. "Danny," Neptune Joe said, "I know what I would do if I was you and really serious about getting better. Get my ass to Chicago Billiards up in Connecticut. Start playing outta there and you'll get a Ph.D. in hustling."

2

HUSTLERS' FINISHING SCHOOL

J UST AS RENAISSANCE painters gravitated to Florence, or
beatnik poets of the 1950s converged on the North Beach
section of San Francisco, the magnet for American pool hustlers in the 1990s was West Haven, Connecticut. Specifically, it
was Chicago Billiards, a dilapidated, cramped, malodorous, now
defunct poolroom nestled in a nondescript strip mall on a nondescript drag of a nondescript American city. There, in a four-thou-
sand-square-foot enclave untouched by time, technology, and
temperance, a generation of the most accomplished pool hustlers
converged to match up and swap spots, money, and, on occasion,
punches.

It was possible to visit the neighboring used-CD store or Chinese restaurant or Indian grocery without realizing that Chicago
even existed. Especially when the pink neon marquee wasn't illuminated, the few indications that the place was a going concern
were the piles of human waste out back (more on this later) and
the assorted out-of-state license plates on the cars and trucks in
the parking lot. But, like a social club that caters to the mob, once
you entered the front door and walked up a steep staircase — past
walls festooned with framed photographs of pool luminaries, including a classic shot of Larry Lisciotti, Danny DiLiberto, and

"King James" Rempe dressed as gangsters — the place blazed to life.

The fifteen pool tables were in perpetual use. Depending on who had commandeered the jukebox, hip-hop or classic rock screamed from the speakers. As many as a half-dozen players slept in the back room. And twenty-four hours a day there was action. Crazy, high-stakes action. "That place was disgusting, just so nasty I can't even describe it. It was filled with degenerates. The ceilings were low, there was always a light bulb burned out or a toilet clogged up," rhapsodizes "Portuguese" George Texiera, an accomplished one-pocket player who spent a significant chunk of his thirties playing pool at Chicago. "But it was the greatest place you could imagine. Like a summer camp for pool players. One of the great action spots of all time. If you want to know a sure way to put a smile on a pool player's face, mention Chicago Billiards. You went there for one night and you came out with stories to last a lifetime."

Chicago's proprietor was Ralph Procopio, a tall, gaunt, terminally unshaven fortysomething millionaire. With hair jutting out at odd angles and tight jeans wrapped like sausage casing around his legs, Procopio was nicknamed "Shaggy" by the clientele, a nod to the *Scooby-Doo* character he closely resembled. Procopio ran a successful bread distribution business in Connecticut and had various other investments in the area. He lived comfortably with his wife and children. Yet somewhere along the line he contracted an unshakable case of the pool jones.

By his own admission, Procopio wasn't much of a player. And as a born-again Christian who neither drank nor smoked — despite the heaping quotients of grief from the resident players, he'd installed Christian-rock CDs on the jukebox — he hardly fit the description of a typical pool-hall owner. But something about the game seduced him, and he had a particular affinity for the road hustler. In the early nineties, Procopio found some commercial space not far from his bread distribution center. He signed a lease, bought a dozen tables from a nearby pool hall that had recently gone out of business, and opened his own parlor. He christened the place Chicago Billiards, not after the city but after the game Chicago, a permutation of rotation pool. At first his patrons were mostly black and Puerto Rican drug dealers from nearby New Haven and Bridgeport. One regular recalls playing a game and struggling to retain his focus as two drug dealers consummated a sale of automatic weapons at the adjacent table.

But word of mouth is the manna of the pool desert, and once the line got out that a benevolent, free-spending millionaire with a bread business had opened a pool hall, Chicago became a sensation. Located a few hundred yards from an I-95 exit ramp, an easy drive from both New York and Boston, Chicago was soon *the* place on the Eastern Seaboard to get action. At one point, Ralph took out a full-page ad in the pool magazines, announcing, ROAD PLAYERS WELCOME. FREE ROOM AND BOARD. FREE POOL. BRING A LOT OF MONEY.

Not that pool was the only source of wagering. For all the self-determination of playing pool, most road hustlers are first and foremost gamblers, lured to uncertainty and odds, with a bottomless appetite for games of chance. At Chicago, patrons would play high-stakes nine-ball for hours, then peer out the upstairs window and bet double or nothing on whether the next car out of the parking lot would turn right or left. A well-pitched quarter or a superior run on the Ms. Pac-Man arcade game would routinely yield a $1,000 payoff. Significant sums of "cheese" were also won and lost over trick shots, eating competitions, and trivia questions. Giving new zest to the phrase "pissing contest," one player was enriched by his heroic ability to urinate out of an upstairs window into a can on the asphalt below.

At least one of Chicago's pool tables had been designated for poker games, which were efficiently run by Ralph's protégé, an African-American kid nicknamed "Chewy," after the *Star Wars* character Chewbacca. Procopio recalls walking in one night in the middle of a high-stakes poker game and seeing that one player was making a small fortune. Fifteen thousand dollars in small bills were scattered in front of him. Procopio offered to help and put away $1,500 in fives and tens for safekeeping, and then he went home. The next day the player called him. "Thanks for taking that fifteen hundred, Ralph! Otherwise I would've really gone bust!" That kind of thing went on every night. One hour, a player had enough money to buy a new car. An hour later, he was in the hole for ten large.

Procopio loved it all: the world-class nine-ball games, the big action, the ambient buzz. And he turned into a sort of mythical figure, a Father Flanagan of the degenerates. Some members of the landed gentry make charitable contributions to orphans and hurricane victims and the malnourished. Procopio used his money to support a different group of misbegotten souls on society's margins. He would give money to any player who asked for it. Paying for table time was unheard of. When there was a lull in the action, Procopio would jump up and put $500 or $1,000 on the table, demanding that two players compete for the loot. Says Texiera: "There were times Ralph would stop by and ask how it's going. I'd be like, 'Not too good, Ralph. I'm down a thousand this week.' He'd give out hundreds like it was candy and say, 'Keep playing!'"

Procopio renovated a back room and filled it with six cots and installed a shower and kitchen, so players could gamble until sunrise, whip up a pot of pasta or similar minimalist cuisine, sleep for a few hours, and then resume playing. (It recalled the old mock-headline joke that hustlers have retailed since the Depression: POOL ROOM BURNS, SEVENTY-FIVE LEFT HOMELESS.) When the beds were filled, Procopio rented efficiency apartments down the road for the patrons.

To the aspiring player, Chicago took on the dimensions of a language-immersion camp. There's no better way to improve your fluency at the pool table than by competing against top players at any of hour of the day. Which is precisely what Chicago offered. Nine-ball, eight-ball, one-pocket, two-pocket, bank pool, straight pool — they played them all. When regulars weren't locked in games, they practiced relentlessly. The hustlers-in-training spent hours before Procopio's video camera, then watched tapes of their strokes, breaking down the smallest technical glitches. At one point, they shimmed the pockets of the two front tables to make them impossibly tight. Just as Kareem Abdul-Jabbar had honed his hook shot on small rims so when he played actual games it would feel as though he were throwing the ball into the ocean, the thinking was that if players knew that they could convert shots in tight pockets, they'd do fine on any table in the country.

The core curriculum at Chicago also included plenty on the black art of hustling. In Philip Roth's novel *Everyman,* a cuckolded spouse says, "Lying is cheap, contemptible control over the other person. It's watching the other person acting on incomplete information." In pool hustling, lying is an occupational qualification. The incomplete information is indispensable. Hustling is in part an athletic endeavor — marksmanship and poise and hand-eye coordination. But it's part three-card monte as well.

At Chicago, the hustlers learned how to lie, how to keep the jackknife out of sight. They learned how to assume false identities and conceal true ones. They learned how to acquire a "sneaky pete," a well-made cue that plays like a Balabushka but, lacking any ornamentation, looks like a cheap house stick — arming themselves with top-rate equipment without arousing suspicion. They learned how to perfect the skill of pocketing balls without revealing their true "speed" (that is, playing position pool but not using any English; when players get "shape" with just speed control it often looks like luck). They taught each other the kinds of trick shots that a sucker in any pool hall would bet $100 they couldn't pull off. They often played "sharking allowed" games. After you've played against an opponent who puts his testicles on the rail or belches in your ear as you're about to shoot, you won't get unmoored by the hotshot opponent in Seattle or Sarasota when he tries to distract you. You went to Chicago and you either got better in a hurry or got out in a hurry.

It was with no small amount of agonizing that Delicious, then barely eighteen, decided to matriculate to Chicago Billiards. As much as he wanted to improve both his stick and his chops as a hustler, he liked the convenience and minimal responsibility that came with living at home with two doting, permissive parents. He had tried, with varying degrees of success, to ignore his ongoing battle with depression, permitting himself a large measure of denial about his fragile mental state. To his way of thinking, facing his depression and treating it with drugs and psychotherapy would have meant owning up to yet another imperfection. His weight was enough of a flaw. He couldn't bear feeling fat *and* crazy. At the same time, he was enough of a realist to recognize that he could scarcely find an environment less conducive to mental health than a pool hall famous for erratic hours, a bawdy cast of regulars, and wild swings of money and momentum.

But in the fall of 1996, Delicious finally massed his courage and told Neptune Joe that he was "ready for pool boot camp." He folded $1,000 in cash into his back pocket, threw a duffel bag of clothes and his cue into the trunk of Neptune Joe's car, pretzeled himself into the shotgun seat, and made the three-hour drive from central Jersey to West Haven. Naturally, Doris and Dave asked their son when he would be coming home. "When my bankroll runs out," he said with a shrug. "Could be days. Could be months."

As it turned out, even his high-end estimate didn't go far enough. When Delicious set up his bedding in the back room of Chicago, any ambivalence melted away. For a gifted player with no girlfriend, few outside interests, and an abiding desire to become a world-class player whose pool legacy would live forever, there was no better place to be. In a small spiral notebook he carried with him everywhere, Delicious would fill page after page with observations. How Ginky would play a ball and position himself perfectly for the next shot. How Texiera would manipulate balls in a one-pocket game as if he were performing surgery. How Larry Lisciotti would psyche out his opponent with a well-timed bathroom break. Delicious' antennae were constantly receiving signals.

Just like at Elite Billiards, status came not from physical appearance or fashion sense but from an ability to direct six-ounce balls into a half-dozen pockets. If anything, an eccentric personality was an entry requirement for Chicago Billiards. Portuguese George was known to dump a cup of coffee over his own head in midconversation and then continue speaking as if nothing had happened. Another player, nicknamed "Bloody," would, after losing a game, punch himself in the face until — hence the name — he drew blood. For as little as $20, another player, Pistol Pete, would sprint at full speed into a wall and knock himself unconscious.

Against that backdrop, Delicious' weight, his ill-fitting pants, and his mental fragility hardly warranted mention.

Apart from an off-center personality, Delicious had the other prerequisite for fitting in at Chicago: an irremediable gambling jones. If players were wagering on a termite race, you could count on Delicious to join in. Too many times to count, he would win a bundle playing pool and lose the money right back, betting that he could eat a stack of saltines without drinking any fluids or that he could name all the members of the Eagles. (Timothy B. Schmit, the bassist, stumps 'em every time.) Like most of the players, Delicious found the chiming and dinging sounds of a casino to be an irresistible siren song. He figures he was winning between $5,000 and $10,000 a month at Chicago; practically none of it stuck to his pocket.

And while he drew the line at hard drugs, he was happy to throw down shots and smoke a J in the parking lot. At a time when his peers were entering college, Delicious' existence wasn't all that different from a freshman in his dorm room, liberated from responsibility, free to experiment as he pleased.

Delicious' pendulous belly almost took on a personality of its own. Two out of three adults in this country may be overweight, but his obesity was a source of endless fascination. The other players would stare at his gut and marvel that a kid with a waist like that could still hold his own. The conventional wisdom is that heavy players are easy pickings, because after ten or twelve hours of playing, their feet will hurt and the pain will break their concentration. "The bigger the opponent, the longer you should make the set," explained Lisciotti. But Delicious' obesity never seemed to affect his stamina. Which only made him more of a curiosity.

Eating and shooting pool were the pursuits he enjoyed most in life, and he approached both with striking similarity. He'd roll up his sleeves, sidle over to the table, and begin a measured, meticulous — religious isn't even a stretch — exercise. Be it a fifty-nine-inch cue or a five-inch fork, the implement appeared to be surgically attached to his arm. He always left the table satisfied. "Danny was famous for eating an entire cake and then still being able to run rack after rack," Ralph Procopio recalls. "Anyone who could do that was going to be just fine at Chicago."

Early in his stay, one of the regulars announced he was making a McDonald's run. "Hey, Kid Ketchup," he said teasingly to Delicious. "How many burgers you think you could eat, anyway?"

"As many as you'll buy me," Delicious shot back. "Hey, I know I'm fat. I like it. If you're gonna try and make me feel bad, I'm not sayin' it can't be done. But you gotta pick on something else besides my weight."

The scene in West Haven laid bare what is perhaps pool's central paradox. The game's most skilled practitioners might often be scoundrels and scalawags, hucksters and hounds, all of them nocturnal creatures. Many resembled Danny McGoorty, the iconic hustler from the city of Chicago whose wife once sent him out to the corner store for a loaf of rye bread. A week later, he called her from a poolroom in Cincinnati: "They don't have rye." But the sport is predicated on meticulousness and discipline and exactitude and attention to detail. Hitting a clean tee shot is nothing compared with sinking the ball of your choice in the pocket of your choice, all the while leaving the cue ball positioned perfectly for your next shot. The Chicago Billiards regulars couldn't be counted on to change their clothes or pay their cable bill or call their kids on their birthdays, but they could spend hours maneuvering a small ball around a table, roughly twice as long as it is wide, with painterly precision. They might eat soup with their hands, but armed with a cue stick, they were as fastidious and painstaking as a jeweler with tiny pliers.

Among the Chicago habitués there was no more accomplished player than Larry Lisciotti, who took great pride in his role as celebrity in residence. Inasmuch as contemporary pool has furnished legends, Lisciotti qualifies, in part because of his achievements in tournaments like the U.S. Open, which he won in 1976, but more for his starring role in countless mythologized stories.

Known as "Oil Can Larry," "Larry the Lizard," and "the Prince of Pool," Lisciotti grew up in central Connecticut, where he was cocaptain of his high school basketball team and a scratch golfer. At seventeen, he was fired from his first job, at a sporting goods store, when the boss — who also happened to be his stepfather — caught him offering to flip dollar bills with customers. A year after that, his number came up for the Vietnam draft. Lisciotti told the Chicago regulars how he had avoided serving. Standing in line for his military physical, he is said to have inserted a black jellybean into his anus. When the examining doctor extracted a small black mound, Lisciotti grabbed it from the doctor's rubber glove and popped it into his mouth.

Instead of reporting to boot camp, the kid packed his cues and set out on the road as a hustler. A 1977 article in *Sports Illustrated*, "A Hustler Meets an Artist," described him this way: "Lisciotti, who has yet to work a day of his life, does not care about games against the big names; any guy he can win a quick $50 from is his favorite opponent." During a tour of duty in Los Angeles in the 1970s, he successfully hustled Hollywood executives and movie actors. Bored with taking their cash, he offered to play them for their cars. As the story goes, before long he had a convoy of seven or eight automobiles.

By the time he arrived at Chicago Billiards, Lisciotti was already in his fifties, but he worked hard to keep up his renegade image. He assumed a regal air, challenging "the motherfucking kids" and using his cue to jab players in the gut without provocation. He slicked back his obsidian hair and maintained his trim, taut physique with what he called a "nicotine-and-booze Zen diet." Once Lisciotti was told by Procopio to stop swigging from his bottle of vodka while he played. Lisciotti stepped outside, transferred the contents into a tumbler, and went back in without missing his turn. A master of trash talk, he would boast of "busting more guys than the Depression." Another favorite line: "I don't count my money, I weigh it."

Late in his stay at Chicago, Lisciotti was diagnosed with lung cancer. Without blinking his bloodshot eyes, he immediately had his teeth capped and bought a fur coat. "If nothing else, I'm gonna go out in style," he announced. When Lisciotti died in February 2004 at the age of fifty-seven, his boyhood friend Randy Smith wrote a pitch-perfect obituary-slash-final-roast in the Manchester, Connecticut, newspaper: "Most boys and girls want a pony. Larry always wanted the winner in the seventh . . . Part of the funeral reading was from Paul's letters to the Corinthians, a curious choice because Larry's letters to the Corinthians were lost in the mail."

On one of Delicious' first nights at Chicago, Lisciotti whipped out a quarter and said, "Hey, fats. Fifty bucks. Heads on the table, I win." Eager for acceptance and intimidated by Lisciotti, Delicious nodded. Lisciotti flipped the coin, and when it landed tails-up on the felt, Delicious politely and passively requested his payment, his cash, his cheese.

Lisciotti shook his head. "I win," he said matter-of-factly.

"How do you figure?" Delicious said, noticing the smiles from the gathering crowd.

"What don't you understand? Heads. On. The. Table. I win," he growled. "Heads landed *on* the table."

"What would have happened if it had landed heads-up?" Delicious asked as he grudgingly paid his fifty bucks, chalking it up to yet another lesson learned.

"I woulda won that too," Lisciotti said, smiling. "Just gauging how much you have to learn."

The Chicago regulars were concerned that Delicious was too nice. The conventional wisdom is that a successful pool player has the heart of an ice-pick murderer. Delicious was severely lacking in this department. He'd destroy a player at the table and then, feeling almost guilty about his triumph, pull up his untucked shirt to expose his belly. "Look at it this way," he would say to the humiliated opponent. "At least you have a better body than I do."

Early on at Chicago, Delicious beat a road player out of a few hundred bucks playing nine-ball. Afterward he confessed that he felt uneasy taking the man's money. To him, this wasn't some preppy college kid or fast-living drug dealer or shark with a well-heeled backer. It was just another guy trying to make a living on the road. "Don't you ever feel guilty hustling a guy out of his money?" he asked the regulars.

"Yeah," Lisciotti said, snorting. "Sometimes I feel so guilty I don't try to screw the guy's girlfriend after I've busted him." He stared hard at Delicious. "You got a lot of stick. But if you're going to make it, you really gotta get in touch with your inner mother-fucker."

Kid Delicious never did channel that inner motherfucker. But late one night, a few weeks into his stay, he became a full-fledged brother in the Chicago fraternity. At the time, Procopio had been backing Billy "the Kid" Lanna, a former junior champion from Rhode Island with abundant native talent but questionable ballast under pressure. To Procopio's way of thinking, if he could just bolster Billy's confidence and see to it that his mental toughness caught up to his shotmaking, he'd have a world champion on his hands.

Billy, though, was having a rough time of it in the money games Ralph was brokering. He would play terrifically in spurts and then inexplicably misfire when it mattered most. As word of his struggles spread across the pool firmament, players from as far as California made the trip to West Haven to try to beat Billy and bust Ralph. At the end of Delicious' first week at Chicago, Puerto Rican Pete and his portly backer, Gypsy — both well-known figures in the pool kingdom — drove up to West Haven from Manhattan. It took Pete, a no-nonsense player with beady eyes, pursed lips, and a laconic manner, just a few hours to beat Billy in a race to ten games and start to head home, $1,000 to the good.

But before Pete and Gypsy reached the door, Procopio offered them a chance to double their winnings by beating the fresh meat — the heavyset kid who'd been watching on the periphery, his shirttail hanging out, his pants pulled halfway up to his sternum. "Why don't you play him?" Procopio suggested, fishing ten hundred-dollar bills out of his pocket. The two visitors responded with a shrug that seemed to say, "Sure, if you insist, Ralph, we're happy to take more of your money."

Using a video camera he had stored under the cash register, Procopio taped the race to ten. It was two in the morning, prime business hours at Chicago Billiards, the joint was crackling with electricity, and a few dozen spectators were perched on surrounding tables to watch. As Delicious ambulated from shot to shot with a goofy smile welded to his face, Procopio, the stakeholder and videographer, provided color commentary. "Ladies and gentlemen," he said in a mock Howard Cosell intonation. "Theeee Kid Delicious RRRrrrrrunnnnNNNNN-out!" Across the room, Puerto Rican Pete seethed.

At nine games apiece, Delicious, still grinning as if he'd just heard a joke that no one else got, calmly ran the rack and guided the final nine ball into the corner pocket. He walked proudly toward Gypsy, who was already unfurling his bankroll to pay up. Pete instructed Ralph to "turn that fucking camera off." Procopio obliged, and so, alas, posterity was deprived of what, according to multiple sources, came next: Pete, enraged by this rare defeat — to an overweight, unknown teenager, no less — chased Delicious around the table, threatening to kill him.

Puerto Rican Pete simmered down before he could assault Delicious. Which was in keeping with the unwritten code of conduct at Chicago Billiards. Despite the flow of testosterone and heavy emotion that came with winning and losing big money, real ugliness was rare. For all the jawing and grief-giving, there was an unmistakable esprit de corps and an unspoken rule of decorum among the regulars. (Another reason for the implied social contract: a visit from local law enforcement could well have sounded the death knell for Chicago.)

As for other vices — gambling notwithstanding — Procopio, the born-again Christian, was intolerant. If players wanted to drink or take a hit of pot, they knew to do it in the parking lot. Nor was theft a problem. There may have been a lot of cash floating around, but only a fool or a masochist would hold up an establishment that attracted so many toughs, drug dealers, and other unsavory types. The same went for inside jobs. During his first week, Delicious slept with his bankroll tucked securely in his underwear. (Plenty of pool players have had their wallets carved out of their pants pockets as they slept.) But he soon realized that his money was safe even if he left it out in broad daylight. Anyone accused of stealing from another regular would be instantly ostracized, and besides, they'd just end up gambling the money away anyway. Plus, with Ralph's infusions of cash, money was essentially irrelevant.

So too was hygiene. In fact, sanitation was so thoroughly neglected that Chicago made a frat house basement look like a Victorian tearoom. The best pool player alive today, Efren Reyes, a superstitious sort, sometimes will not shower during a tournament, fearful that he might wash away his good luck. Some players at Chicago had a more mundane reason for not bathing regularly: they didn't feel like it. Along with the *thwok* of balls and the classic rock on the jukebox, farts, burps, and other bodily noises completed the Chicago soundtrack. The toilet was routinely stopped up, so the live-in players weren't above grabbing a spool of toilet paper and defecating al fresco behind the building.

At one point, every resident who had used the shower contracted athlete's foot. The culprit eventually fessed up, explaining that he'd been afflicted by foot fungus for years but never sought a cure. Why? He claimed that few things in life gave him more pleasure than picking dead skin from toes, even if it made his feet raw. "My mother got mad because I wore out the rug at the top of her stairs from rubbing my feet on them so much," he told the peanut gallery. "If I don't get rid of athlete's foot for my own mother, you think I'm getting rid of it for you guys?"

The various health-code violations — the rancid food in the refrigerator, the unholy accumulation of pubic hair on the bathroom floor, the shower fungus, the occasional rodents — didn't particularly bother anyone. At least not until a well-dressed, well-groomed recent college dropout arrived at this den of dishevelment. It was early 1997 when "Bristol" Bob Begey started parking his Acura in the driveway and swaggering up the stairs.

Handsome, physically fit, and strung tighter than piano wire, Bob was a college freshman, if in name only. In striking contrast to the obese kid from New Jersey who'd dropped out of high school and spent months in mortal combat with his depression — in striking contrast, in fact, to most aspiring pool sharks, who tended to have noirish backstories filled with drug abuse or absentee parents or dire poverty — his background was relentlessly normal.

Bob grew up in a three-bedroom ranch house in Bristol, Connecticut, a sleepy town best known as home to ESPN's worldwide headquarters. In high school he was a popular jock who played on the basketball and soccer teams and went to the prom with a pretty girl. He was an indifferent student, but he passed his classes just fine. His vices didn't extend much beyond sucking down a few cold ones on the weekends. With a slightly conceited, no-bullshit personality and clean-cut good looks, he recalled a Tom Cruise character before the predictable transformation from insufferably cocky jerk to sympathetic hero.

As a freshman at Central Connecticut University, Bob spent the majority of his time playing pool in the basement of the student rec center and on the raggedy tables of student dives. He had just picked up the game, but it fed something in him. He would wile away the hours trying to master the subtleties of pool. The delicate spins and patterns were slow in coming, but on marksmanship alone he could beat just about anyone on campus.

Conventional as his upbringing was, Bob always had a restless streak, an abiding sense that he wouldn't be content living the stable middle-class life of his father, a manager for Southern New England Telephone, or his mother, an administrator for a local doctor. Early in his sophomore year of college, with his grade point average resembling the interest rate on a savings account, Bob took a deep breath and called his parents.

"I think I'm dropping out of college for a while."

"Is everything okay, Robert?" his mother asked.

"Yeah. It's just that I want to pursue my dream."

"And what is that?"

"I'm going to try and make it as a pool player."

A patch of silence descended.

"You told this to your father?"

Bob promised his parents that if he didn't make it in three years, he would return to school and get his degree. He and his father, a stoic former military man, barely exchanged a word when Bob moved out of the dorm and back into his childhood bedroom. His concerned mother couldn't hide her disappointment either.

To pay for his table time, Bob landed a job running the basketball concession at Lake Compounce, a small amusement park in Bristol. When some sap paid his two bucks for a chance to shoot a free throw on a cockeyed goal, Bob would place one of the bills into his apron and tuck the other into his pocket. By the time he'd clocked out, he might have $100 in singles in his pockets. When you're starting out at pool and lining your pockets with an extra $500 in cash every week, it's a good thing. The scam ended, however, when Bob missed a day of work and, curiously enough, the basketball concession grossed twice as much money as usual. When he returned, his boss stationed him at the ring toss, right next to the supervisor's station. He quit that afternoon.

By then, Bob had ventured through the looking glass of pool. He became known as "Bristol Bob," or simply "Bristol," and he worshiped at an altar covered in green felt. A pool hall in Southington, Connecticut, offered a daily special, all you can play for $10. The management didn't figure that anyone would wait for the doors to open at eleven and leave at closing time, thirteen hours later.

Bristol Bob would play a guy for $20 and lose badly. Two weeks later, he would offer to play him again for $50. "Are you nuts?" the mark would ask, unaware that Bristol had practiced every day since their last set. Bristol would beat him, and the sap would think it was a fluke, so he'd want to play again. *Hey, fine with me, pal.* Pretty soon Bristol Bob was making $200 a night hustling.

Bob's disposition was at once ideal for pool and singularly ill suited for pool. A relentless perfectionist, he practiced and re-practiced shots until they became second nature. He was deeply interested in the *process* of pool. He would fixate on his break or his kick shot, deconstructing his mechanics, borrowing the family video camera to study his stroke. *Elbow up, head up, weight shifted just right.* Eventually he'd find that slight glitch — moving his fingers a fraction of an inch up the throat of the cue or transferring his weight to his front foot — and make the necessary alteration. Just as he worked out in the gym, so vigorously that his arms became lined with cables of veins and his body fat dropped to negligible proportions, he assiduously devised regimens and systems to try at the pool table.

Bristol wasn't the most naturally gifted player, and he was disadvantaged by his late start; he didn't begin playing seriously until he was nineteen. But of this he was sure: no one was going to be more dedicated. Pool became an intensely personal obsession. Once outgoing and popular, Bob isolated himself, cutting himself off from his pre-pool existence. Ryan Soucy and the others in Bristol's circle of high school friends witnessed their buddy's almost cult-like devotion to pool and eventually stopped calling to invite him to hang out.

At the same time, competitive to a fault, he couldn't bring himself to play at anything less than full speed. The subtle cadence of the hustle? Bristol simply couldn't abide the thought of letting the other guy win. There was no setting the trap with Bristol. If he played, he wanted to annihilate the other guy. He wasn't going to lie down for anyone, no matter how much it might pay off in the future.

So too was his hair-trigger temper counterproductive. A cardinal rule of pool is that you don't externalize your emotions. Bristol would miss an easy ball — "dogging a hanger," in the vernacular — and, after spraying profanities like AK-47 fire, his eyes would squint in fury and stare at the ball as if to say, *What the fuck are you still doing on the table?* Then, having lost his concentration, he would start to hit balls concussively just to offload some of his rage.

Hustling pool is a lot like making a cold sale: it's vital to establish a rapport with your counterpart. Arthur Miller once wrote of salesmen, "You have to not just be liked, but well-liked." Same in pool. The successful hustler makes everyone in his force field immediately comfortable. When Bob strutted into a pool hall with his tight jeans and well-coifed hair, snorting derisively and refusing to drink a beer or have a smoke, the locals either wanted nothing to do with him or else wanted to kick his ass. When an opponent gave him a lousy rack, he wouldn't just request a rerack. The veins in his neck would bulge and he'd fire off a hail of f-bombs.

In spite of himself, he kept improving and was soon a solid B player. While he wasn't at the pro level, he was fast becoming one of the better sticks in Connecticut. The cue was starting to feel less like an implement and more like an extension of his arm. He had mastered English and draw (essentially, sidespin and back-spin) and subtle tricks for getting out of trouble. He found a run-ning mate in Bob Kobus Sr., an eccentric Connecticut jazz guitar-ist then in his forties who once played with Natalie Cole. Kobus played a mean game of pool and always seemed to know where to get action. For months, the two Bobs drove all over the Northeast, winning $100 in New Haven, $200 in Piscataway, $100 in Bing-hamton. Late at night, driving back to Bristol after a score, Kobus explained to his protégé that the time had come for him to get out of the boat and see if he could swim on his own. "If you really want to get to that next level, Bob," Kobus said, "you gotta start spending time at Chicago Billiards."

Bristol would play through the night and leave Chicago at sunrise and return to his middle-class home an hour away—where the toilet seat wasn't covered in urine, where rancid, half-eaten burg-ers didn't adorn the windowsills. When his parents went off to work, still hoping to hell that their son's devotion to pool was just a bad phase that would soon pass, Bristol slept away the day. In the late afternoon he would rise, shower, and drive back to West Haven.

Bristol was thrilled to find a place where he could always get a game against a better player and learn the sport's black arts. He felt that he was improving his stick nightly. Time and again, he lost $40 games to a kid named Chuck Altomare, but Bristol fig-ured the experience was worth the money. The pool scene was un-beatable; it was Chicago's culture, such as it was, that affronted his sense of fundamental decency. All those degenerates and their bodily noises and their flabby, pasty bodies. And for the life of him he couldn't figure out why rational adults would play world-class pool through the night to win $5,000 and then lose it back by ac-cepting a mindless bet that they couldn't drink a gallon of milk in fifteen minutes without vomiting. (When a road player attempted this feat, it ended, memorably, with a sprint to the bathroom, fol-lowed by a barf to end all barfs.)

Bristol took few pains to bridge the culture gap. While everyone else ate greasy Chinese take-out, Bristol decided that hunger was a more appealing option. (Either that or he'd get into his car and go in search of a nutritious salad, which he'd eat conspicuously — almost tauntingly — in front of the others.) While everyone else slept the day away, Bristol was up early doing sets of push-ups and abdominal crunches. For the first time in his life, he was an outsider. He didn't care. To his thinking, it beat the alternative. The general contempt was mutual. With his devotion to a slick, well-groomed appearance, his college background, his "day student" nonresident status, and the cocky intensity that fueled him while he played, Bristol drew icy stares and cutting remarks. It took barely a week before his last name became a punch line. "Begey. Be gay. Get it?"

If Bristol operated at a frigid remove at Chicago Billiards, he quickly bonded with one player. During one of his first sessions in West Haven, Bristol played a set against Kid Delicious, the well-liked, goofy kid. The two were roughly the same age, among the youngest of the regulars. With the exception of an abiding passion for pool and a deep desire to wring everything they could from the sport, they could not have had less in common. One fought a constant pitched battle with his weight; the other scarcely had any body fat. One was warm and genial; the other, cold and abrasive. One was passive to a fault; the other had the sort of temper that begged for anger management. One, even when he wasn't warding off depression, had a low self-image; the other dripped with confidence.

But as they played, they laughed easily and talked so much they sometimes forgot the score of the set. Constitutionally incapable of disliking anyone to begin with, Delicious immediately pegged Bristol's air of superiority as a mark of insecurity. "He's not quite sure he has the skills to belong here, so he acts like he's better than everyone, like he doesn't need pool as bad as the rest of us do," Delicious once explained to the rest of the rogues' gallery, attempting to defend Bristol. "Get past that and he's a good guy." He admired Bristol's "heart" at the table, his raging competitive nature, his willingness to take on his betters and lose, knowing that it would ultimately make him a stronger player. And he was downright jealous of Bristol's ability to maintain his self-discipline in a den of slackers. What Delicious would give for the will power to eat salads and start the morning with an exercise regimen!

In Delicious, Bristol saw not only a lavishly skilled pool player who fired off balls with ruthless accuracy, but a laid-back kid with a gift for making friends and sucking tension out of a room with his disarming personality. Delicious would miss a shot and betray not the slightest bit of anger; he'd smile that silly smile, crack a joke, and get back to the business of pocketing balls on his next turn. Bristol wondered whether this guy was really so blissfully sweet and naïve, or whether "self-deprecating nice guy" was simply part of Delicious' hustling persona, a ruse to get an opponent to relax before going in for the kill. Regardless, what Bristol would give for that kind of temperament!

Delicious won the set handily. He was a level above Bristol as a pool player and two levels above him as a pool *thinker.* Bristol noticed that while he was thinking one or two shots ahead, Delicious had already conceived a plan for positioning himself for the entire rack. After Delicious pocketed his last ball, they shook hands warmly. After that, without ever formally discussing it, they formed a sort of noncompetition agreement and made a point of never again playing each other for money. Only for fun.

Pool halls tend to come and go with roughly the same half-life as fresh-cut daisies. A law of pool nature: action never clusters in one place for long. One year, it's in Detroit. The next year, Detroit's cleaned out and the big money games move on to Tulsa or Tacoma or Tampa. Sometimes business stinks: if table time runs around $10 an hour, it can take an awful lot of business just to cover the costs of rent and labor. Sometimes the owner needs to liquidate to pay off debts from other business interests. Sometimes a road player busts the regulars, drying up the action that had greased the skids.

In the case of Chicago, well, it's hard to cite a specific cause of death. Like a balloon that slowly and steadily deflates, Chicago gradually lost its vitality. By the end of 1998, the action had all but dried up. Glitzier pool halls opened up in central Connecticut. Foxwoods and Mohegan Sun, the burgeoning, newly opened Indian casinos less than an hour north on I-95, had siphoned off some of the gamblers. But above all, Ralph Procopio seemed to have gotten the pool bug out of his system. He came around less and less often, and the days when he drummed up impromptu tournaments with a few thousand dollars going to the winner were a thing of the past.

Like cockroaches scattering from bright light, the regulars went their separate ways. Some tried to make it as professionals. Others hit the pavement as road players. Portuguese George Texiera, an early convert to the Church of Poker, claims he began making a six-figure income winning online hold 'em tournaments. Bristol girded himself to face his father's disappointment and headed back home. Delicious already felt a wave a depression coming on as he packed up his gear and prepared to return to Jersey and . . . well, shit, he had no idea what he'd do. "It was like we had all graduated from college but didn't have jobs lined up or nothing," he says. "We knew we had to go, but we would have stayed forever if we could've."

So far as revenues ever mattered, Procopio says that the joint was still grossing about $1,000 a week in 1999. But he'd had enough. One day he supposedly pulled Chewy aside and asked whether he would like to take over the business.

"Maybe," Chewy responded. "How much you want for it?"

"I don't want anything," Saint Ralph said. "Just take it."

With that, in the manner of Willy Wonka handing over the chocolate factory to young Charlie, Ralph deeded over Chicago Billiards. For the next few years, Ralph passed by on his way to work every day but seldom went inside. And while Chewy tried his hardest to pump life back into the place that was once ground zero for pool in the Northeast, business continued to flag. By early 2002, Chicago Billiards had been transformed into Chewy's Pool Club. A few months later, it ceased to exist altogether.

Today, a sign for Chicago Billiards remains on the marquee of the West Haven shopping plaza, alongside the Chinese restaurant, the Indian grocery, and the used-CD shop. But otherwise there is no trace of the legendary pool pavilion. As of this writing, there's no tenant in the space where some the best pool players on the planet matched mettle until the sun came up. A For Rent sign resides in the same upstairs window where a group of pool players once leaned out, betting $100 they could direct a stream of piss or a stalactite of phlegm onto the windshield of some unfortunate car below.

3

THE RIBBON OF HIGHWAY

Delicious lost his moorings after he left Chicago Billiards. It wasn't simply that he was out of "work" and had oceans of time to fill while plotting his next move. His entire universe had been upended. He thought he had found his calling playing pool at Chicago. It was an institution of sorts, not unlike the army or college, and everything about the culture appealed to Delicious. He was always comfortable there, and he never thought about what he'd do when the doors shut. Suddenly it was gone, and he was back home in New Jersey, feeling confined and out of place. Everyone woke up at a different time (in the morning!) and spoke a different way and had different ambitions.

In what would become a predictable rhythm, now that he had stopped playing pool, depression paid him an unwanted visit. For the last six months of 1997, after Delicious left Chicago Billiards and returned home, he was locked in a fierce and relentless battle with the doldrums. He would spend hours in the carapace of his room, and was often still in bed when his folks came home from work. He would endure long jags of crying. Cocooned under the covers, he could barely force himself to stand up. A trip from his bedroom to the kitchen to get a bite to eat made for a major achievement; a trip to the shower was akin to running a marathon. He went days without leaving the house, and the weeks were weighted with an unshakable feeling that life wasn't worth living.

Mental illness — which includes depression, bipolar disorder, and social anxiety disorder — remains a largely insoluble riddle and an intensely personal battle. As the author William Styron wrote in his memoir, *Darkness Visible:* "Depression is a disorder of mood, so mysteriously painful and elusive in the way it becomes known to the self as to verge close to being beyond description. It thus remains nearly incomprehensible to those who have not experienced it in its extreme mode."

But this much is known: it is an equal opportunity affliction, a disease that doesn't discriminate on the basis of race, gender, or class. Among the afflicted: Elton John, Robin Williams, Halle Berry, Barbara Bush, and Winston Churchill, who referred to his depression as "my black dog," an unwanted companion that seldom left his side. Abraham Lincoln suffered lifelong depression. Some historians contend that half of the American presidents since 1879 have battled mental illness at some point in their lives.

We know that heredity is a major factor. (In Delicious' case, a number of family members, including his paternal grandfather, who had to be institutionalized, suffered from depression.) And we also know that with a combination of psychotherapy and medication, and with lifestyle choices like exercise and sobriety, mental illness can be successfully managed, if not treated outright. (While Delicious had been diagnosed as a teenager, his mortal fear of physicians caused him forgo treatment, and his fear of "not feeling like myself" caused him to forgo medication.)

When depression enveloped him, Delicious experienced most of the classic symptoms. Persistent sadness? Check. Decreased energy? Check. Irregular appetite and sleep patterns? Check and check. Feelings of emptiness? Check. But beyond that, he had trouble articulating the gloom. Asked to describe a particular cut shot he'd hit a decade ago, Delicious could offer an eloquent disquisition. Asked what depression *feels* like and he'd say, "You feel like shit, basically — that's about as good as I can explain it. Either you have bad feelings or you just don't care about things. You're either upset or you're like 'whatever' about things you know you should care about."

His family would see him lumber out of bed in the afternoon, leaking tears, and they'd ask, "What's wrong?" All they would get in return was a snort or a shrug. Truth was, Delicious didn't know what was wrong. He knew he was suffering from depression. But by being so willfully ignorant and so defiantly opposed to seeking treatment, he had little sense of what that really meant. He knew objectively that he had plenty going for him and that he shouldn't be feeling so low. That he was so low only heightened his self-loathing and his feelings of inadequacy.

To make matters worse, as is the case of many people afflicted with depression, Delicious' mental health was complicated by addictions — in his case, to food and gambling. It had always been unclear what came first. Did his addiction to food and the subsequent weight gain foster his depression? Some psychologists would assert that losing gobs of money by gambling compulsively, or gaining gobs of weight by eating compulsively, leads to low self-esteem and, in turn, depression. Others would contend that depressed individuals have low levels of the neurotransmitter serotonin or dopamine, another neurotransmitter, associated with feelings of joy, reward, and achievement. When Delicious eats or gambles to excess, he is compensating, in effect self-medicating, by replicating the jolt of dopamine. Delicious never much cared about cause and effect. He just saw it all as part of a single vicious cycle.

He understood the irrationality of gambling, at least gambling on games of chance — not on games of pool, where he could control the outcome. But like so many pool players, action at a poker (or craps or blackjack) table could sometimes be as seductive as action at the pool table. So it was that, in late 1997, lacking the rush of pool hustling and the social network of Chicago Billiards, Delicious was making nightly "A.C. runs" — trips to one of the casinos in Atlantic City. He'd leave in the darkness, around one or two A.M., return before dawn, and crash.

In addition to the intoxicating gambling rush, the casino con-

ferred something else: an opportunity for Delicious to be The
Man. Fanning his money, buying drinks, having his car parked
by a valet, it all made him feel like a somebody, a distinction that
had eluded him growing up. For a night, anyway, he'd slip into
character and pretend to be James Bond in Monte Carlo or some
high-rolling Hollywood mogul in Vegas. At the craps table he was
the center of attention, the bon vivant cheering on the other players or good-naturedly taunting the dealers and pit bosses. "How
do you guys stay in business?" he cackled after a successful roll.
Never mind that he'd likely be down hundreds, if not thousands,
at that point.

   Dave and Doris Basavich grew increasingly worried about their
son. Food would disappear from the refrigerator, dirty dishes
would pile up in the sink. Dave would come back from work with
a full tank of gas and it would be half empty by the next morning.
They rarely saw Danny, as he was either asleep or at the casino.
Dave Basavich was so worried about Danny's melancholy that he
stayed up waiting for his son to come home from Atlantic City so
they could have a serious talk. In what was surely a first in the an-
nals of child-parent relations, Dave issued the suggestion, "Maybe
you should go back to trying to play pool for a living."

Mental health professionals tend to gnash their teeth when they
hear the notion that physical activity can cure depression. This ig-
nores the chemical and biological component and implies that if
the mentally ill would just "get their act together" or "buck up"
or hop on a treadmill, all their troubles would disappear into the
ether.

   But Dave Basavich was on to something that night. Pool func-
tioned as Delicious' natural mood elevator. Once he managed to
overcome inertia and get himself to a pool hall, he would instantly
feel an improvement. In December 1997, as the fog of depression
was finally starting to lift a bit, Delicious' cell phone pealed. A
smile formed inside his goatee when he saw the number pop up
on caller ID. "Bristol Bob! How the hell are you, buddy?"

   Like Delicious, Bristol wasn't doing particularly well. He too
was reeling from the closing of Chicago Billiards. He was living at

home, trying to scrounge up whatever action he could in central Connecticut, ignoring his parents' persistent pleas that he place his pool cues on a flaming pyre and get on with his life. Tight as money was, Bristol was determined to resist surrendering himself to convention. The thought of returning to college or getting what his folks called a real job held no appeal.

Delicious and Bristol connected instantly. For hours they talked on the phone, mostly commiserating about their hopeless love affair with pool. They recalled the "cast of freakin' nut jobs" at Chicago Billiards. As ever, their surface differences were dissolved by a mutually held belief in the truth and romance and righteousness and dignity to be found in hitting six-ounce balls across felt-covered slate into a half-dozen unforgiving leather pockets. That and a shared restlessness, a natural tropism for adventure and unpredictability.

Bristol had a proposition. He had signed up to play in a small tournament at Country Club USA in Chelmsford, Massachusetts, a sprawling pool hall near the New Hampshire border, renowned as a spot for action. While it was too late for Delicious to enter, did he want to come up and try to grind out some money, maybe even catch someone big? He could stay with Bristol in a $39-a-night motel down the road from Country Club USA. They'd back each other and see where things stood at the end of the weekend. Flattered by the invitation and thrilled for a reason to flee New Jersey, Delicious gladly accepted and piloted his "grandma-mobile"—a white Cadillac Cimarron his father had recently bequeathed him—to Chelmsford.

Bristol played abysmally in the tournament. Early in his first match, he dogged a gimme shot on the eight ball. He lost his cool and, with it, the match. Not that it much mattered. As so often happens at even the biggest tournaments, when the sanctioned play ends for the evening, the real competition begins. Delicious and Bristol had no problem finding action, mostly against vastly inferior New England players. Back in the mix, back to making games and staying up late and getting up at whatever o'clock, Delicious was having too much fun to notice that his symptoms of depression were no longer bothering him. Without having to sweat much, he and Bristol each made more than $1,000 during their first three nights. When the tournament ended — the champion taking home a purse that was laughably small, especially compared to the amount being wagered in the after-hours action — most of the players stuck around and continued gambling.

Bristol and Delicious knew the drill: the inferior players who had lost money were getting increasingly desperate to recoup their bankrolls. In order to lure the winners back to the table, they either gave up exceedingly generous weight or put odds on the money, offering, say, $1,200 for the chance to win $2,000. Superior players the likes of Bristol and Delicious could clean up. After five days in Chelmsford — accounting for lodging, three meals a day, and Delicious' bar tab — they were up $3,000. Then Scotty Townsend showed up.

Even given the low standards for eccentricity in the pool world, Scotty Townsend cuts a singular figure. With shoulder-length dirty-blond hair, a slightly sinister smile, a large compendium of tattoos, and a beer bottle as a constant companion, Townsend looks more like a Metallica roadie than a pool roadie. Growing up dirt poor, he learned to play on a homemade pool table, six empty coffee cans serving as the pockets.

Townsend is a native of Monroe, Louisiana, and his legend includes stories of wrestling alligators on the bayou. Asked about the veracity of this hobby, he laughs. "Rasslin' gators? Who told you that?" *So we got our facts wrong?* "Hell, I don't rassle 'em. I catch 'em!" More Townsend lore: once, killing time in the parking lot of Herman & Ann's Billiards in Dothan, Alabama, he saw a raccoon scurry into a dumpster. Townsend dropped his conversation and dove into the dumpster. After a symphony of odd noises, he emerged proudly from the detritus gripping the raccoon by the nape. "Caught the rascal!" he said, grinning triumphantly.

Townsend arrived in Chelmsford on a hot streak, fresh from Quebec, where he claimed to have won a wheelbarrow full of Canadian dollars playing against an accomplished French-Canadian player who rivaled Kid Delicious in girth. A local railbird who'd been admiring Delicious' play over the weekend quickly brokered a game between Townsend and Delicious. "Hell," Townsend crowed, "I already beat one fat guy last week. Guess I'll have to beat another this week." They agreed to play six-ahead for $2,000, with the railbird backing Delicious. Bristol took an additional $1,000 in side bets.

Already in-stroke, Delicious ran three racks to start and within an hour had beaten Townsend. Townsend took a long pull on his Budweiser, smiled his Luciferian smile, and demanded a $2,000 rematch. No problem. Delicious was in a groove and happy to continue. Up five games, he hit a clean break and, like a pianist's cadenza, completed the performance with two trick cut shots that displayed his virtuoso gifts. After paying off a gleeful railbird, Delicious and Bristol were now up $4,000.

Townsend banged his beer bottle on the table and demanded another $2,000 race. "Whatever you say, Scotty," Delicious said, a goofy smile frozen solid on his face. This time it was Townsend who was grooving his shots in the beginning. As the match progressed, the momentum swayed, Delicious taking a lead that put him within a few games of running out, only to have Townsend go on a run. Then the reverse occurred, and Townsend closed out the set. "Hell, yeah," he shouted. He took his cash and repaired to the bathroom. Meanwhile, Delicious' backer said he'd had enough. He was $1,000 to the good now and figured he'd quit while he was ahead. He thanked Delicious and disappeared.

Predictably, when Townsend returned from the john, he picked up his cue and demanded to play another set. There's no faster way to run afoul of pool's honor code than to "quit winner," to decline to give the losing player a chance to earn his money back. But Delicious had little choice. "Sorry, Scotty," he said, exaggerating his remorse for dramatic effect. "My backer left."

Townsend slammed down his beer bottle. "Screw that. Put the money over the light and rack 'em."

"Sorry, Scotty, but I'm done."

"What kind of bullshit is this?" Townsend demanded. "What kind of a sissy quits winner?"

Delicious responded meekly, "I guess you're looking at one. Again, I'm really sorry. I'll play you for a few hundred, but I ain't gonna play you without a backer. You can appreciate that, can't you?"

Balling his fists, cartoon puffs of steam practically emanating from his ears, Townsend stared down Delicious. In the corner, Bristol prepared for the melee by removing his watch. Before anyone could throw down, Delicious piped up.

"Look, Scotty," he said. "You could kick my ass. You're built like a brick shithouse and I'm a fat guy who ain't never been in a fight in his life. Or you can let it go tonight, and next time we run into each other, I promise I'll give you a chance to win your money back. I'll come down to Louisiana. You can come to Jersey. I don't care, I'll even meet you halfway. We'll meet up again, you know we will."

Townsend slowly unballed his fists. "I'm coming hard after your fat ass next time I see you."

"I'll be waiting, Scotty," Delicious shot back. "Meanwhile, I'll buy you a beer."

Within minutes, Townsend was at the bar, an arm draped over the opponent he had just wanted to beat to a pulp. Bristol looked on with slack-jawed awe, knowing that if he had been in Delicious' place, they'd be cleaning up the plasma right about now. By his reckoning, he and Delicious had been in business less than a week and had cleared around $5,000.

In what would prove to be a familiar theme in Kid Delicious' pool-playing career, the infusion of wealth was short-lived.

It was after two in the morning when Delicious roused Bristol from a deep sleep. A few of the local bangers Delicious had befriended during the week had just tipped him off to a man named Asian Al, who, they said, had come from Tennessee to play in the Chelmsford tournament. The wire on Al was that he was a slave to a wicked gambling addiction and had lost a bundle playing money games. Now he was desperately looking for a poker game. Delicious heard the word "poker"—code for "still another chance to gamble"—and was immediately enticed. During his stay at Chicago Billiards he had become a pretty fair Texas hold 'em player. But here was the real kicker: Asian Al scarcely knew the rules. He just wanted to gamble. This would be like shooting marlins in a barrel.

Bristol unleashed a hail of f-bombs, but he got up and helped push the beds into a corner so they could set up the poker game in their room. Within an hour, one of the locals stuffed wet towels underneath the door to seal any odor — a trick as familiar to road players as to college freshmen — and circulated a joint. Bristol had little use for drugs, but at a time like this, he took a reluctant hit for the sake of building rapport. Delicious was less ambivalent. He took a long drag. They could both tell that the joint was laced with something far more potent than pot. Bristol collapsed face-down on the bed. Delicious kept playing but felt as though he had been smacked on the head with a frying pan.

As the game progressed, Delicious found himself losing an awful lot of hands. And Asian Al, the novice poker player from Tennessee, was winning plenty. An unkempt man of thirty or so with asymmetrical hair and hopelessly unfashionable clothes, he provoked sympathy. Sometimes he claimed to have only a pair, but when he threw down his cards, the other players would laugh and inform the "lucky son of a bitch" that he actually had a flush. "Sank you!" Al would respond giddily. "Me no even know!" The sun hadn't come up and Delicious was already down more than $1,000.

Eventually the angel dust or the acid, or whatever it was in the joint, wore off. Still face-down on the bed, Bristol came to and was stunned by what he saw. Before the game had started, he had noticed that Asian Al sported oddly elongated nails on both his pinkies. Now, lying on the end of the bed, his head turned at just the right angle, Bristol watched as Al held his cards and, using his long pinkie nails, reached into the space between the buttons of his shirt. With almost subliminal speed, he pulled another card from the inside of his shirt. Clearly, while everyone else had been playing with five cards, Asian Al had his choice of six or seven. Bristol recalled it as one of the slickest moves he'd ever seen. On the one hand, he wanted to kill the motherfucker. On the other hand, he had to respect the guy's skill.

Bristol suppressed the urge to take a swing at Asian Al. Instead, he got up from the bed and demanded that Delicious accompany him to the motel vending machines. As they walked down the hall, he told Delicious what he had just witnessed.

"You sure?" Delicious asked. "I think the guy's just having amazing luck tonight."

"Fuck that. The Chinese guy is cheating, and everyone else is in on it," Bristol snapped. "How are you doing, anyway?"

"I'm down more than a grand," Delicious said sheepishly.

When Delicious and Bristol returned to their motel room, it had gotten considerably more crowded. Asian Al was now flanked by two other Asian men. One of the locals asked if there was a problem.

"Damn right there's a problem," Delicious said, trying his hardest to sound menacing. "My buddy thinks Asian Al is cheating."

The locals offered to examine the deck. Bristol requested that Al shake out his shirt. Al shrugged and stood up, revealing no cards. "Maybe we should call it a night," another of the locals suggested. As everyone left the room, it was clear they had all been in cahoots and were now heading off to divvy up the $1,200 or so they had just scored from the redoubtable Kid Delicious.

"What just happened?" asked Delicious.

"You just got played like a fucking fiddle," Bristol said. "That's what just happened."

It was time for Bristol and Delicious to leave Chelmsford. The question was, where to next? Neither had a compelling reason to return home, especially now that they'd accumulated a respectable bankroll. For Bristol, staying on the road meant a reprieve from his parents, particularly his martinet father, who was growing impatient with his only son's vocational decisions. As for Delicious, he reckoned that it was in the best interest of his mental hygiene to stay active. They decided to leave Bristol's silver Acura Integra in Chelmsford and depart, destination unknown, in Delicious' Cadillac. It was mutually understood — never formalized in a discussion, much less in a contract — that they'd split their winnings and their losses fifty-fifty, split expenses down the middle, and never bet against each other. They'd simply start driving and continue barnstorming until the money ran dry. And thus was consecrated the unlikely union of Bristol and Delicious, Inc., surely one of the more successful partnerships in the history of pool hustling.

It's axiomatic that road players need to win four out of five games to sustain themselves. Winning three out of five won't cover expenses, their "nut." The ratio becomes more dire if the road players in question have no semblance of a game plan. Bristol and Delicious left Chelmsford with designs of hitting Snookers, a well-known room in Providence. But they lacked so much as a map in the glove box, and after missing an exit on the Massachusetts Turnpike, they arrived in Providence much later than they had hoped. They then spent an hour asking strangers, "How do we get to Snookers?" By the time they finally arrived, the money players had left. Their gas, food, and lodging tab for the day hovered around $150. Their winnings totaled $0.00. Rule one: a $10 truckers' road atlas — this being the days before GPS — pays for itself a hundred times over.

As they would later learn, it was a disguised blessing that there was no action to be found in Providence that night. Like an athlete in any other sport, a pool player's state of mind has a direct bearing on performance. You've been sitting in a car for hours, pissed off from driving around and not finding the place you're looking for. You're stressing out because you've spent all this money and you haven't earned a nickel. That's when you get burned. On a day like that, a pool player is better off not even picking up a stick.

The first day of their joint venture, the differences in temperament and lifestyle between Bristol and Delicious quickly surfaced. When they stopped at a McDonald's off I-95, Bristol ate a salad and looked on in horror as Delicious inhaled two bacon, egg, and cheese biscuits, containing fifty-two grams of fat. At the height of his tennis powers, Björn Borg was fearful of gaining a single pound, lest it mess up the mechanics of his stroke. Suffice to say, Kid Delicious didn't share this thinking.

In Bristol's eyes, it often seemed as though Delicious intentionally ordered — over-ordered — the most fat-laden food he could. Ever since they'd left Chicago Billiards a few months back, Bristol noticed that Delicious' belly had expanded like an inflated inner tube. The fattening food sickened Bristol, and he was even more repelled by his partner's complete disdain of discipline. "Watching you eat that shit," Bristol told Delicious, "is like watching someone with lung cancer smoke cigarettes."

When Delicious licked the last vestige of runaway cheese off the wrapper, he tossed the trash into the back seat of the Cimarron. Bristol went ballistic, launching into a tirade about how, if they were going to be spending countless hours in the car, the least they could do was keep it clean. He explained that his partner's lapses in cleanliness spoke to a larger deficiency. "You do stuff like that and it shows that you've got no pride, no dignity," Bristol said, now doing a full-on Bob Knight. "You want to be the best pool player in the world? You gotta respect yourself more." When he looked over at Delicious, he saw a silly grin on his face. Which pissed off Bristol that much more.

Delicious had a philosophical take. *We both treat our bodies like temples. We just worship in different ways. You exercise yours and keep it in shape. Mine, I have to feed mine all the time.* Besides, his weight had no effect on his pool. As for Bristol's complaint that Delicious ordered more food than he could possibly eat, Delicious also had an explanation: "Sometimes I just like to look at food. Just having food nearby comforts me."

Then there was the dispute over music. Delicious' taste was eclectic, and sometimes he grew fond of a song or an album and played it repeatedly. At Chicago Billiards, he would buy a dozen plays on the jukebox, spending them all on a single wretched song, something on the order of Kansas' "Dust in the Wind." His new CD of choice was *The Very Best of Cat Stevens*, which Bristol dismissed as "pussy music." Bristol told him that a fondness for the Led Zeppelin and Doors CDs he'd brought along was not a matter of taste; it was a matter of right and wrong.

After a few small scores in Massachusetts — Delicious took an easy $100 off a Worcester drug dealer with an inflated sense of his pool skill; Bristol took $250 off a kid named Tony P., who had allegedly won a million dollars playing blackjack in a casino and lost it back to the house within a month — Delicious and Bristol decided to drive to Quebec in search of Luc Salvas.

A flashy French Canadian then in his mid-thirties, Salvas — appropriately nicknamed "the Machine Gun" — is known as the world's fastest player, firing balls not with the considered calm of a sniper but with the rat-a-tat of a gangster squeezing off rounds on an Uzi. According to pool lore, he once won a set off the legendary Earl Strickland in ten minutes. Twice Salvas was named the Canadian Player of the Year, but the wire on him was that the longer a set went on, the more likely he was to get burned by his rapid-fire pace. With only the vaguest idea of where to find him, Delicious and Bristol left Boston in the late afternoon, motored up I-93, then I-91, and crossed the Canadian border early the next morning.

On the fringes of Montreal, they checked into a Novotel. Bristol promptly went to work, sweet-talking the blond clerk to reduce the rate — "Hell, yeah, I'm in Triple-A," he lied. "No, I don't have my card, but you believe me, don't you?" — and negotiating a "daily double," a trick he first learned at Chicago Billiards. Because pool players keep vampire hours, if they can finagle an early check-in and a late check-out the following afternoon, they can cram in two intervals of sleep for one low price.

When they woke up in the late afternoon, they explored Montreal. This is the way most pool players see cities — not by going to the usual tourist attractions, but by hanging around bars, strip clubs, pool rooms, and diners that snap to life once the sun sets. The pair had a late-night "breakfast" of "smoked meat," a Montreal version of a pastrami sandwich, and hit the town. At one downtown pool hall, they asked if anyone knew the whereabouts of Luc Salvas. Delicious scribbled on the back of a business card the name of a pool hall Salvas owned in Salaberry-de-Valleyfield, Quebec, forty minutes or so east of Montreal, on the St. Lawrence Seaway. They returned to the hotel, crashed, and woke up late the following afternoon. They promptly checked out — completing the daily double — and went about finding Cool Hand Luc.

If they struggled to find the addresses of pool halls in New England, they were hopeless looking for a spot in a town where the signs were in French. After two hours of driving on snow-lined local roads, they reached a ramshackle joint that resembled a log cabin. The parking lot was filled with pickup trucks, but inside it was surprisingly lifeless. No music warbled from speakers. The conversation at the bar was conducted in low rumbles. The fastest-moving objects were opaque clouds of cigarette smoke. The clientele was exclusively male, mostly bearded French Canadians who looked like a crew of Quebecois lumberjacks.

Bristol and Delicious picked up house cues and banged some balls as they sucked down Molsons. When they went to the bar to reorder, Delicious asked if Luc Salvas, the owner, was anywhere to be found. Everyone had a good laugh. Salvas' place, Dooly's Billiards, was in the opposite direction. After some grumbling in French, one patron in a wool hat with the stocky build of a former athlete who had let his body go to seed, stood up and asked if Delicious wanted to gamble on some pool. Bristol quickly accepted and started walking toward the table. Delicious extended his hand to the local. "I'm Danny. He's Bob. He's happy to meet you, even if he ain't polite enough to say so himself."

It was clear that the local wasn't in Bristol's league. His technique was virtually nonexistent, and his stroke had an awkward hitch that any decent player would have sought to correct. When Bristol suggested they lag for break, the local's ball hit the rail and caromed back almost to the side pocket. When they agreed to race to six for $80 U.S., or $100 Canadian, Delicious was secretly relieved that the poor overmatched local wasn't going to lose big money.

Against all odds, Bristol lost the first game. It occurred to him that maybe his opponent had hustled them and had concealed his speed as they warmed up. But he was more pissed off at his own play. Struggling with his composure, Bristol demanded better racks and then took a break to implore the manager to "turn down the fucking heat." When friends of the local approached the table to watch, Bristol snapped, "If you're gonna stand here, at least shut the fuck up."

Still testy, Bristol had a slight lead when the local took aim at the one ball, but the cue ball was lodged behind the two. He kicked the cue into the rail and, almost simultaneously, it hit the one and the three. "Ball in hand for me," Bristol asserted.

"Bullshit," the local shot back. "It was a good hit."

"Bullshit," Bristol said, flecks of spit coming from the corners of his mouth. "It's ball in hand. It hit the three first."

As the intensity grew, a hush fell over the place. Delicious sidled up to his running mate. "Let it go, Bristol."

"Fuck that. These fuckers are cheating."

"Let. It. Go."

Six or seven buddies of the local, each looking as if he could play for the Montreal Canadiens, were now standing. "Just shut up and play pool," one said.

Bristol spun around. "Which one of you fuckers just said that?"

At that instant, Bristol was blindsided and body-slammed into the wall with a resounding *boom!*

He bounced off the wall and cocked his fist, ready to unleash some fury, but he pulled back when he realized his attacker was his road partner.

"What the fuck are you doing, Danny?"

"I know you took the money and gave it to that bitch!" Delicious screamed in a paint-peeling voice, reaching an octave that he had never before hit.

"What are you even talking about?" Bristol said, dumbfounded.

"Don't lie to me, asshole," Delicious shot back. "I know you gave that bitch my money. We're going back to the hotel to straighten this out."

"I'm in the middle of a set," Bristol whined.

"Screw the set. You're forfeiting."

Delicious then turned to the locals. "Sorry, guys. We gotta go. Nice playin', and you can keep the hundred there under the light. Don't pay attention to this jackass. He didn't take his medication."

Bristol's temper had a way of simmering down as quickly as it flared up. And by the time he and Delicious had finished their shouting and reached the car, he'd come to the conclusion that his comrade's quick thinking had spared them a Canadian-style ass-kicking.

As they screeched out of the lot, Delicious was still livid. "You gotta stop being a jackass, Bristol, or this isn't going to work."

"But that guy was wrong," Bristol said defiantly.

"It doesn't matter who was right and who was wrong," Delicious shot back. "We're in their room. There were eight of them. There are two of us. And one of us has never been in a fight before."

"I was standing up for what was right. Have you *ever* done that in your life?"

Delicious ignored the question.

"You're allowed to get mad sometimes, you know. You're allowed to have a confrontation. It's okay if someone doesn't like you."

Delicious didn't respond, and Bristol filled the vacuum.

"Plus," he said, "you know how close I came to bashing your face in?"

"Fine," Delicious said. "At least that way only one of us would have gotten his ass kicked."

The solicitude struck a chord with Bristol, who exhaled. When he said, "Okay, I hear what you're sayin'," it almost passed for an apology.

"Here's all I'm saying: act like a hothead like that again and you'll need a new road partner."

They drove through the night to Toronto in uninterrupted silence.

Toronto has a reputation for being a sort of lotus land for road warriors. Too many hustlers to count have been stung in Detroit or Buffalo, only to recoup their losses in Canada's largest city. Sloppy as they had been in Montreal, Delicious and Bristol arrived in Toronto with a spot and a plan of action. When Delicious was a teenager, he and a stakehorse took a quick road trip from New Jersey to Buffalo. Delicious acquitted himself well and even won a few hundred off Dennis Hatch, then a young local player who was already being hailed as a future star. But eventually Delicious got busted for $800 by Dale Sweet, a snooker specialist from Toronto.

On this bitterly cold night, as Delicious drove the Cimarron into Ontario, he probed the deep folds of his wallet and found a scrap of paper containing Dale Sweet's phone number. When Delicious reached Sweet, he told him he'd be passing through and was looking for some action, figuring — correctly — that Sweet would recall Delicious as the inexperienced teenager and have no clue just how radically he had improved. "Sure," came the eager response. "You can come by right now if you want."

Since he was a teenager, in the early 1980s, Sweet has owned the Silver Cue, a modest players' room on Toronto's east side. Well liked and well respected in pool circles, Sweet made a habit of giving road players courtesy action, a $100 or $200 set, when they came through town. But, having known Delicious for years, and confident that he knew his opponent's speed, Sweet played for real money, starting at $500 a set. Though he hadn't slept in nearly twenty-four hours, Delicious was in-stroke and won a marathon set. Immediately they agreed to play another for $500.

Clearly chastened by his implosion a few nights earlier in Quebec, Bristol chatted up the railbirds and bought them a few rounds. After the first game, he took them up on their offer of side action, putting $500 on Delicious to win the rematch. In keeping with an unwritten rule that pool-hall owners steer road players away from trouble, Sweet pulled Delicious aside. "Tell your backer buddy not to gamble with those guys."

"How come?" Delicious asked.

"They're gangsters, and they're not going to let you leave with their money."

"Thanks, Dale."

Delicious quietly told Bristol to call off his side bets. Suppressing his urge to argue, Bristol nodded and canceled his bets. The railbirds groaned, but Bristol explained that he'd miscalculated his bankroll. When he bought them another conciliatory round of Labatt Blue, they stopped complaining.

Mainlining coffee to keep awake and alert, Delicious played Sweet for another $500. The set was collegial; in spite of the sketchy characters on the rails, there wasn't a whiff of tension. Again, Delicious' wires were connecting, and he ran out the last three games to take another $500. Almost apologetically, he accepted the greenbacks—salmon- and puce-backs in this case, since the currency was Canadian.

"Don't worry, Dale," he said. "We'll be back."

"Where ya headed?" asked Sweet.

"Off to find a motel," said Delicious.

"Why don't you crash at my place?"

Sweet, it turned out, lived in an apartment a few blocks from the Silver Cue. While Sweet's invitation was a way of making sure Delicious didn't quit him and skip town, it was also an exceptional show of hospitality. Bristol couldn't help but marvel at it all. He would beat guys and they would want to kick his ass. Delicious would beat guys and they would want to invite him to spend the night. "Kid Delicious," Bristol said, slapping his buddy on the back on their way out, "the master of the soft hustle."

Bristol and Delicious crashed on the floor of Sweet's sparsely furnished apartment. When they woke in the afternoon, they were surprised to see a slight, wiry, Filipino kid with a buzzcut and a wispy, starter-kit mustache rummaging around in the kitchen. It was another aspiring pool player, Alex "the Lion" Pagulayan, who had been billeting at Sweet's for months. Delicious and Pagulayan connected immediately. When Sweet left to tend to the poolroom, Delicious, Bristol, and Pagulayan hit Toronto hard, peregrinating from a Filipino karaoke bar to a casino to other nocturnal venues.

Meanwhile, word had spread around Toronto's poolscape that the portly road player had game but was having trouble finding action. Bristol, though, matched up well against local B- and C-level shooters and did the bulk of the playing. While the stakes were never high, he won consistently, bolstering his confidence and his bankroll. After a few weeks in Toronto, lodging for free on Sweet's floor, Delicious and Bristol were up more than $5,000.

Before long, Sweet demanded a rematch against Delicious. Sweet had found some backing and proposed a $1,200 set at the Silver Cue—on a table he knew intimately. Delicious realized that under pool's honor code, he couldn't object, not after the way

Sweet had taken care of him. The following night, with $2,400 resting above the light, they played a lengthy set. Neither player was at his best, but Delicious' conservative, painstakingly slow playing eventually carried the day (the night, actually). As he ran out the last rack with a cold-blooded cut shot and took the money — now $2,400 — he wore a look of guilt.

It had become too awkward to continue crashing at Sweet's apartment. The road players said their goodbyes to Sweet and Pagulayan — whom Delicious would see many more times down the road — and, with a bankroll of more than $10,000, lit out of Ontario and headed back to the States. Riding shotgun, Bristol counted the money, so pleased with the haul that he chose not to point out just how ridiculous his sidekick looked swaying his head to the cheesy Savage Garden tune on the radio.

Their plan was first to stop in Chelmsford, where Bristol's Acura had been sitting for weeks, or so they hoped, in the parking lot of Country Club USA. Then they'd take a few weeks to regroup. They'd work the phones, try to pick up some spots, then sketch out their next odyssey.

As Toronto's skyline receded behind them, Delicious called his parents to announce his return. He hadn't spoken to them in weeks, but he disarmed them as effortlessly as ever. "Sorry I haven't called in a while," he said somberly when they answered. "I've been busy becoming the top-ranked pool player in all of Canada." He looked in the rearview mirror and smiled at his reflection.

4

LIFE ON THE RAIL

THROUGH THE POOL GRAPEVINE, the crew at Elite Billiards had heard about the scores in New England and Canada. When Delicious returned to New Jersey, he was feted like a conquering hero. His first night in the place, he was greeted by a chorus of "You da man, Dan!" and slaps on the back. He had represented his "home" poolroom with honor, and, in a small way, they claimed his victories as their own. Jokingly — but not really — the railbirds at Elite asked Delicious whether they could be his road partner on his next jag.

He got a similarly warm reception at his house. On his first day back, he surreptitiously placed a stack of hundreds in the family vault. He then played Scheherezade for his parents, regaling them into the night with his adventures, glossing over the losses and embellishing the wins.

For years, Dave and Doris Basavich hadn't known quite how to react to their son's pool jones and all that went with it. It sure wasn't the career they'd envisioned for him, especially since they'd moved from their Brooklyn store so that Delicious and his sister, Kimberly, five years his junior, could attend the kind of public schools that send their graduates to college. Delicious rarely called home from the road, but when he did, it was jarring never to know where he was. ("Boise? Last time we talked you were in Baltimore!") On the phone he spared them few details, so Doris and Dave got plenty of guns and bookies and hookers along with the breathless accounts of pool triumphs.

At the same time, the memory of their tormented son's dropping out of Manalapan High and threatening to kill himself had never lost its terror. Pool hustling wasn't their first choice, but the fact that *something* was giving their son such pleasure and inspiration and a reason to get out of bed went a long way toward easing their concerns. They also recognized his exceptional talent. When Delicious was winning local tournaments as a teenager, Dave and Doris showed off the write-ups in the local newspaper. "You'll know he's really made it when he plays pool for money and doesn't ask for a loan," a friend once told them. Well, here Delicious was, a full-time player, and he was doing fine on his own.

If Doris took a whatever-makes-him-happy attitude, her husband went a step further, secretly admiring his son's path. As a young adult, Dave Basavich had had plenty of wanderlust and an appetite for adventure, before it was extinguished by a mortgage and kids. He rarely admitted it, but there was something exceedingly cool about having a pool hustler for a son. Let his tennis partners brag about their kids making dean's list at Rutgers or going off to law school. His kid was threading the back roads, a terrestrial buccaneer, plundering poolrooms. Dave Basavich loved to hear the stories. He had a hard time with the dramatis personae ("I forget, is Frank the Terminator or the Exterminator?") but gorged himself on every last detail. Soon he was referring to himself as "Daddy Delicious."

Those first few days back, Delicious walked around in a state of euphoria. Part of it was the Odysseus-returning-from-his-quest treatment. But there was also an afterglow from his performance on the road. In addition to beating a legion of players — some of them damn good — he'd won an internal battle, proving to himself that he could make a living as a pool player after all. He knew from the guys at Chicago Billiards that it's impossible to hustle forever. Fine with him. He'd go on the road busting as many guys as he could. Then he'd become the best pro in the world. Like a ball kissed with the right amount of English, everything was breaking perfectly.

Then, within days, depression paid him an extended visit. One night he went to bed feeling beset by worries no more profound than what movie he would watch the next night. But he woke feeling as though he were wearing a lead jacket. He retreated into himself, barely able to draw the strength to get out of bed. He would tell himself that he was fat and worthless, liked by no one and mocked by all. Failure, he convinced himself, was his destiny. Hot tears flowed steadily down his cheeks, and suicidal thoughts crept in.

"What's wrong?" he parents and sister asked him repeatedly.

He was never able to formulate an answer.

Pool was at once a blessing and a curse. The sport had always been his refuge. Armed with a maple cue, inhabiting a realm defined by the edges of a table, Delicious felt instant sanctuary. He would arrive at a poolroom with flagging spirits and after a few racks all would be transformed. Delicious refused to submit to psychotherapy or revisit the antidepressants he'd once been prescribed, and the more his parents pressed him, the more resistance he put up. Instead, he told everyone that pool served as his medication. "It makes my head right" is how he once put it to Bristol.

At the same time, if you were to itemize activities that are most conducive to optimal mental health, pool hustling would be near the bottom of the list. After hereditary factors, the biggest risk for depression is stress. Alone on the road, playing high-pressure games of skill for significant sums of money, with little margin to cushion a loss — that might be stress distilled to its essence. What's more, social stability and a solid home life are known to improve mental health. Tethered to nothing but his cue, the road player goes for months without seeing friends; he lives out of a duffel, eats and sleeps in strange places at erratic hours, and seldom has long-term romantic relationships. His sense of place is often nonexistent. All told, you'd be hard-pressed to conceive of a less stable life. "One of the first things we tell depressed patients is to try and end isolative behavior, to try to improve sleep hygiene, to adjust their circadian rhythms," says Dr. Michael Lardon, a prominent sports psychologist. "Basically everything about the lifestyle of a pool hustler would seem to perpetuate mental illness."

Although he doesn't disagree with Lardon's observation, Dr. Eric Hollander, chair of the psychiatry department at Mount Sinai School of Medicine, submits that it's not such an illogical career choice. "Someone with bipolar disorder or impulse control problems often has a hard time functioning in a structured situation. He often ends up in an occupation where, for instance, he doesn't have to report to a boss." In pool hustling, "you're talking about an activity where you can be excellent in brief bursts and rise to the occasion. Then you can crash. I can see why someone with a mood disorder might do okay in that setting."

A few hours north, in Connecticut, Bristol wasn't doing much better. Toward the end of the Canada trip he had loosened up socially and made a conscious effort to plane some of his rough edges; but with that, a layer of self-discipline was stripped away. Back home, with some money in his pocket, he stayed out drinking with the boys. For the first time that he could remember, he started oversleeping, which cut into his practice time. On plenty of afternoons his father would march into Bristol's room and wake his son. "You're sleeping your life away, Bobby," he would bark. Bristol's success on the road had done little to convince his parents that he wasn't hopelessly screwing up his life. *Bet you get a pretty good pension plan out there playing pool, huh, Bobby? They pay for your health insurance too?*

After a few weeks at home, Delicious and Bristol had decided by mutual accord to hit the highway for another hustling jag. They equipped themselves with a fat truckers' atlas, but their itinerary was no more specific than *head west*. It wasn't where they were going that mattered, it was the fact that they were going. Like Jack Kerouac and Neal Cassady, they shared a sense that the road was filled with vast possibilities, an open invitation to craft their own adventure. Somewhere in the folds of their map, deep in the hinterlands, they just knew that the big score was out there.

This time, they headed out in a cherry-red Hyundai Tiburon that Dave Basavich had swapped his son for the Cimarron. The Tiburon was almost laughably impractical, a sleek, petite sports car ill suited to house two grown men — one of them decidedly plus-sized — on an interstate escapade of indeterminate length. But "Daddy Delicious" reckoned that the superior gas mileage would serve two road players well. He also liked the car's pickup; he entertained romantic visions of his son barreling out of a pool-room with the angry, snookered hillbillies hot on his trail. In his mind's eye, Delicious and Bristol would fold themselves into the Tiburon, peel out of the parking lot, and escape the posse.

On their first day, the car's superb pickup did them no favors. On a numbing stretch of the Pennsylvania Turnpike — "This state is the friggin' Texas of the East," Bristol complained — Delicious was doing ninety or so, taking advantage of the V-6, when a siren pierced the air and a police cruiser popped out of the median. "Fuck," Delicious and Bristol yelled in stereo, as the cruiser trailed them and guided their car onto the shoulder.

Mere annoyances for other motorists, speeding tickets are the bane of the road warrior's existence. One careless piece of driving can wipe out the winnings of a successful day of playing. And because road players are so itinerant, they don't appear in court to challenge even the most bogus ticket. Like long-haul truckers, they pick up the tricks — investing in radar detectors, slowing down after weigh stations where cops lie in wait. But occasionally they get clipped. When they do, they rationalize that the speeding ticket is the road player's equivalent of income tax.

Sporting a patchy goatee and radiating insecurity, the young cop approached the car for the license-and-registration drill. Delicious' antennae picked it all up. He addressed the cop in deferential tones, calling him first "sir" and then by the name above his badge. He inflated the cop's ego and made it clear he was conceding the power dynamic.

Delicious got off with a warning. Bristol smiled wryly and shook his head in disbelief.

● ● ●

The rhythms of road playing are maddeningly erratic. The rush of busting a local player and peeling back on the interstate with a swollen grubstake is tempered by days of numbing inactivity, frittering away hours in gloomy rooms. A week into the trip, Delicious and Bristol had yet to find action and had spent more time than they cared to ponder just waiting.

Still, their spirits hadn't flagged much. For partners in any line of work — cops, lawyers, coauthors — there's often a sort of forced intimacy. Delicious and Bristol were never at a loss for conversation, each holding the other in thrall with stories of their childhood. For Delicious it meant recounting the bullying, the depression, the unconventional adolescence, the burden that comes with being obese. For Bristol it meant stories of athletic glory and backseat romances and his relentlessly, if stiflingly, normal upbringing.

Different as they were, a mutual admiration took hold. In Bristol, Delicious saw a trim, good-looking, self-styled badass, plenty comfortable in his own skin. Bristol was firm and assertive in his opinions and tastes. He seemed to possess the owner's manual for life, always saying the right thing, dressing the right way, and getting the girls. At the pool table, his fierce pride and unwavering discipline offset skills that weren't especially remarkable. Delicious reckoned that if he could get Bristol to loosen up and stop acting like a jackass when he played, he could be a hell of a hustler.

Bristol stood in awe of Delicious' pool skills, his ability to read a table and then fire off balls with ruthless accuracy. But he was equally awed by Delicious' comportment during games — his immunity from pressure and his boundless charm. As for Delicious' convex figure, his ability to sleep sixteen straight hours, his personality quirks, and his fragile mental health, Bristol figured it was all part of the guy's endearing overall makeup. "How come I beat a guy out of a hundred bucks and he wants to kick my ass," Bristol once asked, "and you beat a guy out of a thousand and he wants to bring you home for dinner?"

It was lost on neither of them that in another context Bristol could well have been one of the jock bullies who tormented Fat Danny in high school or at the mall. But they were fast friends in the Confederacy of Pool, and they left it at that.

As they sat idly in a pool hall outside Pittsburgh, they were told that the best action in the area was at Starcher's, in Akron, an old-style billiards barn that had been around for decades and had seen every notable player pass through, from Willie Mosconi to Earl Strickland. So Delicious and Bristol hightailed it to northeast Ohio, arriving early in the morning and checking into an Akron Motel 6 in time to pull a daily double.

The choice of lodging was a conscious one. Like eating on the cheap, they had learned the hard way that staying in down-market motels was a bad idea. You might save a few bucks on the room rate, but tossing and turning on a swaybacked mattress or waking up to a domestic disturbance in the next room will exact a hell of a price on your pool. While they weren't about to drop $200 a night at the Hilton, Delicious and Bristol avoided anything south of a Motel 6 on the hostelry food chain. And they would never sleep in the car, no matter how dire the circumstances. They agreed that if they ever got that desperate, it was a sure sign that it was time to pack it in and head home.

Starcher's was an unthreatening blue-collar joint in a blue-collar section of a blue-collar town. But to Delicious and Bristol it might as well have been the St. Louis Arch, a majestic gateway welcoming the East Coast types to the fertile hustling terrain of the heartland. The full parking lot was an encouraging sight. But Delicious and Bristol sensed immediately that the joint was filled with recreational players, groups of teens and twentysomethings, one less skilled than the next, killing a slow night in the Rust Belt. They retreated to a table in the back corner and banged balls, never drilling more than a few in a row on the off chance someone was taking inventory of their speed.

After an hour or so, Bristol had had enough. He rested his cue against the table and, projecting supreme confidence and jangling his keys, approached a table of thickly built young men who looked as though they had just gotten off their shift at a body shop. Delicious followed close behind. Bristol presented himself as "Bob from Connecticut" and said, "Hey, guys, fifty bucks says I can stand here and throw these keys into the far pocket of that table down there." He pointed to a table across the room. The group looked tentatively at one another, not sure what to make of the interloper's proposition. Finally one guy Bristol had pegged as the easy mark took the bet.

Bristol put a fifty on the table and chucked his keys to the designated table. They landed with a thump, hugged the rail, then dropped into the corner pocket. It was a trick he'd learned at Chicago Billiards: the felt on pool tables is darn near frictionless; as long as the keys hit at the right angle, they'd skid down the rail and settle into a corner pocket.

This was pure hustle, and it had the desired effect. The crowd was more curious and enthralled than pissed off. The gambling spigot had been tapped, and now the money, though not flowing, was trickling. Delicious played his complementary role masterfully, waddling over to the crowd and displaying a stack of four quarters. "Who wants to bet me fifty I can chuck these onto the table and have them all land on heads?" With some girls urging them to do it, two suckers took the bet. This too was a trick out of the Chicago Billiards handbook. Flinging the quarters Frisbee style, Delicious could get them to land on heads every time.

When he'd won that bet and sensed he could divorce the kids from still more of their cash, he asked, "Who's the best player among all you guys?" A tall kid wearing an Ohio State Buckeyes football jersey was quick to anoint himself. "Tell you what," Delicious said, smiling. "We're going to play nine-ball for $200, and you play with your cue. I'm going to play with a broomstick." The teenager, now desperate to save face, had no choice but to accept.

Delicious asked the girl at the counter if he could borrow a broom. By this point, dozens of other players had clustered around the table to watch the two hustlers. Delicious let his foil break and even sink a few balls. Then he took his turn. Ignoring the giggles, and gripping the broomstick as if it were a $5,000 Balabushka cue, Delicious nailed ball after ball, before dogging the seven. (The secret: a broomstick has a larger sweet spot than a standard cue, making it more effective for hitting certain shots.)

Hopelessly psyched out, the kid missed the seven, and Delicious ran out. The place erupted with yelps and laughs.

Within an hour, the two roadmen had ground out a few hundred bucks. Sure, in a perfect world they would have each won a few $5,000 sets. But with a little sleight of hand, they had more than covered their expenses for the day, all the while applying the defib paddles to a lifeless pool hall. As a show of good faith, Delicious went to the counter to pay for the kids' table time. When he returned, Bristol had one of the girls perched on his lap. He stood, pulled Delicious aside, and said, "Do me a favor. Give me the keys to the room and stay away for a while."

"What am I gonna do?" Delicious asked.

"I don't know," Bristol said impatiently. "Just work with me here. You can come back at, like, three or four. Just knock first."

So it was that Delicious spent the next four hours in a nearby Denny's, reading the comics in the *Akron Beacon Journal* while Bristol occupied himself with a late-night cardiovascular workout.

When Delicious and Bristol returned to Starcher's the next night, an army was waiting for them. Word had spread. Half of Akron's twentysomething demographic, it seemed, had come to see the hustlers perform their sorcery.

Delicious obliged. He placed the eight ball in the middle of a table and asked a girl named Allison to stand five feet from the table and hold the cue ball aloft. "I'll put up a hundred bucks that if you give me five tries, I can hit the cue ball out of Allison's hand and knock in the eight." When five twenties materialized from various pockets, Delicious slapped his hundred on the table. After two near misses, he nailed the eight ball on the third try. Again, whistles and hollers all around.

Bristol went next, setting up the cue ball on one rail and the eight ball on the opposite rail. "Okay," he said, "I'm putting up a hundred dollars that you can't walk around the table three times and then hit the cue ball into the eight. All you have to do is make contact. Easy, right?"

A kid neither Bristol nor Delicious recognized from the previous night was quick to volunteer. What novice, after all, couldn't hit the cue ball and make it collide with another ball? With girls giggling and his friends razzing him, the poor sap took his three laps, walking as slowly as possible lest the hustlers were trying to mess with his equilibrium. When he finished his stroll, he leaned over the table, took aim at the eight, fired — and watched in horror as his ball squiggled and spun into the side rail.

This was yet another grift mastered at Chicago Billiards. While the poor mook was orbiting the table, Bristol held his cue. As everyone directed their attention to the kid, Bristol slyly wiped all the chalk from the tip of the guy's cue. Meanwhile, Delicious hid the chalk in his palm. Not only were the East Coast hustlers already up $100; the very people who were getting fleeced were eating it up.

They would have kept coming with more tricks were they not interrupted by a middle-aged black man in an ill-fitting sports jacket who introduced himself as "One-Pocket Harry." Harry had a mountainous afro and wore sunglasses that covered a face with deep creases and crevices. He said that he owned a poolroom in South Carolina, but he had family around Akron and was a regular at Starcher's. He challenged the out-of-towners — "young bloods," he called them — to a $50 game of one-pocket.

All tactics and defense and safeties and subtle bank shots, one-pocket is pool's answer to chess. Players rack fifteen balls, as in eight-ball, but then choose one of two adjacent corner pockets and spend the next few hours maneuvering and nudging their eight balls toward the mouth of the designated pocket in such a way as to prevent the opponent from having an unobstructed shot. It's a cat-and-mouse game.

Like a classically trained musician who specializes in one instrument but can play several others, Delicious was a nine-ball player by nature but could more than hold his own at one-pocket. He accepted the challenge, figuring that he could string Harry along, then go for the jugular when the stakes were sufficiently high.

He figured wrong. Harry played competently, if unremarkably, in the first game. Careful not to reveal too much speed, Delicious shot erratically and lost the set. "Good playin', young blood," Harry said with a cordial nod.

When Delicious asked to play again, for "real money," Harry shook his head. "We can play for fifty bucks," he said, "but that's it." This made little sense to Delicious. The guy had just beaten him comprehensively. Why wouldn't he want to up the ante? But Delicious nodded and racked the balls. By two in the morning, he had won the set, and both players were no better or worse off than when they began hours earlier. "Let's play for some real money now," Delicious all but begged. Harry declined, but agreed to return the following night.

To Bristol's astonishment, Delicious returned directly to the motel, forgoing his usual late-night contribution to the local fast-food economy. Smiling as he patted his belly, Delicious explained to his partner that he was on the road to "six-pack abs" and no longer craved cheeseburgers and fries.

Bristol considered it just the latest indication that his partner was finally adopting some self-restraint. He'd already noticed that their car was no longer littered with empty coffee cups and beef jerky wrappers and spent Red Bull cans. That he hadn't pissed in the sink of a motel bathroom during the entire trip. And he hadn't once requested to make a detour to a casino. Bristol noticed that when his sidekick started to lose weight, the rest of his unfortunate habits began to disappear as well.

Delicious betrayed still more of this newfound discipline the following night. He hoped that Harry had spent the day rounding up backers and was now looking to play one-pocket for some serious timber. When Delicious returned to Starcher's, Harry was waiting for him, but was unwilling to play him even, demanding two balls in weight plus all the breaks.

Negotiating the rules of engagement is a preamble to playing —the foreplay prior to the sex—that can sometimes be as long and as intense as the game itself. Often, one player is either hungrier to gamble or simply more desperate than the other, and capitulates. (That player is usually the one who has to pay for the hotel room later.) Time was, Delicious would have agreed to Harry's handicap just to be in action. On this night, however, he stood his ground. His mantra became: We play even or we don't play at all. Back and forth they went, neither budging from his position. "Come back tomorrow," Harry said, "and see if you've changed your mind."

On the third night, Delicious returned. He hadn't changed his mind. When the impasse persisted, Harry tried another tack. He told Delicious and Bristol that if they really wanted to make big money, they ought to go to Columbus and hunt down a guy named Chris Bartram, who was a big bettor and, according to Harry, "a terrible player." With no better alternative, Delicious peeled a twenty off his bankroll and handed it to Harry, a token of gratitude for the spot.

But Harry wasn't through. "You'll never find the place on your own. Take me with you. I'll get you there and get you a game with Bartram. You give me ten percent, pay my hotel, and pay my way home. It's win-win-win. We have a deal, young bloods?"

Grudgingly, they agreed, and for two hours they sped down I-71, watching the Ohio landscape turn from industrial to rural, listening to One-Pocket Harry hold forth on topics ranging from the virtues of hip-hop to the need for more government spy cameras. The first indication that Harry may have been less than forthright came when they arrived at their destination, Cornfed Red's. For one thing, the place wasn't exactly hard to find, just a few miles off the highway on the south side of Columbus, in a congested strip mall. Far from a hole in the wall, Cornfed's was a massive, twenty-four-hour joint with an array of tables, a full bar, and its own signature hamburger.

Harry's credibility was further undercut when Delicious and Bristol got their first glimpse of Chris Bartram. Baby-faced and built like a young bull, Bartram was by far the best player in the joint. Smart and methodical, he played one-pocket and nine-ball with equal skill. He also wore a thick beard — he would later earn the nickname "Fifty," for his likeness to Ulysses S. Grant's mug on the fifty-dollar bill—which Delicious correctly read as the mark of a hustler who'd become well enough known that he needed to alter his appearance. Bartram, Delicious would later learn, even had his own backer, who staked him in big action.

Practicing on one of the three Brunswick Gold Crown tables with impossibly tight pockets in a corner of Cornfed Red's, Bartram was making easy work of "the Crow," a player so named because, after having suffered a stroke, he'd pull his off-hand from his cue in the manor of a bird with a gnarled talon.

Bristol and Delicious had been steered to Columbus, and their "easy mark" turned out to be an A-level player. For bringing these two Yankee "young bloods" into town, Harry was surely going to get a piece of Bartram's action. By all appearances, Harry had hustled them. (For the record, Bartram steadfastly denies that he and Harry were ever in cahoots.)

Bristol seethed and plotted ways to beat the shit out of Harry, who had, not surprisingly, disappeared. Delicious had another approach. By professional necessity, a road player develops a sixth sense for determining the speed of an opponent and then does a split-second calculus of how they would match up. Delicious reckoned that he could play fairly evenly with Bartram, and that Bristol was better than the Crow. Worst-case scenario, they would break even. Without consulting his wingman, Delicious departed from hustler artifice. "Hey, man, my name is Danny Basavich, and my partner here is Bob Begey," he told Bartram. "I'm from New Jersey, and Bob is from Connecticut. We'd like to play you."

Bartram nodded slowly, and within five minutes they were playing for $500 a set, Bob and Crow on one table, Delicious taking on Bartram on another. Six or so hours later, Bob was down $1,000 and Delicious was up $1,000. Sweating profusely, his face flushed red, Delicious announced he was quitting. "I feel like shit, guys," he said. Bartram interpreted this as a plea to increase the stakes, but Delicious shook his head. "I gotta go back to the hotel and rest. Don't worry, I'll be back."

When he reached the hotel, the Knight's Inn, Delicious collapsed on the bed as if he had been shot. Rivulets of sweat ran down his body. Illness and injury are the Scylla and Charybdis of serious players. They don't just take you out of action; they can cost you a bundle. Like all too many Americans, it is the rare road warrior who carries health insurance, and even the most perfunctory trip to a health clinic can cost hundreds of dollars. Itinerant players often recite the cautionary tale of Ronny Wiseman, a popular road veteran from Detroit who was severely beaten in a Florida hotel's parking lot late one night after a big score. The medical bills totaled close to $20,000 and nearly wrecked him. Knowing that a serious illness would either bankrupt him or force him to confront his phobia of doctors, Delicious came prepared. He rifled through his bag for a bottle of Nyquil, which he guzzled as if it were water.

Meanwhile, at Cornfed Red's ego was getting the best of Bristol. He had promised his ailing partner that he wouldn't put much of their bankroll into action and that he'd quit if he started losing. But it wasn't working out that way. Bristol, playing poorly, lost a few more nine-ball racks to the Crow, at $100 per. Then Chris Bartram tried to rope Bristol into a $500 race to ten, giving up the eight as weight.

Bristol foolishly agreed. When Bartram took a 4–0 lead, Bristol came to the realization that he was out of his league, so he made an offer: "Let me pay $250 and quit you right now." Bartram, not surprisingly, was having none of it. Bristol slammed down his cue and sat in the corner, refusing to continue. It wasn't until an hour later, when Bartram and his backers were reduced to threatening bodily harm, that Bristol played out the set and lost the full amount. By the time he had forked over the last of the twenties, he was thoroughly humiliated.

It was late in the afternoon when Bristol charged into the room at the Knight's Inn. He chucked his cue case onto a chair and kicked the bottom of Delicious' mattress. Aware of Delicious' rich history of hypochondria, he was particularly unsympathetic. "Motherfucker, I don't care how sick you are!" he yelled. "You're going to get your fat ass out of that bed, go back to Cornfed's, and beat those guys."

After he calmed down, Bristol ashamedly explained that he had gotten in over his head and blown $1,000. "You gotta fuckin' bail us out, Dan," he pleaded. Looking like John Belushi after a week-long bender, Delicious stirred himself and lumbered into Corn-fed Red's. Bartram was smiling: he had expected the return visit. "You wanna play a little? Try and win back some of your buddy's money?"

"Sure, but I'm gonna need the eight ball," Delicious said.

"No way, big fella," Bartram said, smirking. "Play me even."

"I need the eight ball. You beat my partner, and we're the same level. You're too good."

For an hour, they negotiated back and forth as if hammering out the terms of a hostage release. They both wanted weight and danced a familiar dance, appealing first to fairness ("It's your home table"), then to a sense of honor ("Be a man and play me on the square"), and finally to creativity ("Give me the eight and play me on the Olhausen table, but you can't combo on the break"). Neither budged. Still, the potential windfall was too great for either to walk away.

Like most road players, Delicious lacked a college education and committed his share of crimes against grammar and diction. But out of occupational necessity, he'd always had a savant-like gift for math and probability. Delicious seized on an idea to break the stalemate: rather than give up weight, they would play even, but Bartram would put odds on the money. They would play ten-ahead. Delicious would put up $3,300 — the entire bankroll, save enough gas money to return to the East Coast. Bartram would put up $4,000. Bartram excused himself to call his backer, Chili — a man so named for his recent success in a local chili cook-off — and returned to announce that they had a deal.

A set of ten-ahead ends when one player achieves a ten-game lead over his opponent. The momentum can seesaw back and forth, and two closely matched opponents might play for days before a winner emerges. In this case, the race barely took an hour. Already feeling like shit, Delicious knew that he wouldn't have much stamina. So — as if it were no more difficult than this — he went on autopilot. Grinning with a sort of clinical detachment, so fatigued that his eyelids were at half-mast, he ran six straight racks and quickly built an eight-, nine-, then a ten-game lead.

"It was as good a run as I've ever seen anyone go on," says Bartram.

Through it all, Delicious was "in the moment," as sports psychologists like to call it. He had no conflicting thoughts rattling around his brain, just the single-minded purpose of making the next ball. He might as well have been in a sensory-deprivation chamber. His opponent, his partner, the railbirds, the money, everything became irrelevant. He no longer heard the music on the jukebox or saw the hottie at the adjacent table or smelled the odors of the poolroom. His pattern of play was simply obvious, all intuition. His liquid stroke was all muscle memory. As he potted ball after ball, there was no suspense. He was going to win, the same way an actor finishes a play or an artist completes a painting. The drama didn't reside in the outcome; it resided in the ways his genius expressed itself.

It's often difficult to describe pool virtuosity. We can visualize a diving catch by a shortstop in foul territory, or a birdie putt on a par-three hole, or a three-pointer from the right baseline. But pool is so heavily predicated on position, it's nearly impossible to appreciate a shot without knowing the precise coordinates of the other balls on the table. An eight ball in the corner pocket is much different from an eight ball in the corner pocket when the cue ball is pinned against a rail with three balls obscuring the object. Even diagrams of a table seldom convey the degree of difficulty or the delicate spins and speed.

At one point, Delicious was compelled to hit the five ball, which was buried behind a cluster. It was an exercise akin to getting from, say, Washington State to California without passing through Oregon. Delicious took his time — as ever — squinting and staring at the diamonds on the table that help advanced players do their geometric calculations. When he slowly reared back, squinting like a marksman, he kicked the cue ball off the opposite rail. After the carom, it circled back — *I was going to go straight, but I thought better of it,* the ball seemed to be saying — and collided with the five ball. The five squiggled through a small chasm and found a home in the bottom of the side pocket. The cue ball kept moving until it clicked the cluster like a chaperone breaking up a party. When the balls came to rest, the cue was directly in front of the six. The others had scattered. "Holy shit," said Bartram, in brief summary.

Suddenly, Bristol and Delicious, Inc., went from financial dire straits to winning $3,000 in Columbus. Beyond the new ration of cash, the victory meant that their road trip could continue. Even before Bartram shook Delicious' hand in admiration, there was a rapport between the two. Something about Bartram — his unassuming suaveness, his professionalism and poise at the table, his mix of quiet dignity and hustler sensibility — appealed to Delicious.

With his action now officially dead in Columbus, Delicious asked Bartram for a new spot. "There's some good action in Toledo," Bartram said.

"Thanks, Chris," Delicious said. "Maybe we'll run into each other again sometime."

While Bristol was grateful that his partner had practically risen from his "deathbed," as Delicious (hyper)dramatically described it, to bail them out against Chris Bartram, self-doubt gnawed at him. His spotty play and spottier gambling judgment at Cornfed Red's had punctured his confidence. With Delicious still weak and exhausted from the cold he'd caught in Columbus, Bristol operated as a solo practitioner in Toledo. It was the perfect rehabilitation.

Toledo resembles a sort of Baja Detroit, a small midwestern city with a decidedly working-class, industrial vibe. So, not surprisingly, it's chock-full of poolrooms. For years it was home to the Glass City Open, once one of the better-organized and highly anticipated events on the pro billiards tour. It's easy to get a fix of action in Toledo, and Bristol found his at Glass City Billiards, a somewhat sullen outpost not far from the room he and Delicious were sharing at the Red Roof Inn.

Once asked whether he enjoyed his craft, Willie Mosconi, perhaps the most skilled practitioner ever to have picked up a cue, is said to have responded, "I would no more play pool in my spare time than a headwaiter would wait tables on his day off." Neither

Bristol nor Delicious shared this attitude. Every rack was practically throbbing with possibility and promise. Even when they practiced alone, without the gambler's rush of a potential payoff, pool never lost its appeal. On a table autographed by Johnny "the Scorpion" Archer — who seemed to make an annual ritual of winning the Glass City Open each November — Bristol spent hours limbering up, trying to get back in dead stroke. Playing by himself, illuminated by gauzy light, he cut a Hopperesque figure as he went through his routine, setting down the cue ball here and there, working on the shots that had bedeviled him in Columbus.

Like Starcher's in Akron, Glass City Billiards drew a young clientele. But these weren't giggly, harmless teenagers and young adults, cowed and impressed by a pair of road hustlers. The kids in Glass City wore do-rags and cockeyed baseball caps and copious jewelry and baggy clothes and wispy mustaches — trying like hell to appear like menacing urban toughs and not the white heartlanders they were. Bristol immediately took them for low-level drug dealers, an assumption supported when, one by one, they unfurled wads of bills.

The gambling conditions were ideal: no one was better than a C-level player, but there was an abundance of testosterone and ego coursing through the place. After getting himself in-stroke, Bristol did some reconnaissance work and scoped one local — compactly built, with a straw-blond mustache and a tattoo on his neck — who looked particularly game. He played quickly and cracked balls with unnecessary violence. They were the earmarks of a rank amateur, but the look-at-me attitude suggested the guy thought he'd mastered the sport.

Five minutes later, they were playing nine-ball for $500. The action came with a caveat. Bristol had to play on the local's table of choice. He picked a barbox that was a parody of a pool table, a slick, frictionless surface that had its own laws of physics. In the Gilbert and Sullivan comic opera *The Mikado*, a character is consigned to play "on a cloth untrue, with a twisted cue, and elliptical billiard balls." Bristol could relate. The local knew the quirks of the table, which pockets were tight and which rails were unforgiving. But it's part of the gig: road players — the good ones, anyway — know they're surrendering the equivalent of home court advantage and take that into account when making their games.

Even after hitting some dead rails and watching a few balls skid awkwardly away from their intended targets, Bristol closed out the local without exerting much effort. The loser handed over the five C-notes with a casualness that made it clear he wasn't going to miss the money too much. In the inevitable rematch, Bristol won another $500, as well as an invitation to return the following evening for more action.

Bristol saved some of his best work for later that night. During the set, he had noticed a sweet young thing intently watching him play. Her face was adequately cute, and her outfit — jeans and a T-shirt that appeared to be aerosoled onto her body, calling attention to a tattoo on her back — suggested a woman of obliging virtue. A typical poolroom groupie, Bristol thought. The out-of-town road player had a certain cachet and no-strings-attached appeal. As if it were no less routine or taxing than tying his shoes, Bristol went through his ritual:

Step 1. Seek out said groupie.
Step 2. Bring over "his and hers" bottles of Bud Lite.
Step 3. Make cursory small talk while drinking the beer.
Step 4. Invite said groupie back to the Red Roof Inn, an
         invitation she was sure to accept.
Step 5. Close the deal.

Displeased as Delicious was to have been "sexiled" from his room — especially while nursing a fever — he marveled at his partner's skill with the ladies. Delicious may have lacked inhibition with guys, but around women, painfully conscious of his physique, he'd stutter and sweat and look into their eyes and assume they had no interest in him. Bristol was fearless. He was good-looking and he knew it. He approached a woman with an attitude of *You know we're getting together tonight. It's just a matter of how, when, and where.* The same way Delicious once watched better players execute five-rail kick shots — taking mental notes and envisioning himself in that position one day — he internalized everything he observed of Bristol's pickup moves.

The week in Toledo was good to both Delicious and Bristol. The former recovered from his mega-cold without having to confront his mortal fear of seeing a physician. The latter won more than $2,500, restored his confidence, and still had time to keep up an active social life. By good fortune, as his action was drying up at Glass City Billiards, Bristol caught wind of a small tournament coming up in a few days in the northwest corner of Indiana. On a grim Thursday morning, shrouded by curtains of rain, they motored across the Hoosier State, and before sundown they arrived at Top Notch Billiards, in the Chicago bedroom community of Merrillville.

Unsure whether they would enter the tournament or just troll for after-hours action, Bristol and Delicious tried to be as inconspicuous as possible as they practiced on a back table while angling to get a read on the competition. Delicious hadn't hit a ball in nearly a week, and it was like running into an old friend. There was something instantly familiar, gratifying, and comforting about holding a cue in his hands again and snapping off shots. After an hour or so, a harsh-featured player in a satin plumbing-supply jacket approached him. "Greg Smith wants to have lunch with you tomorrow. Two o'clock in the booth over there."

"Who the hell's Greg Smith?" Delicious asked.

"You'll find out tomorrow, I guess."

5

THE WARSAW PACT

W ITH HIS THROATY Chi-CAW-go accent, slicked-back hair, jowly face, and a gut that had accepted its share of kielbasa and amber-colored beverages, Greg Smith could have passed for a character from the old "Da Bears" skits on *Saturday Night Live*. As his jangling bracelets reflected the overheard light, he spoke to Bristol and Delicious with a strange cadence, his voice suddenly shooting up as he emphasized words that didn't necessarily merit emphasis. Hard as he may have tried to play the part of tough-talking badass — "I'm DEAD SERIOUS here," he kept saying, pounding on the table — it soon became clear that he was another of those endearing, nonthreatening types that populate the pool universe.

Hustlers' road stories often have the ring of classic myths, replete with heroic acts, winding odysseys, fatal flaws, changing fates, and hubris-inspired downfalls. So it's fitting that road sagas also have an oracular *deus ex machina* figure. Smith identified himself as a "pool detective," and before explaining what precisely that meant, he gave Delicious and Bristol an impromptu quiz.

"So if me and youse're playing for five hundred A RACK and you bust me and walk out with five thousand, how many racks have you beat me?"

"Uh, ten," Delicious replied.

"Wrong," Smith growled. "Eleven. KNOW why? Because if you're a REAL POOL PLAYER, you give the guy a free game. A gapper, a walking stick, CALL IT whatever you want. You beat him outta five large and you say, 'This one's on me. Beat me, and I pay you five hundred. I beat you, and you owe me nothing.'"

"Why would you do that?" Bristol asked.

"Two reasons. First, out of respect. He had the heart to gamble with you. He's another pool player trying to make a living. He got kids that NEED FOOD AND DIAPERS, a car that needs gas. Second, your reputation is crucial. You never know when you're going to bump into him again, when you might need a spot or a loan or whatever. Treat people right and you get PAID BACK in spades."

Delicious and Bristol exchanged looks: *This guy is a trip, but he's making sense.*

"Okay, here's another one," Smith said. "If you see me playing and think you can beat me, WHAT'S DA FIRST thing you say to me?"

"Know anyone here who likes to play for a little money?" Delicious offered timidly.

Bristol suggested, "Know anyone who likes to play some pool and make it interesting?"

"Not bad," Smith said. "But you just gave yourself away as a guy who talks the talk. You say something goofy — 'Know if there's any MONEY STICKS in here?' — and they'll think you're such a DOO-FUS they'll be linin' up to play ya!"

Then, with the passion of a tent preacher, Smith recounted the story of one California Jack, a road hustler based in San Francisco, famous for getting the name of a rainmaker — a guy who thinks nothing of losing a six-figure fortune — and thoroughly researching the guy. Jack then moves to the guy's town and meticulously sets his trap.

A favorite ruse: he poses as a disheveled, unemployed schoolteacher and spends weeks getting to know his whale at the local diner or VFW hall, never mentioning pool, much less venturing into a poolroom. Before long, the whale grows comfortable with his nerdy schoolteacher friend and mentions in passing that he plays pool for money. "That's funny," schoolteacher Jack will say, "I used to play decently myself, years back. Love that sport." Just to be polite, the whale invites Jack to play for fun. A few weeks later, they play for a little money. A few weeks after that, they play for a bigger sum. Finally, when the stakes are sufficiently high — and Jack has insinuated himself so deeply into the community that it is inconceivable to think he's a hustler — he plays full speed and busts the guy for $100,000.

"That guy made more money than anyone because HE WAS smart," Smith asserted, now unaccountably screaming. "You know what he looks like? No? Neither do I. Know why? Because he only shows up when he knows THERE'S ACTION."

After this long prologue, Smith offered his sales pitch to Bristol and Delicious. Through his network of trusted sources, he had been tipped off to the pair. Most recently, a veteran road player from Toledo had gushed that "a nice, heavy kid from New Jersey with un-friggin'-believable skills and his buddy, who also plays pretty good," were on a barnstorming tour of the country. "It's obvious you guys have talent and can make some real money," Smith said matter-of-factly. "But it's also obvious that you don't know what DA HECK you're doing out here."

Smith told them how stupid it was to have grifted the locals at Starcher's Billiards in Akron. "You probably made five hundred bucks and pissed away the chance to earn ten thousand." He explained that walking into a pool hall "all willy-nilly" and playing locals in the wrong order can cost a road player thousands of dollars. "You gotta be smart. You gotta KNOW in what ORDER to play guys. You gotta KNOW who to stay away from. You gotta KNOW who has the big backers and who doesn't. A few bad decisions and you're DONE."

Delicious was dumbfounded. "How'd you hear —"

"Don't worry about it," Smith said. "I hear all sorts of things."

Delicious tried to explain that grinding out a few hundred bucks in Akron was their only option.

Smith cut him off again. "Ya gotta be patient. And one UTTER TING — you don't walk into a place with YOUR OWN cue! Ya give yourself away before you hit your FIRST BALL! Use a house cue! Whattaya do if the house CUES are shit? Ya get someone to fetch your cue outta your car. They PRETEND it's theirs and then YA ask them to borrow it."

He looked at Delicious and scolded him for showing his face at the Merrillville tournament. "You know how many guys are here that you'll want to hustle one day? They're all gonna REC-A-NIZE you now!" At some level, Bristol and Delicious knew the central tenet of road playing, but it had never completely crystallized. Now Smith spelled it out in unambiguous terms. "In other sports you want to be known. In this one, once you're known, the jig is up. The clock IS TICKIN', always tickin'. You can make a lot of money or a little money. It's UP TA you."

Finally Delicious took the bait. "What are you gonna do to help us?"

A self-described "star high school athlete" in Illinois in the 1970s, Greg Smith has spent the past forty years on the fringes of sports. One of his many "best friends" is a top harness racer at the famed Arlington Park raceway, outside Chicago. Smith is often at the track, making use of inside information. Another purported best friend, Chico Walker, formerly a Cubs outfielder of minor distinction, once tried to get Smith a job in the clubhouse at Wrigley Field. Smith has worked in the locker rooms of various posh golf clubs around Chicago, where, he claims, NBA players would regularly tip him hundreds.

Early on, Smith discovered that his real talent lay in handicapping pool. He always played a decent game, certainly well enough to know what to look for. One glimpse of a player and he could not only assess the guy's talent level but also his ballast under pressure, his stamina, his temperament. Plus, Smith was sociable, with an easy manner and an ability to chat up anyone. He gleaned plenty of information about other players—who was looking for action, who had just come into money, who was playing well, who was getting divorced or drinking too much or had a habit of giving too much weight—without arousing suspicion.

Before long, Smith became a one-man clearinghouse for information about the Chicago pool scene — what's player X's true speed, what's player Y's game of choice, what's player Z's gambling weakness. In time his territory expanded to all of Illinois, then to the rest of the Midwest, and finally the entire country. Smith didn't even need to set foot inside a pool hall. By working the phones, cultivating a network of bird dogs, and housing countless road players as they passed through Chicago, he became, at least in his circumscribed world, all-knowing. When big action rolled into Oklahoma City, Smith heard about it. When that rich kid in Atlanta was burning through his inheritance playing nine-ball games, Smith was on the case. "When I call myself the pool detective, I mean it," he boasts. "I got eyes and ears in every pool hall in the damn country."

Intelligence and inside information have value in every industry. Pool is no different. With a spot book — a pool Rolodex of sorts — the size of the Manhattan phone book, Smith has a real cottage industry going. A kind of pool lodestar, he steers players to action. When they win, he gets a percentage of the bounty. In the rare event that they lose, he has risked nothing. "But that don't never happen," he says. "Go where I send you, you play who I tell ya to play, and you don't lose."

How does Smith know whether he is being properly compensated? "Like I say, I got eyes and ears in every pool hall. A guy wins five grand and tells me he only won two thousand, I'm gonna find out real fast what really happened. I'm not gonna do anything crazy to get my money. But I'm not gonna take his calls again. But honestly, there have only been a few times I ever got stiffed. These guys are pretty honest. At least when it comes to me."

For Bristol and Delicious both, their interest was piqued, and Smith could sense as much. "Here's how it works with me: the games are won before you ever set foot in the place. You just do as I tell you, play everyone in the order I tell you, and don't do anything stupid once you win a little money, and everyone wins."

"How much of a cut do you get?" Bristol asked.

"Twenty percent jellyroll."

"What if we lose?"

"Do what I say and you ain't gonna lose. These ain't FIFTY-

FIFTY propositions. They're EIGHTY-TWENTY propositions. At WORST."

"How do we know you're not working for someone else and setting us up?"

Like a drug dealer who gives a potential client his initial hit of crystal meth for free, Smith offered Delicious a "no-obligation" spot. "Warsaw, Indiana. Small town not far from Fort Wayne. Take you just a few hours to get there from here. Nice place. Went there the summer before last. Did some fishing by a lake during the day and won a bunch of money playing STRAIGHT POOL and nine-ball at night. Guy named Earl owns a pool hall. Loves to gamble. Guy from Ohio, Bucky Bell, has been playin' at Earl's hall for weeks. Bucky's been around forever, and he used to play great, beat everyone in the country on a bar table. Now he's showing HIS AGE. But over there at Earl's, everyone thinks he's the Tiger Woods OF POOL. There's a Chinaman backer who's won a few grand with Bucky and thinks he's automatic money.

"Here's what you do. Check into THE MOTEL down the road from the pool hall. Bucky is living there too, so be careful not to make yourselves known. Have yourselves a nice dinner. Get down to Earl's. Delicious, you can play a little, but don't show no speed. Act like Bristol's the real player and you're just his backer. Have Bristol get a game real fast against DEM KIDS always hanging out there. Win a little money, maybe twenty bucks. Bucky'll get his backer and come back wanting some action. He won't want you, Bristol. He'll look to make easy money off of Delicious. Set up a game, try to get some weight, and then beat up on ol' Bucky. Then get the hell outta Warsaw."

When he was finished, Bristol and Delicious held each other's gaze. They didn't need to confer.

"You got a deal," Bristol said. "How do we pay you when we've won? Western Union?"

"SCREW WESTERN Union!" said Smith. "They take like ten percent. It'll cost you a hundred bucks to send me a thousand. Just go to DA POST OFFICE. Fill out a money order and send it overnight. It'll COST YA a few bucks."

A pause.

"What do we call you, anyway?" Danny asked.

"Whatever you want, long as you pay me."

"How about 007?"

Bristol and Delicious slept into the early afternoon and then motored back across northern Indiana, bound for Warsaw. The view from the various state roads was all patchwork farms, cornfields, and water towers. Still shaking their heads over 007, they shared a measure of skepticism, but figured they were risking little. And reluctant as they were to admit it, a pool detective was precisely what they needed. They both had ironclad confidence in their abilities, but they also knew that their relative inexperience could bite them in the ass. Bouncing around the country like so many pinballs, popping into pool halls without much of a game plan, was hardly a blueprint for longevity — never mind success — on the road. If 007 was half as good as he claimed to be, he was worth twenty percent.

America can sometimes seem like a sterile, homogeneous monoculture of fast-food franchises, big-box stores, and outlet malls. A travel writer recently noted that it's possible to drive from Maine to California and eat every meal in the same crappy restaurant chain, fill your car with the same brand of gas, and sleep at different franchises of the same hotel. This doesn't hold for pool hustlers. Rooting their way through the country's subcutaneous layer — all those backwaters and remote outposts — keeping odd hours, traveling county roads that run beside hand-lettered signs for yard sales, hustlers get a taste of the true American soul and character. They meet the natives. They drink the local beer at the local dive bars. They eat at the local barbecue pits and seafood shacks.

Bristol and Delicious arrived in Warsaw, quintessential small-town America, a blink-and-you-miss-it hamlet in the northeast corner of Indiana, roughly halfway between South Bend and Fort Wayne. Warsaw boasted a modest main drag, a few mom-and-pop stores, and a complement of family-owned restaurants. They stopped into one for a late lunch. Bristol ordered his customary salad and a grilled chicken sandwich. When Delicious asked the waitress if there were any Indiana delicacies on the menu — "Give me something I can't eat nowhere else in America," he said enthusiastically — she responded that the tenderloin sandwich was the house specialty. A few minutes later, a pork loin, pounded out to the size of a small pizza and then deep-fried, arrived.

The sandwich was just the kind of cholesterol-heavy, artery-clogging mucilage that Delicious would once have devoured with pleasure. He summoned the waitress and handed back the tenderloin, stealing a glance at her nametag. "Sorry, Shannon," he said. "Go ahead and charge me for this, honey, but can I have a salad instead?" Bristol looked on, smiling approvingly. He didn't even mind when the bill came and Delicious, upon realizing that Shannon hadn't charged him for the tenderloin, left a $20 tip.

They then checked into a nondescript motel. With a few hours to kill before heading over to Earl's, Bristol suggested they go for a jog. Delicious' response was short and to the point: "Fuck off."

With uncharacteristic patience, Bristol explained that if Delicious was serious about losing weight, he'd have to exercise as well as eat better. And so they started their jog. Though Delicious barely made it beyond the parking lot before sucking wind and quitting, he had to admit that it felt good to be doing something active. His face lashed with sweat, he went back to the room and tried to squeeze off as many push-ups and sit-ups as he could.

When Bristol returned from his run, he was smiling. "How'd you like running, Big D?"

"It sucked," Delicious said.

"Fine. We'll buy tennis rackets and exercise that way instead."

Later that night, they made their way to Earl's, which was like no other pool hall either had ever entered. A spare structure, it contained a half-dozen coin-operated barboxes and a single nine-foot table. The lights were dim, the floor was uneven, the ceilings were low. Save for a poster on the wall of a squirrel adorned with a witticism about having a big pair of nuts, Earl's had no décor to speak of. How Earl, a pleasant, soft-spoken man with a back condition, ever expected to make money on the place was a mystery.

Bristol handed Earl his Connecticut driver's license as a security deposit for the table time, and he and Delicious grabbed cues off the wall. They noticed that several of the house cues had been autographed by Bucky Bell. Delicious turned to Earl at the counter.

"Hey, who's Bucky Bell?" Delicious asked.

"Player who stops in here from time to time," Earl casually responded.

"He any good?"

"Ain't bad," said Earl, practically pulling a muscle in his arm as he reached for the phone to summon Bucky to get his ass over and take down a pair of out-of-town suckers.

Even at the age of fifty-six, Clarence "Bucky" Bell was better than "ain't bad." A lifelong road player, Bell had trolled the Midwest for action since the sixties and partnered with hustling legends the likes of Billy "Cornbread Red" Burge and Clem Metz. Bucky was born in rural Booneville County, in eastern Kentucky, where his father was a judge. If you were under eighteen, you needed a permit to play pool. When Bucky was eleven, his father wrote him a permit to play one game of pool at the local poolroom. Bucky doctored the permit and kept returning. Soon he was gambling, winning everything from twenty-four gallon jugs of molasses — "I sold them to the A&P manager for two bucks a gallon!" he says, cackling — to a field of cucumbers.

As a teenager, he commandeered a friend's truck and drove from Booneville to the big city of Cincinnati to play a prearranged game. His opponent, though, had gotten into a fight the night before the match and been carted off to jail. With no high-stakes match, Bucky wiled away the day playing the locals. He won enough money to buy his own truck and has lived on the road ever since.

Bell was particularly adept on bar tables, the preferred equipment in the Midwest. He says he made a small fortune in Jackson, Michigan, in the 1970s, beating a string of Detroit drug dealers. Asked about the score, Bell neither confirms nor denies it. "It's just money. One day you have it, the next day you don't. In pool, money is just a token. But I'll tell ya this, for a long time not nobody could beat ol' Bucky Bell."

For all his years on the road, Bucky never lost his country roots. He made no attempt to curb an accent that verged on unintelligible when he crossed the Kentucky state line. A small, sinewy man who weighed 130 pounds on a full stomach, he dressed in sausage-casing-tight Wrangler jeans and a flannel shirt. His features were hard and craggy, his nose beaky, his face pleated by years of hard living. Behind a pair of unfashionable glasses that resembled two windshields, his eyes were strikingly close together, and they almost appeared crossed as he squinted to concentrate on the table. He lived by a certain old-time code of honor. He never did drugs or drank to excess. Although age and failing eyesight exacted a price on his game, he didn't turn down many challenges to play for money. And on the rare occasions when he lost, he always paid up. "Bucky is that rare road player," says Bob Flinders, the proprietor of Rhinos Billiards in Cincinnati and a longtime friend of Bell's. "If you lend him a few hundred bucks, eventually you'll get it back."

Bucky had found an ideal situation in Warsaw. The cost of living was not high: he could rent a motel room down the road from the pool hall for around $25 a night. Plenty of action passed through town, and there was an abundant supply of the hustler's oxygen — backer money. Bucky's reputation as a reliable road player preceded him, and after that first night at Earl's, locals lined up to subsidize his games.

Traditionally, backers front the money and split the winnings with their player, fifty-fifty. This may not seem like a savvy investment, but most backers are so confident in their players' abilities that they're willing to wager a dollar to win fifty cents. In recent years, especially as "dumping" games became increasingly fashionable, some backers have wised up. While they still front the money, if the player loses, he's in arrears for half the amount, collectible the next time he wins. In other words, time was, a player who lost $1,000 and then won $1,000 still went home with $500. Under the new rule, when a player loses a grand and wins a grand, he leaves with nothing. Fortunately for Bucky, this trend had yet to hit Warsaw. He wasn't putting up a dime of his own money for the chance to earn half of the cash resting above the light. So for all intents and purposes, he was playing with house money.

Just as road partners do an elaborate shuffle when they walk into a joint, often the locals have their own well-choreographed dance. A scouting team of lesser players is deployed to help get a read on the visitors' games. As Bristol and Delicious practiced on the large table — Delicious taking pains to miss balls and gripping the cue awkwardly — within minutes they were approached by a tough-looking kid with dirty-blond hair, a nascent blond mustache, and a Metallica T-shirt. The kid challenged Bristol at the "just for fun" rate of ten bucks a rack on one of the bar tables. Delicious, playing the role of clueless backer, consented on his buddy's behalf.

Metallica wasn't near Bristol's phylum as a player, and Bristol did little to camouflage just how good he was. He broke concussively and ran entire racks and walked authoritatively around the table. With Bristol up $40, Metallica quit. The kid was out some money, but he had done his job as a scout for the estimable Bucky Bell. While Bristol put a beating on the kid, Delicious and Earl struck up an amiable conversation.

"You just passing through?" Earl asked.

"Yeah," Delicious said.

"Where ya headed?"

"Back east, Earl. We were visiting my uncle outside Chicago."

"How come you got off the interstate?" Earl asked, no doubt sensing that these were two roadmen.

Delicious didn't miss a beat. "Highway driving gets boring. Figured I'd rather see the real America, even if it takes longer."

"What'd y'all do back east?"

"To be honest, Bob plays pool, and I back him from time to time."

"Really," Earl said. "Wanna play a little?"

"Nah. I don't really play."

"Me neither. Just for, like, fifty bucks."

"Okay," Delicious said. "I think I can afford to lose that."

Kid Delicious playing Earl of Earl's Billiards on a coin-operated bar table was akin to Shaquille O'Neal playing a lunchtime pickup game at the YMCA. But Delicious kept it close, missing shots that he was capable of drilling in his sleep, attempting ridiculous combinations, and taking forever to study the simplest shots. All the while he relished his own performance, muttering "Damn!" when he missed and asking amateurish questions. He did just enough to win the first set, and then obliged Earl's offer of a rematch, and promptly lost.

"Guess we play about even," Earl said, reclaiming the same two twenties and a ten he had surrendered.

"Guess so, Earl."

Around this time, Bucky Bell arrived with his backer in tow. With his avian features and tough, leathery skin, Bucky looked every bit the hard-boiled veteran hustler as he strutted into the hall. As 007 had predicted with almost frightening accuracy, Bucky wasted no time issuing a challenge, wheeling and staring at Delicious. "So, we gonna play a little, big boy?"

Bristol jumped in. "Why don't you play me?"

Bucky continued to fix his gaze on Delicious. "I wanna play the big guy."

"Aw, Danny?" Bristol said. "He don't hardly play. He's just my backer."

"I play about as good as Earl," Delicious volunteered. "You'd destroy me."

Bucky didn't let up. "So," he hissed, "are you small time or big time, buddy?"

"Depends what big time is," Delicious said quietly.

"Thousand bucks a rack."

Bristol laughed dismissively. Then he feigned interest. "If you play him, you're going to have to give him a ton of weight."

"Weight is the last thing your boy needs," Bucky said.

After tense negotiations, the parties agreed that Bucky would give Delicious the last three balls in a six-ahead set. It was a sizable handicap — Delicious essentially needed to hit only the seven ball to win, but he still had to run it out — that is, he couldn't win on a combo. Bristol knew that Bucky had an advantage on the bar table, where breaks are meaningless and you're seldom faced with a long shot, so he demanded that they play on the nine-footer.

Bucky reluctantly agreed to that too. Together, the weight and the table gave Delicious a huge advantage. And Bucky, the veteran roadman, had broken one of the cardinal rules of hustling: don't give up a handicap to a player before you've seen him play at his true speed.

Staying in character, Delicious turned to Bristol. "I'll play Bucky, but you can't get pissed off at me if I lose."

Figuring that Delicious was already intimidated, Bucky tried to fan the flames. "There's some fury up here, boy," he said. "I'm going drill your ass, son. There's fury up in here."

In the end, all of Bucky's sound and fury signified nothing. As with athletes in any sport, pool players reach an age when they begin to decline, their skills irretrievably deserting them. But even in his mid-fifties, with fading eyesight and plenty of miles on his pool odometer, Bucky Bell was a hell of a player, capable of beating ninety-nine percent of his opponents. The problem was, Kid Delicious was in that other one percent. Pitting him against Bucky was a mismatch. Pitting him against Bucky and giving him the last three balls on a big table was verging on a joke.

It took only a few balls for Bucky, Earl, the backer, and the other railbirds to realize that they'd been snookered. Delicious bellied up to the table and, now playing at full speed, put on a clinic, making the balls behave with a logic that was at once ruthless and elusive. After the second rack, there were audible groans from the gallery.

Bucky didn't go down without resistance, summoning every trick he could to take up residence in Delicious' head. At one point, after Delicious had racked the balls perfectly, Bucky angrily slammed his cue and demanded a rerack. Had Bristol been the opponent, fisticuffs would likely have followed. Delicious smiled. "Whatever you say, Bucky."

Within half an hour, Delicious was "on the hill" and needed only to sink the seven ball to end the set. As he lined up the shot, Bucky stood directly in behind the pocket. One of the unwritten rules of road playing is that you don't complain too vociferously about such sharking. It's partly practical: you're on someone else's turf, and grousing to the gallery will be met with indifference at best. But there's also a tacit understanding that the road player has to concede the equivalent of a home court advantage. Sharking is pool's equivalent of the home team fans who paint their faces and clap those horrible ThunderStix noisemakers when the visiting team shoots free throws.

Bucky, of course, had no way of knowing that Delicious was fully prepared for this kind of distraction. When you've had to nail pressure-packed shots during the "sharking allowed" games at Chicago Billiards, with one guy belching in your face and another rubbing his crotch against the rail, Bucky's maneuvers were hardly going to rattle Delicious.

Beyond that, Delicious had always been impervious to choking, immune to collapsing mentally under the weight of the occasion. It wasn't necessarily that he elevated his game when the stakes were high. It was simply that he didn't let himself acknowledge the significance. To him, it was all just pool. Playing for thousands of dollars in an unstylish hall in rural Indiana was no different from playing against himself on the table in the family basement.

"Bucky, you can do whatever you want," Delicious said without looking up. "I'm not missing this shot."

Bucky did, and Delicious didn't. When the last ball descended out of sight, Earl was silent.

Bristol and Delicious took their $4,000. "We'll be back tomorrow, and maybe we'll play on the bar table," Bristol said, neither meaning it nor, for that matter, expecting anyone to believe he had.

The pair quickly folded themselves into the Tiburon and peeled out of the parking lot, kicking up a plume of dust. Daddy Delicious would have been proud of the maneuver. In the car, they couldn't suppress their giddiness. Never mind that the $4,000 was far and away their biggest haul thus far. They had pulled off a real sting, combining their table skills with their skills for deception. They were now experiencing a "hustle high." As they sped down Warsaw's main drag (such as it was), they slapped five, pounded the dashboard, and let out euphoric shrieks. "That was some old-school shit," Bristol bellowed. Delicious whipped out his cell phone to call Greg Smith, their new shaman, with the news.

Delicious recalls the conversation bearing a resemblance to Charlie's Angels when they talked to their inscrutable boss.

"You're awesome, 007! We just —"

"I heard. Four grand."

"How the hell did you already hear —"

"Don't worry about it. Good work. Told you we would DO RIGHT by each other."

The two-man carnival rolled on to the next town. Wired from the adrenaline rush that came with pulling off a textbook hustle, they barreled down a lonely state road toward South Bend. "That was freakin' classic, Danny!" Bristol yelled, slapping the steering wheel. Delicious was glowing too, charged up not only from the theatrics but from his exceptional play under tense circumstances. He assumed that hustling wasn't going to last forever, but damn, he told Bristol, "I could really get used to living this life."

Bucky Bell knew it was time to move on as well. His local backers had been cleaned out, and his star had dimmed considerably in tiny Warsaw. They all agreed that Kid Delicious was a hell of a player. When asked where he was going next, Bucky told the gang at Earl's that he would lie low for a while, head home to Cincinnati or drive to Chicago and stay with a buddy who might steer him to some good action: Greg Smith, who called himself a pool detective.

Danny Basavich, aka "Kid Delicious," in 2005

Danny Basavich,
age fourteen

Danny's parents, Dave and Doris Basavich

The newly
christened Kid
Delicious dazzles
the railbirds.

Diana Hoppe

Clay Patrick McBride

Kid Delicious awaits his turn at the table.

"Bristol Bob" Begey, Kid Delicious's setup man

Bristol Bob, looking as intense as ever

Greg Smith, aka "007," conducts his detective work.

An excerpt from Greg Smith's "spot book," in which he lists the places to go and people to see, ensuring success to a hustler on the road. (Names have been concealed to protect privacy.)

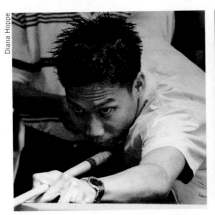

Alex Pagulayan, one of the most skilled shooters in pool's firmament

The estimable Efren Reyes, universally regarded as the best pool player alive today

Five-time U.S. Open winner Earl "the Pearl" Strickland, an icon of Pool Nation

Carlos Santos, aka "the Peruvian Prince," and a slimmed-down Delicious, after Delicious won the inaugural Billiards Channel Challenge pro event in 2001

Carlos Santos, Kid Delicious, ESPN pool commentator Allen Hopkins, and Tanya Harig

Little John Macias, of Hattiesburg, Mississippi, a notoriously high-stakes gambler, takes aim at the cue ball.

Chris Bartram, gambler extraordinaire and one-time road partner of Kid Delicious

Kid Delicious experiences the rollercoaster emotions of the hustling life.

Kid Delicious and his girlfriend, Danielle

6

KINGS OF THE ROAD

THE UNACCEPTABILITY of failure formed one of the cornerstones of Bristol Bob's code. After a lousy night of playing, he would often punish himself. Sometimes it meant going out for a run designed to brutalize his body. Sometimes he deprived himself of a movie he wanted to see, or forbade himself from watching a favorite TV show. Most of all, he practiced. If, for instance, he missed a "spot shot" during a match, he would spend hours at the table perfecting the shot he had botched, no matter how hungry he got.

This creed had a converse: successes were to be celebrated. After a big score or a well-played set, he made a point of rewarding himself with a treat, which could be anything from a milkshake to a woman. Driving west toward Chicago, still buzzing from the "textbook, fucking textbook" hustle in Warsaw, Bristol decided it was time to take his partner on a shopping spree. They drove through the night and, when dawn broke, dutifully stopped at a post office and wired 007 his jellyroll. Then Bristol parked the Tiburon in the parking lot of a Chicagoland mall.

"What the fuck are you doing?" Delicious asked.

"We're gonna sleep for a little bit," Bristol replied. "When we wake up, I'm taking your ass inside to buy new clothes."

A few hours later, Bristol tried to roust his running buddy. When Delicious insisted on continuing to sleep, Bristol took out a cube of cobalt-colored chalk from his case and began painting a mustache on Delicious' face. After taking a clumsy swing at Bristol, Delicious finally woke up and the two walked to the nearest clothing store, the Gap. "We're getting my friend out of these homeboy baggy-ass pants," Bristol announced to one of the salesgirls. "We're going to prove to him that he can get clothes from a regular store and not some big-and-fat store."

Self-conscious about his body, Delicious had always taken a minimalist approach to fashion. Someone once said, "Dressing a pool player in a tuxedo is like putting whipped cream on a hot dog," and Delicious wholeheartedly agreed. He couldn't remember the last time he'd been shopping for clothes and had no idea what size pants he wore. For as long as he could recall, his parents had shopped for him, bringing home shirts and pants from plus-size outlets. To Delicious, the spared embarrassment trumped the unfashionable clothes. "Whatever they brought out, it never fit," he remembered, "and they had to come back with something bigger." He tried to tell Bristol that he'd always simply worn the clothes that made him comfortable. "I don't want to hear it, Danny," Bristol shot back. "You feel better when you look better. That's just fact."

As Bristol made trip after trip to the dressing room, trying on sweaters and khakis and dress shirts, Delicious halfheartedly pawed through the racks. When he came upon a stack of extra-large fleece vests, he tried one on. To his surprise, it fit snugly. It was a minor milestone, the first time in years he could recall finding something off the rack in his size. He thought that he had been losing weight in recent weeks — the benefit of the salads and the exercise — but this confirmed it. He looked approvingly at his reflection in the mirror. "Give me a bunch of them," he told the salesgirl. She picked out five fleece vests, each in a different color, and added them to Bristol's inventory.

In all, they had racked up six hundred dollars' worth of apparel, which Bristol paid for in cash. When the girl at the register asked if they wanted their clothes in separate bags, Delicious

said, "It don't matter, we'll sort it out when we get to the hotel."
They headed out — Delicious to find a salad for lunch and Bristol
to find a tanning bed — leaving the puzzled suburban Gap girls to
speculate among themselves as to the nature of their relationship.

After the Warsaw heist, 007 vowed to ride his new charges "like
friggin' thoroughbreds." And that was just fine by Delicious and
Bristol. Their rap was a good one: Bristol would be the setup man,
playing the shortstops and triggering the gambling. After winning
or losing a bit, the locals would demand to play "the big dude,"
or "your backer friend with the goofy smile on his face." Bristol
would decline, holding out until the locals gave up some weight.
Then Delicious would play lights-out pool. Soon they were operating in seamless tandem, two parts of the same machine.

Now all they needed were spots as fruitful as the one in Warsaw. Over the next few months, 007 steered them to action, and,
like balls on the rail, they caromed from Watervliet, Michigan, to
Kenosha, Wisconsin, to Olathe, Kansas, and a dozen other backwaters in between. They hit yuppie billiards clubs and chrome-
and-leather biker bars. They hustled kids and they hustled senior
citizens. Soon they were grossing a few thousand a week.

In southern Ohio, Bristol suggested that they depart from the
cadence and choreography of their usual hustle and pull a pool
sting so time-honored it had its own name: the Two Strangers.
The setup Bristol envisioned was blissfully simple. Delicious
would wander into the pool hall while Bristol stayed behind at the
motel. Delicious would beat some locals out of $5 and $10 racks.
He'd take the money and buy drinks for the house and charm everyone with the force of his personality. He'd explain that he was
a road player and regale the boys with his escapades. He'd return
the next night, affable as ever. After an hour or so, in would walk
Bristol at his imperious best. "I don't fuck around with hustling.
I take the direct approach," he would announce. "I'm Bob Begey. I have two thousand dollars in my pocket. I want to put it
up against the best player in this town." The locals, thinking they
had a world-class road player in their midst, would gladly back
Delicious against this cocky interloper. Delicious would play well

enough to douse any suspicions of a conspiracy, but he'd leave a few balls short and Bristol would beat him, just barely, in a race to ten. Bristol would take his money and walk back to the motel. Delicious would stick around the poolroom and drink his "sorrows" away, before reconvening with Bob at the motel. Then they'd gleefully get the hell out of town.

Delicious, though, was having none of it. He would willingly concoct stories and play under a pseudonym and splatter cake on his shirt to deceive everyone into thinking he was a fat slob. But he'd never dump a game — lose on purpose and split the money with the victor later. In his moral universe, throwing a match and double-crossing your backers brought dishonor to the sport in a way that lying about your identity or concealing your speed didn't. It was his version of Edgar Allan Poe's telltale heart: he knew that if he were ever to dump a game, he wouldn't be able to live with the secret. "I've never dumped and I never will," he insisted to Bristol. "I couldn't bear having that as a reputation." To Bristol it made no sense: "What's the difference between dumping and lying about who you are? Hustling is hustling." Still, they never attempted the Two Strangers sting.

Delicious, in fact, often showed uncommon conscience for a hustler. If he sensed he was truly busting another player, he sometimes refused the man's money. "Buy me a beer and we'll call it even." Once, in Richmond, Virginia, Bristol played through the night against the best player in town, a strikingly tall lefty. They finished even and agreed to resume the next night. Bristol figured if he could battle with Lefty, Delicious could also handle him, no problem. "I'm gonna say I'm not feeling good," Bristol schemed. "You show up and play him instead."

The plan went as designed. With his partner back at the motel, Delicious proposed a game. "Sure," said Lefty, "I was going to play with this other guy, but he just called in sick, so let's me and you play." Soon Delicious was winning by a substantial margin. In the middle of a set he phoned Bristol.

"Hey, it's me."

"What's up, Danny?"

"This don't feel right. I'm scared."

"What the fuck! How come?"

"I feel like I'm hustling this guy."

"You *are* hustling him."

"Well, if he finds out we're together, he's gonna be pissed."

Delicious let Lefty pull even. Then he quit.

But overall, Bristol and Delicious began accumulating money and stories in equal measure. There was the time they played against a roomful of hillbillies at a Manchester, Kentucky, social club that had a dirt floor and a "no women allowed" policy. "That place was straight out of *Deliverance*," Bristol announced when they were safely back in the car. It was a joint reminiscent of the old Marx Brothers joke: *They were missing teeth and spitting tobacco juice right on the floor — and you should have seen the men!* They left there with $1,000.

They met a man in Wheeling, West Virginia, who couldn't play pool for a lick but won some of his money back by betting successfully that he could urinate across a two-lane highway. ("I swear," Delicious said later, "he had like a double-jointed penis.") They played a woman in Tennessee who lost $200 to Delicious and asked, with a sugary voice and an unmistakable wink, "Is there *anything* I might be able to do to get it back?" "Sure, honey," he said. "Play me another set."

They ate food they had never tried before and heard accents they thought existed only in movies. At an age when their peers were taking those quintessentially collegiate cross-country road trips, they were also taking part in that American ritual. Only the circumstances were just a little less conventional.

Apart from the pool and the winning, Bristol and Delicious were enjoying the role-playing that hustling required. Both had a facility for slipping into a character. One night they were cousins who happened to be in town for a family funeral. Another night they were fraternity brothers on spring break driving out to Las Vegas. Their collusion in these improv acts — what the less charitable might call lies — went a long way toward solidifying their bond.

All the while, Delicious was eating little besides salads and exercising every day. As they plotted their itinerary, Bristol made sure their motel had either a swimming pool or a tennis court. Before eating breakfast, they would swim laps or play a few sets of tennis; before going to sleep, they would dutifully do their push-ups and sit-ups. Delicious' body seemed to be melting. In wasn't just that his belly was starting to resemble a balloon slowly losing air. His legs, his neck, even his fingers were getting thinner.

His jeans became so comically baggy that Bristol referred to him as Kid Hip-Hop, before demanding that he buy a few new pairs. While Delicious never set foot on a scale — an amenity missing from the bathrooms at the Red Roof Inn and the Holiday Inn Express — photographs taken at the time suggest he lost between fifty and seventy-five pounds. It's also hard not to notice that in each shot, he's smiling. "People who aren't fat think it's about having a big gut or a big ass," says Delicious. "But it affects everything. Telling me to eat less was like telling an alcoholic to only have one glass of Scotch. I couldn't help myself. Then, all of a sudden, I was in control. That felt so good."

Four months after Bristol and Delicious had left the East Coast, they were riding strong. Even after sending 007 his commissions, periodically mailing money orders home to their folks, and generously remunerating exotic dancers for their creative gyrations on brass poles, their bankroll still exceeded $10,000. Then 007 told them they could double that amount with a successful romp through St. Louis.

For decades, the Gateway City and surrounding towns on both sides of the Mississippi have formed a sort of fertile crescent for high-rolling players. The exemplar is the late "St. Louie" Louie Roberts, a legendary shotmaker whose appetite for action remains the standard against which all others are measured. An Elvis look-alike, Roberts was a character of the first order — each year, the Derby City Classic event confers a Louie Roberts Action/ Entertainment Award on the most prolific gambler. The anthology of Roberts stories is a thick one. (One has him winning a bet by jumping off a diving board into a hotel pool with no water in it.) But the hard living caught up with him, and he died in the early 1990s at the age of forty.

In an authoritative tone, 007 outlined what he called "OP-

ERATION Saint LOUIE." The ultimate goal was to "snap off" a teenage kid named Andy Quinn, playing out of the Break in Cahokia, Illinois, who was busting every player who came through the heartland. But before getting to Quinn, Bristol and Delicious were to take down a raft of lesser players who frequented poolrooms in the area. They checked into a La Quinta Inn on the outskirts of St. Louis and promptly put the plan into action, grinding out $100 one night, $250 the next.

Delicious noticed that wherever he and Bristol gambled, a squat, unimposing-looking man in his early forties always seemed to be lurking, surreptitiously watching them from the corner of the room. At first he chalked it up to coincidence, but it became clear that the man was getting a read on them. The third or fourth time they crossed paths, the man approached and introduced himself.

His name was Gary Lutman, and he owned Sharkey's Billiards in nearby Maryville, Illinois, and, say, did Delicious want to play for money sometime? Delicious instantly recognized the name of the poolroom from 007's list. Lutman not only loved pool action, he loved action, period—he had recently lost a few grand shooting free throws against the girlfriend of an Indianapolis road player. ("I come to find out later," Lutman recalls, "she's one of the best high school players in the history of Indiana girls' basketball.") Delicious shrugged, nodded genially, and said he'd be happy to play Lutman a little.

Lutman had one condition, however. He had just lost a sack of money to a pair of young road players, Gabe Owen and Jeremy Jones. Lutman thought he'd lost in part because there were too many distractions at Sharkey's. If he and Delicious were going to play, they would have to play elsewhere. Again Delicious shrugged, thinking, *You don't want to play me at your own poolroom, it's fine by me, dude.*

Lutman and Delicious met the next night at a trendy afterhours nightclub in Sauget, Illinois. The two players found a table and played for $200 a rack. While Lutman had obvious chops, he was no match for Delicious, who, for all the times Lutman had been observing him, had yet to show his full speed. When Lutman was down ten racks, he quit. At least Delicious claims it was ten racks. Asked later whether this figure matched his recollection, Lutman paused and chuckled. "Sounds about right. After watching that guy shoot pool, who am I to question his accuracy about anything."

All the time spent watching Delicious work a room was finally having a transformative effect on Bristol. Suppressing his natural intensity, he was growing more sociable and laid-back; he was quicker to make small talk and slower to pass judgment. Now when he played, his emotional temperature, once so volatile, was much steadier. (Delicious had introduced him to marijuana, and Bristol surmised that the weed also played a role in his mellowing.)

Displaying his newfound charm, he was consistently winning bets by making trick shots and jump shots. Some road players consider it beneath their dignity to grind out cash; Bristol grew to revel in it. His specialty was a game called six hangers. Bristol would place a ball on the lip of each corner pocket, and for the side pockets the balls would sit just to the left and the right. Then he would challenge another player to pocket all six balls in six shots. The catch was that Bristol would call the pockets. A player who didn't position the cue ball right in the center of the table soon realized that the game was much harder than it looked.

Another grift entailed Bristol's balancing the cue ball on the lip of the table where the felt meets the wood and betting he could not only hit the cue ball cleanly but pocket the eight ball, which was placed in the middle of the table on the opposite end — a shot that looks far more difficult than it in fact is. Bristol also wasn't above betting kids they couldn't eat eight saltines in ninety seconds without drinking water. As he saw it, if he picked up $100 a night this way, shit, it paid for the hotel and meals. Then, whatever they cleared playing sets would be pure profit.

Late one night, two road players from Alabama sauntered into the Break, and one of them challenged Bristol to high-stakes nine-ball on a bar table. Delicious suggested that Bristol play for $50 a rack, not exactly a strong vote of confidence in his partner's abilities. One well-heeled railbird had grown fond of Bristol, and he came out from behind the counter and offered to back him for $300 a rack. Emboldened by the support, Bristol played some of the best pool of his life. When he was up six racks, $1,800 in the black, the Alabaman's backer made his guy quit.

Delicious felt guilty that he might have shown a lack of trust in his partner. "You don't have to split that with me, Bob," Delicious said by way of apology. "You really earned that money."

"Fuck that. We split everything down the middle," Bristol said. Then he smiled and added, "Besides, maybe you can use the money to buy some fucking confidence in me."

For the only time in the partnership, Bristol and Delicious played tourist. In St. Louis one day, they took a tram to the top of the Gateway Arch and visited the local zoo. But they also put in countless hours practicing. Instead of — or in addition to — patronizing the strip clubs, they used their dead time fortifying their strokes. The Break was open twenty-four hours a day, but it tended to clear out at around three in the morning, at which point the partners would walk in and conduct a five-hour boot camp.

On a back table, Delicious worked with Bristol on the finer points of aiming sequences and position patterns. Particularly when he was under pressure, Bristol had a habit of what pool players call cinching — focusing solely on making the object ball. In Delicious' eyes, Bristol was always a skilled shooter, but his positioning was horrible. He would make the eight ball but then have a terrible leave on the nine. Players are taught to split their focus fifty-fifty between making the object ball and positioning the next shot. With Bristol it was more like ninety-ten. So for the next few days Delicious put him through the positioning paces.

He also helped Bristol with his mental game, telling his partner to think of pool as a sport similar to golf. Instead of water hazards and sand traps, the obstacles are other balls blocking yours. Instead of a bad lie behind a tree, the object ball might be pinned against a rail. But, as in golf, it's the way you handle adversity, the way you temper aggression with prudence, that makes all the difference. "If you sink an amazing birdie putt but get so jacked that you blow up on your next hole, it don't do you much good,"

Delicious explained. "If your attitude stays consistent, your shooting will too."

With his eye for detail and his love of the *process* — "That whole anal side of him," Delicious calls it — Bristol watched his partner break and then deconstructed the mechanics. He noted that Delicious put too much weight on his back foot, a holdover from when he was much heavier and less nimble. He also observed that Delicious jerked his cue back rather than letting it glide. "People think the faster you take your stick back, the harder the break," Bristol told him. "But it's like a golf stroke. You come back firmly and then accelerate through." The analysis was spot-on, and within days Delicious' break had improved dramatically, to the point where he was routinely potting three balls off the break. For a full month, they coached each other every night as they waited for action like patient fishermen.

At last, Andy Quinn walked into the Break. Tall, thin, blond, athletic-looking, and oozing enough confidence to shame even Bristol, Quinn looked like the kind of popular kid who'd made Delicious' life miserable in high school. He offered to play Delicious even, eight-ahead for $2,000.

"No way," Delicious said, recoiling. "I know who you are, Andy. You're a friggin' legend. I can't beat you even. Give me some weight."

Quinn didn't flinch. "You got the seven. Get up there and play."

Delicious avoided eye contact with Bristol for fear he would crack up. He was thinking, *The way I'm playing right now, I can beat anyone. Here's some kid who I never even heard of until a few weeks ago — he's giving me the seven? That's just stealing money.* He figured that, short of a tornado flattening the pool hall, there was no way he wasn't walking out of there with $10,000 that night.

Quinn, though, lived up to his billing. Playing on his home table, a Gold Crown with fast felt stretched taut and tight pockets, the kid rarely missed a ball. A game of eight-ahead with two pro-level players can sometimes take as long as twelve hours. Quinn won in less than an hour. "That's one lucky motherfucker," Bristol muttered. Naturally, owing to the combination of his gambling addiction and his hubris, Delicious demanded that they play again. This time, he asked for a two-game lead in a race to thirteen — in other words, the best of twenty-five games — and the seven ball as a handicap. Quinn smiled and agreed.

Again Quinn played as though the pockets were as wide as buckets. He guided the cue ball as if by remote control, directing it into the object ball, and then, as his target dropped into the pocket and out of sight, the cue rolled to a halt in perfect alignment with the next ball.

Delicious could barely make a game of it and felt a mix of frustration and apprehension. When a pool player enters "the zone," the cozy space where he can do no wrong and every pattern is glaringly obvious, he often forgets that he's sharing the table with another person. Like a lone golfer playing against the course, you're just playing against the table. But when your opponent is in the zone, you're keenly aware of him. In this case, knowing that Quinn was playing jam-up, Delicious stroked every ball with the burden of knowing that if he was anything less than perfect, his counterpart was likely to get up from his seat and run the table. Through his expert play, Quinn was applying pressure — pressure that was breaking Delicious' back. Devastated, he whined to Bristol, "I feel like one of them boxers who beats up guys in his own gym but then gets a pro fight and boom-boom-boom gets flattened."

Bristol alternated between being a cheerleader and the voice of reason, urging his partner to cut bait. No matter. Twice more Delicious and Quinn played. Again the same result. Had Delicious been misfiring, he could rationalize the losses. *Lucky son of a bitch caught me on an off night.* But this was infinitely more demoralizing. He complained to Bristol that his vision was blurry, that he was having a hell of a time reading the table. In truth, he was playing just fine; Quinn was simply better. Dawn hadn't broken yet and Delicious was down $8,000, spraying money like a busted fire hose. Quinn played it cool, calmly taking his wages, figuring he was pasting a deluded road player who was desperate for action and betting higher than he should have been.

Inconsolable, Delicious repaired to the La Quinta and quickly broke training, numbing his pain with a six-pack. While no pool player relishes losing, for Delicious it took on the dimensions of an existential crisis. He had lost before, of course, but he'd never gotten rocked quite like that. Gutted as he felt, the financial hit didn't have much to do with it. Losing eight large would make plenty of other roadmen head out on a hemlock run. But Delicious' relationship with pool had always gone to a layer deeper than the money. When he won, sure he enjoyed the payoff, but the satisfaction of victory was the real high. Likewise, when he lost, the sting of defeat went far beyond the change in his economic fortunes.

By this point, Delicious was convinced that pool was his oxygen, his reason for living. If it was possible for him to be crushed four straight times — and not playing even! and against a guy younger than he was! — maybe he wasn't destined to become the next Mosconi after all. It wasn't just his confidence that was in tatters, it was suddenly his will to live. He started the day feeling invincible; now he tossed on his bed, feeling the familiar numbness that came with the onslaught of depression. He was sweating through his clothes and becoming short of breath. He looked at his body and convinced himself that every freckle was a cancerous growth. Thoughts of suicide flitted in and out of his mind. "I'm so fucked up in the head right now," he said over and over.

Lying on the adjacent motel bed, Bristol tried to recall the inspirational words of sports coaches past. *Everyone has a bad day. You'll get 'em next time. You show your character by how you respond to defeat.* But he knew that for Delicious, this drubbing was about much more than a few sets of pool. Neither of them slept that night.

Bristol figured that if they cut their losses and left town, his partner might be irreparably wounded. If Delicious could get a rematch, he might lose a fifth game — which would completely bust them — but he might also win and thereby restore some self-esteem. Bristol had overheard a comment that when Quinn left the comfort of the Break, his play dropped a level, so he called Quinn's backer and made a game. Quinn would still stake Delicious two games on the wire in a $2,000 race to thirteen and give him the seven. Except this time they would play at Billiards on Broadway, a predominantly black poolroom in St. Louis.

Harold Johnson, the proprietor of Billiards on Broadway and a longtime railbird, surmised that Delicious had purposely lost the previous night and was setting Quinn up. "Dang, you're a smart hustler," he whispered to Delicious before encouraging the regulars to place side bets on the "crazy fella." Delicious didn't bother telling Harold that if he lost this $2,000 game, he would be dead broke.

Quinn continued his hot play, but Delicious was instantly more comfortable on the table at Harold's. He found his stroke, and after two hours they were tied at eleven games. As Quinn racked the balls, Bristol put Motown on the jukebox, the Temptations' "Papa Was a Rolling Stone," a tune Delicious loved as much as Bristol despised.

Delicious looked up and smiled at his partner. Like medicine kicking in, the music soothed him. Two games from going home broke, Delicious ran out the last two racks and won $2,000. "That's the power of the Temptations," Delicious said to the railbirds, playfully slapping five with a cluster of African-American men who had just made some nice cash betting on "that crazy fella."

In a complete role reversal from the previous night across the river in Cahokia, Delicious had commandeered the table's mojo, and Quinn all but begged to continue playing. To the delight of Bristol, Harold, and the railbirds who were betting big with Quinn's backer, Delicious caught fire and won the next race to thirteen. He then agreed to play Quinn even, and won again, then again.

Quinn decided to call it a night. In a matter of hours Delicious had wiped out an $8,000 deficit, and more important, his self-belief was again boiling. While he would have happily continued, he shook Quinn's hand and thanked him for the opportunity to win his money back, and, without saying as much, for the lesson about the fickle nature of momentum.

When Delicious called 007 to tell him the news, the pool detective could hardly contain his disappointment. "You played Andy Quinn even?" he said. "Shoot, Danny, I thought you was callin' to tell me you had won five or ten large."

"Nope," said Delicious, trying to sound appropriately forlorn. "Just even."

He didn't let on that, all things considered, he was positively thrilled. A few bad breaks and he could easily have been in the hole for ten large. Still, he took it as a sign. Like a rock band reaching the end of a tour, Bristol and Delicious decided, after more than six months on the road, it was time to take a break from the road.

7

PHILADELPHIA STORY

RISTOL AND DELICIOUS were barely home for a week when they heard the siren song of the road. Or, more precisely, they heard the throaty, clipped voice of 007, speaking excitedly about "HUGE friggin' money down in DEM CAROLINAS! Columbia, Charlotte, Myrtle Beach—they're playin' REAL HIGH down there." Within a day, Bristol had finagled a ride from Connecticut to the Basavich home in New Jersey, which he called "Casa de Delicious."

Bristol spent the night there and, after hearing Dave Basavich tell a string of dirty jokes, realized where his road partner had gotten his winning personality. "You remind me so much of Woody friggin' Allen," Bristol told Dave. He was surprised that Dave spoke so casually about Delicious' depression, sharing his pet term for his son's episodes, "full-moon phases." The topic would have been a conversational no-fly zone in his own household, but Bristol admired the Basavich family's openness.

He was also envious of the wide berth that "Mom and Dad Delicious" gave their son with respect to his road play. By then, most of their concerns over their son's entry into the pool world had melted away. Delicious was seeing the country, he was thinner than he'd been in years, he was making money, and above all, he seemed genuinely happy again. Sure, they conformed to the parental cliché and wished he called home from the road more often. But they weren't about to intrude when their kid was doing the one thing in life that gave him the most pleasure.

The next afternoon, Bristol and Delicious jammed their bags into the back of the tiny Tiburon. Delicious, convert to physical fitness that he was, threw a pair of tennis rackets into the back seat. Like parents sending their kids off to summer camp, albeit one of indeterminate length with no fixed address, Dave and Doris wished the guys well on their next tour of duty and waved as they drove out of sight.

They zipped down the New Jersey Turnpike, encouraged by the warbling of Axl Rose at full blast, comforted to be back on the road. An hour into the trip, Delicious made the impetuous suggestion that they pull off and try to hustle some action in Philadelphia. Like cooking and fashion and music, pool has its regional differences. The Philly–South Jersey pocket has long been known for skilled practitioners — the great Willie Mosconi, "Spanish" Mike Lebron, Jimmy Fusco and his cousin Petey — with businesslike, no-bullshit dispositions. The mirth and endearing quirkiness that fill pool pavilions in other parts of the country are seldom in evidence, replaced in the many halls of Philly by a faintly sinister current. More often than not, the popular image of gloomy, gauzily lit, smoke-filled poolrooms awash in shadowy characters and hard-boiled sharks bears little resemblance to reality. In Philly, that perception is reality.

Delicious and Bristol first hit Tacony Billiards, a well-known action spot near the banks of the Delaware River. As they walked in, a veteran Philly hustler known as Peter Rabbit nearly came to blows with another player who'd been teasing Peter by putting a paper straw wrapper in his ear. (An immutable law of pool: players who get bored waiting for action will find new and creative ways to annoy each other while passing the time.) Otherwise, the place was dormant. So Bristol and Delicious drove on through a decidedly working-class neighborhood and hit a hall with a wonderfully ironic name, the Boulevard Social and Billiards Club. Billiards? Yes. Social? Um, not so much.

A sprawling hall above a Blockbuster video store that offered dozens of tables, most of them older Gold Crowns, the Boulevard was a popular haunt for several gangbangers and low-level soldiers in the Philly mob. (Which is why a few of the characters here will bear pseudonyms.) A pervasive gloom overwhelmed the low-wattage bulbs and fluorescent panels. On more than one occasion, chalk outlines and police tape have adorned the premises, an interesting complement to the yellowed posters of dogs playing pool.

As the sun was setting, Delicious and Bristol trundled up the stairs of the Boulevard, oblivious to any danger. Standing alongside the counter, a young pool junkie named Dale recognized the two from some small tournaments in the Northeast. A Hispanic kid in his early twenties, Dale knew immediately they had come seeking action, and he made a game with Bristol for $1,000. A few players nearby stopped banging balls to watch. Even though he'd been consciously trying for months to tone down some of his more grating mannerisms — the biceps flexing, the swaggering, the cursing at the railbirds — Bristol projected too much self-satisfaction for the Boulevard's habitués. By the time he had beaten Dale out of his money, there was a palpable uneasiness in the room. The railbirds didn't like Bristol, and they didn't like it that Dale had just lost to him.

Spotting Dale the seven ball, Delicious played next. He not only won but managed to undo some of the bad vibes his partner had created. Trying to defuse the tension, Delicious cracked jokes at his own expense and made nice with the growing legion of railbirds. Addressing his opponent by his first name — "That's good playing, Dale," "Wow, you almost pulled off a killer shot there, Dale" — he put the kid he was beating at ease. At one point, Delicious called for a "cheesesteak break," his desire to show deference to the locals trumping his goal to eat healthily. He repaired to the snack bar and came back with two sandwiches, one for himself, one for Dale. When Bristol asked where his sandwich was, Delicious shot back, "Stop acting like a jackass and maybe I'll buy you one later."

As Delicious was putting the finishing touches on Dale, he

noticed a menacing, heavily muscled, heavily bejeweled railbird speaking softly on his cell phone. In the interest of authorial safety, we'll call him "Wally Paulnuts." He was a hulking Puerto Rican and was allegedly a ranking member of the Philly mob and a big-time drug dealer who invested a huge chunk of his income backing pool players. He was on the phone with a promising player, Ray Seckel. Wally, who clearly ruled the roost, had conscripted Seckel to come down to the Boulevard and beat the road players. When Delicious pocketed his $1,000 from Dale, Wally closed in on him.

"I know you want to put that money back into action," Wally said. "I know you ain't quitting winner." He then brandished a black nylon bag filled with hundreds — easily five hundred C-notes. "Keep playing and you can win a lot of this. I got a guy coming over right now."

Bristol let loose his trademark dismissive cluck. Delicious smiled agreeably. Within minutes, Seckel arrived. Spotting him the seven ball in a race to thirteen for $2,000, Delicious played dead-on pool and ran out by a wide margin. What had begun as a fun, impulsive detour had netted the team $4,000. But Wally wasn't about to let them leave. With an edge in his voice now, he announced that he had already made another game. Whether he liked it or not, Delicious would play for $7,000 against Eddie Abraham, the best young player in Philly, giving Abraham the eight ball in another race to thirteen. Though it was the middle of the night, Abraham was awake when Wally called him.

"I need you to come down here and get in the box, Eddie."

"Who's the guy I gotta play against?" Abraham asked.

"Danny something. They call him Kid Delicious."

"Aw, I know that guy," Abraham said. "I can't beat him, even getting the eight."

"Get in the box anyway."

This kind of dance is typical. The most powerful figures in contemporary pool are the stakehorses, the backers whose financial resources drive the action. A backed player risks nothing but his pride for a chance to win a portion of the money — usually half—above the light. (If the horse pays less than half, there's too much incentive for the player to dump. That is, if player A is getting only twenty-five percent to win, player B will offer half the booty to player A to lose on purpose.) On its face, it's a can't-lose proposition for the player. But the Faustian bargain is that the player is subject to the whims of his sponsor. If a Wally Paulnuts figure summons you to the table and you decline to appear, you can forget about his support in the future.

It was well into the early morning by now—the television in the corner was tuned to an infomercial—and Delicious was, in his words, "fried." Eddie Abraham arrived looking surprisingly fresh. A thick, powerfully built kid with a baseball cap pulled low over his head and an abundance of tattoos—"basically a totem pole to people I knew who passed away," he says—Abraham avoided eye contact with Delicious as he screwed his cue together. He was a hired gun, ready to discharge his duties with the detachment of a mercenary. There were now more than a hundred railbirds, including several with known ties to Joe "Skinny Joey" Merlino, then the head of the Philly mob, who would soon thereafter begin serving a prison term for racketeering.

For all his success as a hustler divorcing suckers from their money, Delicious had never been in a fistfight, much less a gunfight. On the occasions when he caught the faintest whiff of danger, he deployed a fail-safe strategy: he threw the game or played his opponent even and then quit. Marty Reisman, the great table-tennis hustler, famous for beating opponents using a trash can lid or a Coke bottle or a shoe as a paddle, lived by a simple gambling philosophy: "Take a little, give a little." As long as you're coming out ahead, why get greedy? Why humiliate your opponent? Why push him to the brink of receivership? Delicious lived by the same credo. Since he didn't know how to throw a punch, he wasn't about to get into a beef over a few hundred bucks. By the same token, he wasn't about to lose to Abraham on purpose either.

Indifferent to the pressure, he jumped to an early lead over Abraham and never relinquished his grip. Despite the high stakes and the high danger factor, Delicious played with his usual poise.

Whenever Abraham won a rack, Delicious graciously threw out a compliment: "That's strong, Eddie!" Then he'd respond with his own flourish. The suspense was gone long before Delicious ran out at 12–4. He was now up $11,000, but, fearful to appear to be gloating, he suppressed his smile.

As Delicious scanned the rail, he saw firearms in plain view. Other bystanders had obvious bulges in their pockets. As always, Delicious was armed only with a boundless reservoir of charm. But it was an effective weapon, the equivalent of a stun gun. When he potted his last nine ball against Abraham, he announced that he needed to smoke a joint to relax, and anyone who wanted to join him was welcome. A small crowd, including one of the players he had just beaten, gathered around Delicious, sharing his weed. With his endearing accent and self-deprecating jokes and generosity of spirit, it was impossible for the thugs to summon much dislike for the guy. Even as he was robbing them.

Nevertheless, Wally was now "in some heat," and that's when backers — all gamblers, really — get into trouble. Wally kept summoning players as if pulling out Russian nesting dolls, each one brighter and better than the next, but his bag of cash was steadily losing heft. Delicious knew well that he couldn't quit winner and leave. And Wally had one last card to play.

He called Spanish Mike Lebron to the Boulevard. Though he was in his mid-sixties, with a creased face, rubbery jowls, thick glasses, and graying temples, Lebron was still winning professional events and was one of the most accomplished players ever to pick up a cue. It seemed like months ago that the night had begun, with Delicious playing the kid working the counter; now he was matching up against Lebron, a former U.S. Open champ who had mentored the incomparable Efren Reyes. It was akin to a sandbagger in golf winning a few holes from the boys at the country club and then finding himself playing for big timber against Arnold Palmer.

All traces of playfulness gone from his voice, Wally set the terms: they would play even for $7,500 in another race to nine. Wally could have pummeled Delicious to a pulp with one hand tied behind his back. But for maximum effect he approached Delicious flanked by mobster henchmen. Bristol had been a huge source of encouragement for Delicious the entire night, but now his mask of confidence was gone. Pulling him aside, Bristol said, only half jokingly, "You know you're getting on the wrong side of the Philly mob. You do know that, right?"

"Should I just lose to Spanish Mike on purpose?" Delicious asked. "We'll still be up like five large."

"You can't do that, Dan," Bristol responded. "A whole bunch of guys on the rail are betting *for* you now."

Delicious began to panic. He was screwed either way, and his internal danger detector was blaring. An old trick of road players entails repairing to the bathroom, leaving a cue leaning against the table as tacit collateral, and sneaking out the window. But Delicious remembered seeing that the bathroom window had been barred, which suggested to him that others in a similar position had tried this escape hatch before.

Suddenly he was the most scared he'd ever been in a poolroom. "Like check-your-underwear-for-stains scared," as he described it to Bristol. He'd beaten three solid players, and now a raft of mobsters was betting for him and against Spanish Mike. He was dead tired. His stomach hurt from the cheesesteaks he'd eaten. He was sweating so much he kept grabbing stacks of napkins from the snack bar. He was a mess.

Spanish Mike arrived looking puffy and dignified and not particularly Spanish. In keeping with the flinty Philadelphia pool culture, Lebron barely acknowledged his opponent and limbered up with casual efficiency for a few minutes before lagging with Delicious to see who would break first. Feeling every last ounce of the tension, Delicious played tentatively, as though he had been shot with a tranquilizer gun. Before he knew it, Lebron was up five games to none. Standing next to the table, Wally was smiling smugly, figuring that between winning back his $7,500 and winning all of his side action, he might finish the night ahead.

Waving Bristol off, Delicious retreated alone to the bathroom. Sitting on a toilet seat, slivers of daylight poking through the window, Delicious began to cry. The sleep deprivation, the stress, the grease-laden food he'd inhaled, the impending loss of $7,500, and, not least, the very real fear of death — it all converged on him. He recognized it as the onset of a panic attack, many of the same symptoms he felt when a depressive episode was coming on. But then, as he sat on the toilet seat in a dank bathroom, he was, for one of the few times in his life, overcome by rage. *Fuck Wally the bully and the rest of the fucking Philly gangsters and gangbangers on the rail. I'm going back out there. I might lose, but I'm going to fight like a motherfucker.*

Delicious returned to the table, his eyes no longer at half-mast, and broke to start the sixth game. Shrouded in a state of calm, he "caught a gear" and played jam-up pool. Within twenty minutes, it was 5–5, and the railbirds, half of them anyway, were clapping and wolf-whistling. When Delicious squiggled a near-impossible massé shot around the four ball in the thirteenth game, the place crackled with energy. Lebron ran a hand through his close-cropped hair and smiled ever so slightly.

By seven A.M., a full twelve hours from the time he'd walked in the door, Delicious was a game away from winning, and the railbirds, most of them awfully well oiled, were going nuts. Lebron broke but failed to make a ball. Dripping with sweat, Delicious stood, hiked up his pants, and methodically ran out the rack. As half the railbirds got paid and the other half cursed the road player who had improbably taken down Spanish Mike, Bristol bear-hugged his partner. Between the four games and the side betting, Bristol and Delicious, Inc., had grossed nearly $20,000 for the night. Including the side action, Wally must have lost $40,000. Supposedly a few months removed from going to jail on a drug charge, Wally slapped seventy-five hundred-dollar bills into Delicious' sweat-soaked palm, sneered at him, and, with at least a trace of admiration, barked, "Now get the fuck out of here."

The partners flew down the stairs, their pockets overstuffed with cash. "Holy fucking shit," Bristol screamed when they were safely inside the Tiburon. "We just made twenty fucking grand. Off the fucking mob!" Delicious was plenty happy about the loot, but he was thrilled for other reasons too. For one, he knew he'd shown immense heart, winning four straight races against increasingly stronger opponents, the last of them Mike Lebron, a pool legend by anyone's definition. What's more, he had escaped the Boulevard unscathed. He'd been in a situation that invited ugliness. And once again he had slain everybody with kindness.

8

BRISTOLICIOUS, INC.

Between the size and the circumstances of the Philly score, Delicious and Bristol were riding a wave of adrenaline as they left town, shimmying south on I-95. Bristol counted the money over and over, and yes, they really had managed to take more than $20,000 from Philly's finest. Delicious' face froze in a smile as he bobbed his head to the Cat Stevens number emanating from the speakers and kept the beat on the steering wheel, ignoring his wingman's requests, and soon demands, for a classic-rock station.

At a rest stop in Delaware, they sat in the car and divvied up the money as any savvy road players would. Time and again, hustlers would make a big score and, as word of their new riches quickly spread, they'd be robbed a few nights later. Delicious and Bristol sprinkled the cash in various pockets, the glove box of the Tiburon, the sides of their cue cases, the pouches of their suitcases. If they were going to be held up, at least the assailant was going to get only a fraction of their cash.

By midmorning, their collective high had worn off and they looked for a place to crash. Their glorious achievement called for a suite at the Four Seasons; they settled for a $39.99 single with two queen beds at a Motel 6 outside Baltimore. Pulling off the daily double, finagling an early check-in and a late check-out the following day, they promptly fell into the grip of Morpheus and slept until close to midnight. When they woke up, they decided it was too late to embark on a long drive to South Carolina, so they might as well put some of their Philadelphia riches into action.

Although Baltimore isn't known as a particularly fertile pool town, it does have one of the better action spots on the East Coast, the Jack & Jill Cue Club, a pared-down joint not far from BWI Airport, in the blue-collar suburb of Glen Burnie, Maryland. Like a good many pool halls around the country, Jack & Jill's is tucked away off the main drag in a grimy industrial park, alongside auto body shops and warehouses. It's safe to assume that lots of locals don't know the place exists, much less that there are pool players who are willing to cross time zones — oceans even — to converge there.

Jack & Jill's is the quintessential seamy action joint. It's shrouded in stale cigarette smoke, open twenty-four hours, and populated by crusty regulars who play cards at the snack bar to kill time between money games on the twenty-two tables. The walls are covered with black-and-white pool posters, including one of a baby brandishing a cue, with the caption "Misspent Youth." The obligatory wink-wink "No Gambling" and "No Loitering" signs hang on the wall. The fluorescent light above one table is adorned with the message "Just Say No." One gets the sense that all of the various directives are disregarded in equal measure.

Delicious and Bristol ducked in around midnight, just as business was starting to pick up. Feeling impregnable, they didn't bother with their usual routine, Bristol playing setup man and Delicious cleaning up. They just made games, flipped a coin to determine who would break, and got down to business.

Delicious kept up his torrid playing, taking on all comers in the game of their choice. He beat them all, seldom having to summon his full speed. On one of the first nights, he ran roughshod over

Eric Durbin, a young, tortured-looking roadman from outside Cincinnati who would go on to become one of the better-known action players in the pool world. Delicious gave up the seven, the eight, and the break, and still won $4,000 from Durbin.

Channeling his partner's success, Bristol did plenty of winning too, mostly at one-pocket. All the while he deployed his newfound reserves of charm, making friends with the crew of regulars — some of whom slept on mattresses in a back room — smoking weed with them in the parking lot, and buying them hot dogs and Cokes at the snack bar. Having learned from Delicious, Bristol came to see that small talk really was big talk, that shelling out a few bucks for a stranger's snack was a sound investment if it improved the odds of getting the guy to gamble later that night.

The two also maintained their physical fitness regimen. They would wake up in the early afternoon and leave the Motel 6 to exercise, usually playing tennis or sweet-talking their way into a nearby community swimming pool. They would eat a healthful dinner, maybe a turkey sandwich at a Subway or a grilled chicken salad at a chain restaurant the likes of T.G.I. Friday's. ("Nothing with fucking cheese, Danny," Bristol commanded nightly.) They would clock in to work at Jack & Jill's, and when their shift ended, they would exercise once more in the room — one hundred push-ups and one hundred sit-ups — before bed. For Bristol it was a matter of sustaining his sculpted physique. For Delicious it was transformative. He weight was skidding downward to 180 pounds, the lightest he'd been since his early teenage years. And with his weight and self-esteem moving in opposite directions, he was feeling damn good about life.

Unlike most pool halls, Jack & Jill's wasn't run by the owner. In fact, the proprietor, Cliff Macklin, made only cameo appearances, leaving the counter duties to a crew of loyal employees. A silver-haired, avuncular type with a thick Bal'mer accent, Macklin was cloaked in mystery. Jack & Jill lore had it that Macklin had once made a mint in a high-stakes poker game, winning several six-figure hands off blue-suited inside-the-beltway types. Fearful of possible recriminations by the unhappy losers, Macklin rarely went out in public, managing two pool halls and his Factory Discount Billiard Supply from his home.

The truth about Macklin was something altogether different.

Even as a boy growing up in Maryland, Macklin seemed to have an invisible umbilical cord connecting him to action, be it at a pool table, a card table, a racetrack, or a golf course. He was thrown out of school at thirteen and, playing under the nickname "Hummer," turned into a pool shark and embarked on a career as a road player. Hummer eventually landed in Vegas and was drafted into a "bust-out crew" by the casinos. When a high roller came in, it fell to Macklin and the other guys in the crew to bust him — that is, to make sure the guy didn't leave with the house's money.

There isn't a gambling ruse Cliff Macklin hasn't perfected, a grift he hasn't seen. Give him a deck of cards and his sleight-of-hand moves would make David Copperfield's jaw plummet. Make a bet with him and he'll add a seemingly irrelevant condition that will shift the math to his advantage. Put a maple pool cue in his hands and he can hold his own against anyone. "I was just one of those guys who was born to hustle," he says with a what-can-I-do-about-it? cadence.

But like so many itinerant gambling men, the stress came to overwhelm him. Macklin had smoked four packs of Marlboros a day, popped Xanax like they were Tic Tacs, had a heart attack in his mid-thirties. By his late forties, he had developed a fear — sometimes a paralyzing fear — of social situations. While he was happy to talk on the phone, he could go for months without seeing another person aside from his wife. The mere possibility of a social encounter was unbearable. He claims to have had great success operating his businesses from home. "I became a multimillionaire from my bed," he asserts. "Running a poolroom is a nickel-and-dime business, but it can add up fast."

From his self-imposed exile, Macklin still managed to keep his pool antennae finely tuned. If someone won a big score in California, he would find out about it before the sun came up. If two players had a dispute in Texas, he knew the backstory. One day a friend of Macklin's called, gushing about a heavyset road player from New Jersey who "sure didn't act like a pool hustler" but played as well as anyone he'd ever seen. When Macklin was told the player's nickname, he laughed out loud. "I thought I had heard them all, but 'Kid Delicious'? That's as good as it gets." When, just a few months later, Kid Delicious showed up at Jack & Jill's, Macklin, as he put it, "loaded for bear." He didn't tip anyone off that he had the wire. Instead, working the phone like a madman, he took whatever side action he could get, betting big on Kid Delicious.

After a week or so, under the pretext of wanting to be a backer, Macklin invited Delicious to his house for dinner. "It was a con," Macklin concedes. "What I really wanted was to meet this guy, see what he was about, and pick up a few tricks from him. I wanted to see him play pool, but I also wanted to see for myself why everyone liked him so much. I had never come across a road player with his reputation. He was a mensch and a winner. You don't hear that said about too many guys in pool."

Road players might develop friendships at the pool hall, but there's usually a firm social barrier in place dividing work and home. If two players break bread together, you can bet it's a snack-bar hot dog sweating with grease, not a home-cooked meal. To borrow a phrase from Las Vegas, what happens at the pool hall stays at the pool hall.

Flattered to be invited, Delicious agreed and took down directions to Macklin's house, in Glendale, Maryland, half an hour from Jack & Jill's. When he pulled up, he was stunned by the place, a sprawling property on a golf course with a circular driveway filled with vintage cars and Vespas.

Macklin and his wife, Sandi Jo, greeted Delicious and served a feast. The conversation flowed, mostly Macklin and Delicious swapping road stories. After dinner, Sandi Jo left the two men, who went down to an immense basement, fitted out with a Gold Crown and a casino-sized craps table. They played a relaxed game of nine-ball, Macklin asking his guest for pointers, which Delicious was happy to dispense.

Immediately, Macklin says, he saw a level of talent that distinguished Delicious from other elite players. "You know how, when you watch a cowboy movie, you see wild horses? The one at the front of the pack has an electricity and confidence the others don't. He carries himself differently. The frontrunner knows he's the best, the others know he's the best, and there's no need to bullshit. That's what I saw in Danny."

Neither man told the other of his psychological struggles, but they both sensed that they shared more than a passion for pool. An unmistakable warmth passed between the two. To Delicious, this kindly man with a shock of gray hair was savvy, but he also appeared uncommonly trustworthy and unusually genuine. Likewise, Macklin was struck by Delicious' authenticity. His only worry was that Delicious might be a little naïve.

When they finished playing nine-ball, they moved on to the craps table. Macklin gripped a pair of clear dice. "You like craps, Kid Delicious?"

"You kidding? I love craps."

"What number do you want me to roll?"

"I dunno. Eleven?"

Macklin shrugged and rolled a six and a five.

"Holy shit, how'd you do that?"

Macklin handed him the dice. "Whatever you do, don't roll a seven. Anything but a seven."

Delicious tossed the dice: a five and a two.

"Unbelievable," he said, his eyes wide as saucers.

Next Macklin picked up a casino-style shoe filled with six decks of cards. He dealt Delicious a poker hand, face down, then proceeded to tell him the five cards he was holding.

Delicious looked at his cards and smiled. "Man, you're good. How did you know that?"

First, Macklin explained that dice, even clear ones, can be weighted and magnetized. Some tables even have a switch that the dealer can use to increase or decrease the magnetism to the house's advantage. Also, dead spots on the table could trigger the magnets. He had picked up this insider info during his Vegas days. As for the poker sorcery, while the deck was unmarked, the corners were coded in slightly raised felt, not unlike Braille. An experienced dealer could, with the most subtle brush of his forefinger, "read" the cards and bet accordingly.

"They really do this at the casino?" Delicious asked, his mouth forming a perfect O.

Macklin wasn't trying to teach Delicious how to become a card cheat. He was imparting a more general lesson about games of chance: *There's always the possibility that someone is putting one over on you. Stick with pool: you have the skill and you control the outcome.* "I was just giving him the information," Macklin said later. "What he chose to do with it was his own business."

After two weeks in Baltimore, Delicious hadn't lost a set, although the competition got progressively stiffer. By the time he beat the best player in town, a lanky guy in his twenties, Max Schlothauer, known to everyone as Baltimore Max, Delicious and Bristol were up nearly $10,000. But even the best road hustler can overstay his welcome. Either the locals will call in a new stick who can beat him, or the roadie will grow careless and agree to ill-considered games. In Baltimore, the partners got careless.

Having lost decisively, but not disgracefully, at nine-ball, Baltimore Max proposed that he and Delicious play high-stakes one-pocket, say $400 a rack. Max wanted a spot, though. Riding the wave of invincibility that comes when you're on a winning streak, Delicious obliged without blinking. When Max asked for the nine-seven spot — he would need to bury only seven balls in his designated pocket, while Delicious would have to make nine — Delicious put up no resistance. "Sure, Max. If that's what it'll take."

Unbeknownst to Delicious, Max was a one-pocket specialist. When the game began, Max had a sizable entourage in tow: a backer, several friends, and a statuesque blonde wearing an outfit so tight it looked shrink-wrapped to her body. "She wasn't my girlfriend or nothing," Max said later. "She was just a girl I was hanging out with, partying with. I don't remember if she was a stripper, but she might have been."

Whatever she was, Delicious noticed her immediately. "Look at them great tits," he whispered to Bristol. "And have you ever seen a rounder ass?" His confidence still inflated like a bagpipe, he flirted with her. "If Baltimore Max ain't satisfying you and you want to get with a real man, let me know," he told her, albeit with a goofy smile and enough sarcasm so that no one took offense.

Three hours had elapsed, and the momentum had wafted back and forth like a gentle breeze. Delicious would win two games, Baltimore Max would win three. Delicious would win three, Max would counter with a mini-streak of his own. With Max up $400, Delicious suggested that they up the ante to $800 a rack. Conferring first with his backer, Max agreed. The next game was fiercely tight, with both contenders playing the defensive, heavily strategic pool that one-pocket demands.

One ball away from winning, Delicious lined up his shot and heard giggling. He turned to find Max's bombshell companion standing near the edge of the table. The peanut gallery hooted as she struck a sex-kitten pose, licked her lips, and proceeded to remove her top. She then reached into a pocket, removed the eight ball, and lodged it between her double-D's. Delicious played along: "I've been sharked before, honey, but never quite like this."

Just as he prepared to shoot, he stole another look at the woman's substantial chest. Then, his concentration not so much broken as shattered, he backed away. This went on for a few minutes. Finally he shot, and the misguided eight ball went straight into the rail. He pronounced it "one of the worst shots I've ever taken." The crowd cracked up and slapped five with the woman, who had not only given everyone a nice show but had also changed the outcome of the match. Delicious, no matter how pissed off he felt, had to laugh along with everyone else.

Nothing went right for him after that. On his turn, Max deposited his seventh ball in his pocket to win the game. Then he won again. Now Delicious was down $2,000. Like many gamblers, pool players in the midst of action can lose all grasp of the value of money and the variables of reason. The same person who will go miles out of his way to avoid paying a fifty-cent toll will, when desperate, put thousands of dollars on a dubious wager.

And so Delicious invited Baltimore Max back the following night, and promptly lost another $2,000. It was obvious to anyone watching that Max had taken up tenancy in Delicious' head. The time had come to concede defeat and move on. But Delicious demanded a second rematch the next night. Usually the conscience of the partnership, Bristol was torn between common sense and a desperate desire for Delicious to return to his winning ways. He chose to stand silent. Max gleefully obliged and won yet another $2,000. Then he took $2,000 once again on the fourth night.

After blowing more than eight grand — nearly all their winnings in Baltimore — Delicious finally quit. Financially they were doing okay: although he had been positively drilled by Baltimore Max, he and Bristol had still broken even for Baltimore and hadn't dipped into their Philadelphia war chest. But Delicious' psyche, ironclad a few nights earlier, was now in tatters. He kept repeating to Bristol, "This game will fuck with your head worse than any girl."

Bristol, meanwhile, was having problems of his own. A few weeks earlier, he had won $1,200 from a middle-aged Asian man who frequented Jack & Jill's. The Asian had had only $600 on him, but since he was known to everyone on the rail, Bristol assumed he was good for the rest. But weeks went by without the man settling his tab. While Delicious wouldn't have given the unpaid money a second thought, breezily chalking it up to the cost of doing business, Bristol seethed a little more with each passing day. "It's the fucking principle," he explained when Delicious urged him to forget about it.

One night at Jack & Jill's, Bristol had gotten word that the Asian was playing at another poolroom. He tore off to find the place and promptly got lost on the sinuous routes and beltways of Maryland, which only inflamed his temper. When he finally arrived, the Asian was hanging out at the counter. "Where's my fucking six hundred dollars?" Bristol said.

"Don't have it," the Asian said.

"The fuck you don't," Bristol shot back.

The Asian got up to leave, and Bristol followed him to the parking lot, fearful that the guy was going to either drive off or return with a gun. Standing between the man and his car, Bristol informed the debtor that he wasn't getting away until he paid off.

"I don't have the money," the man said repeatedly, each time sounding increasingly desperate. He then came up with an offer: he would give Bristol his cue instead.

Bristol glanced at the cue. It was a Tim Scruggs custom stick that retailed for two grand.

"Fine," he said, grabbing the stick and walking off.

When Bristol returned to Jack & Jill's, he remembered that a road player named Wayne, who was bivouacking in the back room, had recently asked for a "gapper." Wayne had proffered a sob story about losing his money gambling, which prevented him from going home to his family for Christmas. Bristol sought out Wayne and tossed him the cue. "Here," he said. "Sell this to someone and go see your family."

Bristol then turned to Delicious, who was planted at the snack bar. "Shit, Danny, I'm starting to act like you," he said. It was the last sign they needed. It was time to get out of Baltimore.

Bristol could never quite relate to his partner's battle with depression but had grown skilled at predicting when Delicious was about to venture into his wilderness and enter his full-moon phase. He would retreat into himself, stop cracking jokes, and become indifferent to the music on the car radio or their money situation. He'd go off his diet and order obscene amounts of food, sometimes finishing the portions, sometimes just admiring his french fries or ice cream as if it were a pretty, unattainable girl.

Now, Bristol understood that with Delicious' fragile mental state, he was in no position to gamble for big stakes in the Carolinas. He suggested that they make a detour to Virginia Beach, Virginia, where Delicious could relax and get his head right playing for low stakes. They headed to Q-Masters Billiards, a twenty-thousand-square-foot place with reliable action, not far from the site of the annual U.S. Open.

Q-Masters is owned by Barry Behrman, the convivial U.S. Open promoter, a natural-born charmer whose silver Mercedes convertible bears the vanity plate US9-BALL. A bona fide character even by the limbo-bar standards of the pool world, Behrman recently had to ask a judge to release him on bail so that he could run the U.S. Open. Behrman had been arrested on assorted charges that he was running a casino out of his spacious bachelor pad. ("It looked like a little Vegas in there," a police lieutenant had told the local newspaper.) On the night of the bust, Behrman, ever the bon vivant, invited the cops to return for his upcoming New Year's Eve party.

Behrman was nowhere to be seen at Q-Masters, and after a few slow days in the area, Delicious made a game against a reed-thin, baby-faced kid with a caesar haircut. From the start, Bristol could tell that his partner was on a mental vacation. Caesar played well and was soon up a few hundred bucks, but Delicious looked as though he were about to dissolve in a puddle of tears.

"Come on, Danny," Bristol implored. "What's wrong?"

"I feel like shit," Delicious said.

"Just take your break," Bristol said. "I'll get you a Coke or something."

Delicious waved him off. "I have cancer," he said, straight-faced.

Bristol froze, trying his best to stifle laughter. "Sorry? Did you just say you have cancer?"

"I swear. I'm dying of cancer. I can feel it."

Delicious went on to explain that while he hadn't wanted to say anything, he had felt a knot in the back of his head. Then, earlier in the day, his big toe had gone numb. He recalled reading somewhere that the big toe and the brain were connected and — he knew it, just knew it — the numbness in his toe indicated that the cancerous brain tumor had metastasized.

Bristol had long known that Delicious was a world-class hypochondriac — he once told Bristol of how, as a child, he was so terrified of getting a standard immunization that he ran away from home and slept in the woods for two days — but this took the prize. Still trying his best not to giggle, Bristol calmly tried to assure him that his toe could have gone numb for any of a hundred reasons having nothing to do with cancer or any other fatal disease. He patted the back of Delicious' melon and felt no knot. "If anything, it's a zit," Bristol said, trying to lighten the mood.

Delicious was adamant. "Trust me. I know my body. It's cancer."

The game continued, but soon Delicious quit, apologizing as he paid Caesar $800. "Sorry," he said, "but I'm having a panic attack. I think I need to go to a hospital."

Unwilling to continue playing the role of enabler, Bristol announced that he was staying at Q-Master and made a game with Caesar, who by this point was, understandably, more than a little confused. This puzzled Delicious too. If Caesar had beaten him, the odds were overwhelming that he was going to beat Bristol as well. Why would Bristol make that game? On the other hand, he was a dying man—what did he care if his road partner lost a few hundred bucks?

Overcoming his fear of hospitals and physicians, Delicious drove himself to a local clinic and, after a long wait, complained to a doctor about his cancerous toe, his brain tumor, and his panic attack. The doctor gamely examined his patient. ("They even put them stickers on my chest and hooked me up to the machines," Delicious recalled.) Without cracking a smile or mentioning hypochondria or a hyperactive imagination, the doctor pronounced Delicious perfectly healthy. His heart was fine. His vital signs were normal. The big toe may simply have gone numb from sitting too long. The "tumor" was probably a pimple or an ingrown hair.

Delicious was ecstatic, feeling as though he had been given a second life. For good measure, from a deep recess of his wallet he pulled out a copy of his father's Blue Cross card. He presented it and, much to his pleasant surprise, was eligible for coverage. "I'm a survivor!" he shouted to himself as he drove back to the pool hall.

Back at Q-Masters, Bristol had won a $300 set against Caesar, a considerable upset, and was now "hill-hill" (tied heading into the decisive game) for a second set. "That's my boy!" screamed Delicious, who looked nothing like the unstable wreck he had been only hours earlier.

Perhaps distracted by his partner's rapid recovery, Bristol lost the set. Still, he had played even with a superior opponent, conjuring some of the best pool of his life. And Delicious was back in good spirits. Then his cell phone rang.

"How come Y'AINT in da Carolinas yet?" the voice on the phone bellowed.

"We're almost there, 007," Delicious said. "We just took a detour."

"Start driving to TOBACCO ROAD, and don't stop until you get there."

"Okay, okay. We're going, we're going."

When Bristol and Delicious arrived at the Sports Palace in Columbia, South Carolina — more than a month after they had initially anticipated — the scene exceeded their high expectations. Half sports bar, half roadhouse, the place was teeming with action. Classic-rock standbys blasted from the speakers. Jack Daniel's flowed like water. Baseball and football games played on big-screen televisions. And there was big action on every table in the house.

When Delicious got to the pit area, he fixed his gaze on some of the leading lights of professional pool: Shannon "the Cannon" Daulton, Tony "the Hurricane" Ellin, Jimmy Wales, Tony Watson, Steve Moore, Benny Conway, all were playing for big money. Delicious soon learned that Johnny "the Scorpion" Archer and Earl "the Pearl" Strickland, two prominent members of the pool ecosystem, had recently been by too.

A look of awe was pasted on Delicious' face, and he whipped out his bankroll and challenged anyone who was up to it. For months now, all the sweaters — from Harold in St. Louis, to 007, to Cliff Macklin in Baltimore — had been telling Delicious that he played as well as any pro. Quietly, he thought so too. Here was an opportunity to prove to it to everyone, not least himself.

The road adventure was a way to stay one step ahead of his depression, and if it yielded some money, so much the better. But he'd always grasped that the life he'd chosen was a zero-sum game: as he got better and better, he'd gain more and more renown, but that meant he'd get less and less action — and he was fine with that.

His ultimate goal was to be the best, his generation's Willie Mosconi. He'd always envisioned himself as a pro, winning tournaments and holding up trophies while his parents and friends watched on TV. He didn't dream of walking out to the parking lot of a poolroom in Podunk at five in the morning with a bankroll after he'd hustled some hillbilly. What's the fun of being the best at something if no one gives you credit or recognition for it? If he could get one of the pros to the table and take him down, he'd start to make a name for himself.

That was his id speaking to him. His superego, though, told him something entirely different. Namely, if he gave a Tony Watson or an Earl Strickland a run for his bankroll, his career as an anonymous road hustler would screech to an halt. Was he really ready to give up his career as a roadman?

The internal battle was fierce, but common sense won out. Delicious spent night after night in Columbia unobtrusively lingering on the periphery, watching the pros. He took meticulous mental notes, pregnant with confidence that he'd be busting them all one day soon. There it was, Delicious thought: the clearest example yet that he had listened when 007 had extolled "FRIGGIN' PATIENCE" and when Bristol had sermonized about "having fucking discipline."

It turned out that the throngs of pros had gravitated to South Carolina's capital city for good reason. The owner of the Sports Palace was a cackling, genial, silver-haired southerner called Harry the Hat. Harry had once owned a manufacturing plant that produced shirts for Reebok and Umbro before it was put out of business by NAFTA. Harry, though, had done well for himself and was known around Columbia as a high roller. He says that in the late 1990s he bought the Sports Palace not so much because it was a viable business but because of the potential for action.

By day, Harry the Hat was a scratch golfer, happy to take part in a skins game on the courses around town. By night, he would put the money he'd won on the tables of his pool hall. Harry was a capable pool player, but he was nowhere near the level of the pros. Still, he'd throw caution to the sweet southern breeze and, after taking a negligible spot, would play some of the most skilled pool practitioners in the world. One veteran pro recalled that it was as though Harry had been trying to lose his money.

Because his identity and skill level are matters of public record, a top professional player can go for months without getting action — at least not without giving up a preposterous amount of weight. So when word of high-rolling Harry passed on the wire, the players circled like vultures. When Harry finally stopped playing, the pros picked at the carcass by convincing him to back them. Time and again, Harry would back a pro for $5,000 or $10,000. Business would sometimes take Harry away from the table, and when he returned, the player he'd backed would be wearing a sheepish look. "Played him real close, but he made a lucky cut shot and beat me. Sorry, boss." Harry didn't want to believe that his player had "dumped," so he would back the player in a rematch. "Them guys was ruthless!" Harry recalls, with more amusement than anger. "All of them must have taken me for a hundred grand!"

Unable to make a game with Harry, and unwilling to challenge the big names, Delicious and Bristol were consigned to the sidelines, and if they got lucky, they'd gamble a few hundred bucks, trying to snap off the B-level players from the Carolinas. Sometimes they won. Sometimes they gave up too big a spot and lost. But their meager winnings were vastly outstripped by their "nut" — easily $200 a night between their room and their meals. At least they were having a hell of a good time.

Staying at a Quality Inn not far from the poolroom, Delicious and Bristol kept up their fitness routine. Bristol, the natural athlete, had gotten the hang of tennis and could beat his partner on most days. Still, Delicious swelled with pride as he walked off the court drenched in sweat. ("That endorphin thing ain't no bullshit," he says.) They ate all their meals at an Applebee's restaurant, Bristol standing sentry over Delicious' caloric intake, making sure his sidekick drank only Diet Coke and steered clear of fried food and desserts.

Bristol began regularly "seeing" — his euphemism — one of the waitresses at the Sports Palace after her shift. And it wasn't his only relationship. As he relaxed by the Quality Inn pool one afternoon, his reverie was interrupted when a girl in a bikini sat down near him. She was a bubbly, busty blond teen who resembled a slightly naughty Wisconsin milkmaid. Her only physical flaw was a nasty black mark on her right foot the size of a quarter.

Bristol turned on the charm, putting her at ease. He learned that she was traveling with her mother, who was in Columbia attending a sales conference. No, she didn't have a boyfriend. She was a senior in high school. Without asking, Bristol made the assumption that she wasn't exactly college material, a supposition further solidified when he asked about the origin of the unsightly mark on her foot. "Oh, I accidentally shot myself with a BB gun," she said without a trace of shame or embarrassment.

Bristol laughed out loud.

"I know," she said sheepishly. "I'm clumsy like that. Another time, I tried to open a tube of Krazy Glue with my teeth and the paramedics had to come and pry my mouth open."

No matter. She was sufficiently appealing to Bristol. It would take more than stunning stupidity to stop him from squiring her up to the room. Which he did.

Delicious was also productive in Columbia. Watching the pros, he struck up a conversation with Amy, one of the Sports Palace bartenders. She had a toothy smile and an endearing southern drawl. She had just turned twenty-one but had the look of a party girl who'd seen the sun come up plenty of times. When she was on her shift, she let Delicious drink for free, and she chatted with him on her breaks. Chastened by past experience — and, disconnected from his corporeal self, forgetting that he no longer weighed three hundred pounds — Delicious assumed she wasn't sexually attracted to him. He was sure she just thought he was sweet and would want to treat him like a brother or a friend, or another of the let-him-down-easy buzzwords he'd heard plenty of times before. Bristol, though, saw the way Amy always warmed to Delicious and held his wrist when they were talking or sweating the action. "Danny, trust me," he said, "she's yours for the taking."

Delicious may have been socially fearless at the pool table, but it took weeks for him to make his move. When Amy's shift ended, at two in the morning, Delicious asked if she would like to return with him to the Quality Inn. As if she had been waiting for the invite, she nodded and said that she'd grab some beer on her way out and bring it over. With Bristol out smoking weed with some of the players — something he seemed to do with near-nightly frequency — Delicious had their motel room to himself. He tidied up (which is to say, he shoved his dirty clothes under the bed) and drenched himself in cologne. By the time Amy arrived, Delicious was reduced to a nervous teenager. Fortunately, she remembered the beer.

They took pulls on their Bud Lights, and Amy, perhaps sensing Delicious' jellied nerves, suggested they play a drinking game, quarters. (If a player manages to bounce a quarter off the table and into a shot glass, the others at the table have to open their gullets and drink.) Quarters was a ritual on college campuses, and it was also in vogue at the place where Delicious got his higher education, Chicago Billiards. Recalling the tricks he learned playing quarters on slow nights in Connecticut, he made shot after shot, which had a devastating effect on Amy's sobriety. By the time Bristol knocked on the door, around noon the next day, Kid Delicious, age twenty-one, was a virgin no more.

Early one morning at the Sports Palace, as sunlight was starting to muscle out the darkness of night, Delicious massed the courage to try to make a game with Tony Ellin, a longtime pro player. Delicious had known about Ellin for years and, from a distance anyway, greatly admired him. Though he was overweight, Ellin was a serious athlete, able to supplement his pool income by playing tennis, golf, and basketball for money. The wire was that he played big-money H-O-R-S-E, a basketball shooters' game. Because of his flabby physique, he would receive a generous spot. Then, with the same exquisite touch and dexterity he displayed playing pool, he'd pull off the basketball equivalent of the massé, swishing half-court shots and tossing in spin-laden reverse lay-ups. At the pool table, Ellin was a dynamic player whose nickname, "the Hurricane," was an allusion to his monstrously powerful break. Blasting the cue ball with a sound that echoed throughout the room, he could reliably sink two or three balls off the break and then run the rack. All the while, a soft smile managed to steal across his face.

Ellin vaguely recognized the outgoing kid with the squawky voice and the decidedly Yankee accent who'd been loitering at the Sports Palace for weeks. But he had no idea that Delicious was his equal, if not his superior, as a player. Ellin claimed to be dead tired and agreed to shoot for $5 a rack. No problem, Delicious said; if the stakes were low, no one was going to pay attention to the outcome and get suspicious about his identity. In keeping with the size of the stakes, they played casually, chatting between shots and drinking liberally. After a few hours, Delicious was up ten racks. By then it was around nine A.M., and they agreed to call it a night.

For Ellin, the session was undoubtedly forgettable, a few hours of pool against an outgoing kid from up north who hit some nifty shots and sure asked a lot of questions. For Delicious, however, the session was fraught with significance. The stakes may have been low and the pressure nonexistent and his opponent exhausted, but the fact remained that Delicious had just beaten a well-known, well-regarded pro. He felt validated. He didn't care that it was only for fifty bucks. He had just beaten a guy whose picture he had seen in *Billiards Digest*. He was in a state of euphoria for days after that.

(The story has a tragic epilogue. Not even a year later, in the summer of 2000, Ellin was driving to his home in Ladson, South Carolina. A few blocks from his front door, he tried to beat an oncoming train to a railroad crossing. Ellin collided with the train and was killed on impact. At age thirty-five, he left behind a wife and young daughter. An obituary in the *Charleston Post and Courier* spoke to the brutal economics of playing legitimate pool for a living: "Ellin was ranked No. 51 last year in the Camel Pro Billiards Series with tournament winnings of $1,200.")

For all the road players who go bust, the majority exhaust their bankrolls simply by earning less than they spend. After three months — rollicking, fun-saturated months, to be sure — Team

Bristolicious was nearing bankruptcy. They had blown most of their wad of cash just by eating, drinking, sleeping in motels, and paying for gas. It didn't help their finances any when, late in their stay, as they were doing their wash at a laundromat, a bandit made off with their clothes. They took some compensatory comfort picturing the thief's look of revulsion as he fingered Delicious' underwear.

Over the months, Delicious had befriended Harry the Hat, the free-spending proprietor of the Sports Palace. Having learned of Delicious' identity and level of play, Harry tried again and again to back him in big action against one of the prominent players. Delicious declined and declined. But as finances grew dire, he agreed to let Harry back him. His opponent was California Jack, the San Francisco road player who would go to heroic lengths to stalk a lucrative mark. His eyes hidden behind a pair of black plastic "geek chic" glasses, Jack barely said a word. The game was simple: Delicious and Jack would alternate between nine-ball and one-pocket, playing for $1,000 a rack. They would quit when one player was up $6,000.

It was a vintage California Jack hustle. Delicious was a superior nine-ball player, and Jack was an expert one-pocket player. The difference was that a rack of nine-ball can last five minutes, whereas a game of one-pocket can take hours. All "pokes and strokes," one-pocket is notorious for screwing up a player's facility for other forms of pool. (On the other hand, a quick game of nine-ball will do little to detract from a person's ability to play one-pocket.) Back and forth they went, Delicious quickly winning the nine-ball racks, Jack winning the tortuous one-pocket games. For a few hours, neither managed to commandeer much momentum or consolidate a decent lead. For eight, nine, ten hours, they kept at it.

Delicious hadn't been in serious action for months, since he'd concealed his identity in Columbia. He hadn't even practiced at full speed, lest he tip his hand. Eventually fatigue set in. Bone-tired from playing for so long, wrung out from all the time spent on the road, and addled by the demands of one-pocket, Delicious dogged an easy carom. Even at the B level, pool is often more about the misses than the "makes." Wily hustler that he was, Jack took advantage of the opportunity and at the end walked away $6,000 wealthier.

It fell to Delicious to tell Harry that, once again, he had backed a loser. With bags like steamer trunks under his eyes, his face sweat-soaked and flushed, Delicious explained what had happened. "That's okay," sighed Harry, who just a few weeks later would cut his losses, shutter the Sports Palace, and return to playing golf every day. "I can tell by looking at you that you didn't dump. That differentiates you from everyone else I've backed."

For Delicious, having been hustled by California Jack was no unique feat. In fact, it constituted a sort of rite of passage. Still, with his identity no longer concealed, his wallet emaciated, and his underwear missing, he didn't need to study the tea leaves too closely to recognize that the tour of duty in South Carolina had just ended.

9

FLYING SOLO

IN THE LATE 1990s, before Google and the online poker boom, there was still something wonderfully anachronistic about pool hustling. Consider how radically other sports have changed over the years, how advances in equipment, training, and arenas have thoroughly transformed the product. Pitted against today's leviathans, the great George Mikan, for instance, would be only a mediocre player in today's NBA. The NFL of Vince Lombardi's era bears just the vaguest resemblance to the league's current incarnation. Lofting a tennis ball with her racket made of lumber, Chris Evert played an entirely different sport from Venus and Serena Williams with their high-tech thunder sticks.

But in pool, time largely stood still. In some ways the sport had evolved since its inception as "pocket billiards" in the 1800s, when the balls were made of rubber, then ivory, and now are made of plastic. But over the past fifty years, say, the changes were barely perceptible: the rules, the table dimensions, the required skill set were all virtually unchanged. Willie Mosconi would have been a redoubtable English billiards player in nineteenth-century Britain, just as he would be winning serious currency were he playing today.

As far as hustling went, sure, part of the landscape had changed over the past decades. Most of the best halls had come and gone. A room at the Motel 6 cost a hell of a lot more than $6, and Lord knows, gas no longer cost less than a buck a gallon. Speeding tickets weren't so easily covered by slipping the local patrolman a ten-spot. But, overall, the drill was largely the same as it had been in the early days of Eisenhower's brainchild, the Interstate Highway System, which made it easy to motor from here to there, thus ushering in the golden age of road hustling. Backers and "horses" still drove the action. Success was determined partly by guile and partly by native ability. Most roadmen still hit the pavement with little more than their sticks, their maps, and their smokes — if they had a cell phone, it was likely their only piece of equipment containing a circuit board. Players still came off the road without much heft in their wallets, but they were rich in experiences and stories.

Technology, though, was starting to bring about a drastic change in the pool culture. Thanks largely to the Internet, the "wire" was beginning to move at warp speed. A player would make a nice score in some jerkwater town, and within hours backers were getting calls, and sweaters were reading about it on the message boards of AZBilliards.com. Even a stealth hustler like California Jack couldn't escape the tentacles of Google.

If this trend has generally been a bane for road players who complain their action is being knocked too easily, it can be a boon to those controlling the purse strings. Like Wall Street speculators who discover a little-known company before it goes public, a welter of well-connected backers have made an art of finding little-known players before they "blow up," and putting them in action.

So it was that in late 1999, shortly after his return from South Carolina, Delicious received a call from a stakehorse in South Florida we'll call Lopez. The proposition: Lopez wanted to back him in a nine-ball game for $10,000, playing eight-ahead against another young player, Charlie "the Korean Dragon" Williams. Then twenty-two, Williams was already a fledgling pro, regarded as the best player in Florida. But Lopez felt that his "ringer from Jersey" was just as good. If Delicious won, he and Lopez would split the ten large, fifty-fifty. This wasn't hustling; it was gambling. The match was already made. It was just a question of who was going to lay claim to the money.

These kinds of prearranged, high-stakes matches erode a player's ability to go incognito on the road. Word of the result inevitably flits across the pool radar. But Delicious was enticed by the size of the bet—the chance to win $5,000 without putting up a dime of his own money—and the challenge of matching up against Williams. If he was now a pool mercenary, playing at the behest of a stakehorse, so be it.

His one reservation was a reluctance to make another long drive. When he conveyed this to Lopez, the man laughed. "Shit, don't worry about that," he said. "I'll fly you down, get you a motel. I pay all your expenses."

"Okay. Then I'll play."

No sooner had the words left his mouth than Delicious felt a stab of guilt. What about Bristol Bob? They were partners and went everywhere together. Delicious asked if Lopez could also fly Bristol down to Florida.

"Sure, Bristol can come," Lopez said, "but why should I pay for him? You're the one I want to put in action."

Delicious was nervous about telling his partner that he had signed up to play a solo gig. But when he did, Bristol could scarcely have been more supportive. "Go down there and bust his balls, Danny," he said. "A guy's staking you for ten thousand, you gotta go." In truth, Bristol was relieved for the downtime.

Though never explicitly discussed, at some level Delicious and Bristol both knew it was time to put their joint venture on hold. There had been no epic blowup or battle royal over money, as there usually is when road partnerships dissolve. One apocryphal (but nonetheless illustrative) story recounts how players A and B parted bitterly after a successful road partnership. A accused B of stealing from their bankroll and vowed revenge. The two happened to be playing in the same tournament. A approached B claiming that all was forgiven, and they ought to have a beer and rehash some of their scores on the road. They drank until morning and rekindled their friendship. The next night, A went further in his generosity, hiring a prostitute to service B. Deep in the night, with dozens of players gambling in an action room, a voluptuous blonde walked seductively up to B, sat on his lap, and ran a hand through his hair. B suggested they leave the place, but the prostitute insisted on ministering orally to him in the corner. With the blonde's face buried in B's crotch, A told the other players to "watch this." He walked up to the blonde and yanked off her wig. The prostitute that A had hired for his former road partner was a transvestite. A had gotten his revenge, and B had been thoroughly humiliated.

Suffice it to say, Delicious and Bristol were divorcing on considerably more amicable terms. In fact, they weren't really divorcing at all. They were merely separating, with plans of reuniting in a few months for another adventure, maybe out west.

Still, it was clear that their partnership had hit its expiration date. For one thing, Delicious had improved so radically that he now played far better than his partner. While Bristol never showed jealousy, the growing chasm separating their levels of play had changed the chemistry of their hustling. Also, Bristol, once fiercely devoted to self-discipline, was smoking pot early and often, drinking too much, and keeping crazy hours. All that time observing Delicious' ice-breaking personality and his "if it feels good, do it" philosophy had resulted in Bristol's dialing back his intensity and loosening up. But now he slacked off too much.

Besides that, Bristol had tired of the lying that hustling required. It was fun at first — the bullshit stories, the improvisational lines, the pseudonyms, the guises, the concealed speed. But it started exacting a price. As Bristol saw it, he'd spent so much time being someone else that he had damn near forgotten who he was. The author Kurt Vonnegut once observed, "Be careful what you pretend to be, because you are what you pretend to be." Bristol understood all too well. He felt that his entire self was becoming counterfeit.

Delicious arrived in Miami on a Wednesday night. Slicing through the skies on a plane to reach his pool destination was a novel experience. Lopez picked him up at the airport and took him to a motel not far from the Coconut Grove poolroom, where he was to play against Charlie Williams. The first time Delicious had met Williams, years before, he did a double take. Williams was not, as Delicious had initially assumed, a burly Florida redneck, but rather a sinewy, slightly built Korean who'd harbored a desire to become a minister before contracting the pool bug. (He was born Heoun Ho Kim in Seoul, but came to the United States when he was eight weeks old and later chose to Americanize his name.) They had run into each other over the years and had always gotten along. Now, like two boxers who were about to do combat to appease their promoters but couldn't muster any authentic animus toward each other, they talked easily before their match and even swapped a few spots.

As Williams took his last practice strokes, Lopez sat in front of a slot machine on the far side of the room. He whistled to Delicious. "Come here, Danny."

Delicious walked over. Lopez whispered, "Stand right here in front of me." Delicious did as told and turned around to see Lopez discreetly inserting a laminated twenty-dollar bill on a string into the slot machine and then pulling it out. Delicious was oblivious, but he would soon learn that the "laminated twenty" is one of the secret scams of the pool world. When cut at precisely the right angle, the laminated bill can trick a machine into registering the money. Yet when the schemer yanks the bill out of the slot with the string, the cash credit remains. For whatever reason, the change machines at automatic car washes are particularly susceptible to this scam—put in your laminated twenty, the machine spits out four fives; pull back your laminated bill, and you're $20 wealthier.

Here Lopez was working over the slot machine, inserting the bill again and again while Delicious inadvertently blocked everyone's view. Each time, another $20 credit registered. Finally Lopez yelped and sprinted to the counter. "Holy shit," he said. "I just hit three cherries. I won five hundred! Let me cash out!" The poolroom owner walked over to the slot machine, saw the $500 credit with his own eyes, and dutifully paid off Lopez. Delicious no longer wondered where such an unkempt guy came up with the money to front $10,000 on a set of pool.

The match started problematically for Delicious. Feeling sluggish, perhaps from the travel, he played passively. With Williams making his shots and controlling the cue masterfully — offering a glimpse of the fine pro career that would await him — it looked as if Lopez was going to need to spend more time with the laminated bill to pay off his debt. By two A.M., Williams was seven-ahead and a few balls from wrapping up a wildly profitable night.

Sitting in his chair, Delicious was nearly comatose, done in by exhaustion and disappointment. Reflexively, he would turn to look at Bristol for support, as he had done so many times before, only to realize he was alone.

Perhaps having lowered his guard, since he had such a commanding lead, Williams dogged a shot on the seven ball that he'd ordinarily make ten times out of ten. Delicious took a break to step outside and suck on a joint. Then he returned to nail a crazy cut shot, bury the eight, and run out the rack. With that small opening, he'd turned the set around. Within ninety minutes, he had pulled even. They agreed to return the following night, and again, Williams held a comfortable lead but couldn't close out Delicious.

On the third night, the backers agreed to sweeten the pot, changing the set to ten-ahead. After six hours, Williams was up nine games, on the brink of winning a nice chunk of cash. In a virtual repeat of the first night, he dogged a shot at the nine. Delicious rose from his chair and, with the exception of a few safeties (defensive shots that afford the opponent no chance to score), never sat down again, erasing the deficit and then winning the set. It was another referendum on his mettle, his "heart," as pool players call it. Williams was impressed, too, with Delicious' endurance. "I remembered him from earlier as a big fat guy, and I kept telling myself he would get tired out," says Williams. "That never happened. He was the underdog, but it was like he made up his mind he wasn't going to lose, and that was that."

With sweat flowing from his brow and down his back, Delicious shook Williams' hand before getting mobbed by his jubilant backer. To Delicious, the money could hardly have mattered less. Naturally, the first person he called to relay the news of his great conquest was Bristol Bob, who was genuinely thrilled for his partner. But as Bristol listened to Delicious exult in victory, it was not lost on him that "I" and not "we" was the operative pronoun.

Marooned in New Jersey, Bristol seized on an idea. Lately he'd been growing obsessed with the Filipino style of pool. To a man, the Filipinos played with a sort of effortless elegance, a seamlessness that made everything they hit look so damned easy. This combination of poise and equipoise was apparent in their dispositions too. Sure, Filipinos could be hustlers: Efren Reyes, for example, barnstormed Texas roadhouses under the alias of "Cesar Morales," a Mexican immigrant allegedly busting the poker legend Amarillo Slim for $200,000. None of the stresses of the profession seemed to fluster them. What Bristol would give for the constitution of Reyes or José Parica or Francisco Bustamante, players whose moods, outwardly anyway, were unchanged whether they were shooting exquisitely or terribly.

Bristol contacted Al Lapena, a Filipino veteran who'd helped mentor Delicious when the kid was just starting out. Bristol and Lapena made low-stakes games that Bristol had little hope of winning. But for the cost of a $20 or $50 set, he would get to observe Lapena and make abundant mental notes on the niceties of "Filipino pool." Exhilarated, Bristol spent most of his waking hours at Action Billiards, in Old Bridge, New Jersey, "donating" to Lapena — it was way cheaper than private lessons, he reasoned — and picking up on every subtlety and inflection. Soon Bristol was gripping the cue differently, planting his feet differently, even reading the table differently.

Bristol had been driving around in a spiffy Ford Bronco that he had purchased with road winnings. His designer clothes and his $150 Nike Shox were also tokens of the successful nights playing alongside Kid Delicious. But now, without any income to speak of, Bristol was running short of cash. He ate as sparingly and inexpensively as possible — sometimes a Cup-O-Noodles comprised his only meal of the day. When he didn't fall asleep in the back room at Action Billiards, he couch-surfed, crashing with various acquaintances, one more distant than the next. He fell for an Asian cutie, and they went out a few times. But, ultimately, Bristol was so transfixed by Filipino-style pool and all its intricacies that he had neither the time nor the emotional reserves for a serious girlfriend.

Not unlike a tennis player switching from a two-handed to a one-handed backhand, or a pitcher trying to transform himself from a flame-throwing ace into a cunning knuckleballer, Bristol struggled with the changes, trying to undo years of habits and muscle memory. The adjustments he was making in order to play like a Filipino felt awkward and unnatural. His stroke was suddenly filled with indecisive hitches. When he would grow frustrated and revert to his familiar stroke and playing style, that too felt strange. And as a player whose mood had always moved in lockstep with how well he was stroking the ball, Bristol was, by his own admission, "a total basket case." If he was a borderline A player when he started, he was now steadily working his way down the alphabet.

On one particularly dismal night, Bristol was practicing alone at a poolroom in Jersey City — a gritty, vaguely sinister town at the lip of the Holland Tunnel, at once a stone's throw and a million cultural miles from Manhattan — and growing increasingly frustrated. He'd noticed a handsome hipster at a nearby table, an Asian man who looked as if he were ready to bite through his cue as he dogged one ball after another. Now the man sidled up to Bristol.

"Want to play better?"

"Fuck yeah, I want to play better," Bristol snapped.

The Asian, maybe forty, with a jack-o'-lantern smile and an oval for a head, led Bristol to a landing in the back of the pool hall and unwrapped a small cellophane bag packed with what appeared to be crystals of rock salt. The man took a sheet of aluminum foil, placed a few crystals on top, and made a little canoe with the foil. Then he lit the foil from underneath and gently eased it back and forth. The burning crystals turned waxy, and the man tilted the foil at an angle. As the wax oozed down, it left a trail of smoke. Taking out a rolled-up dollar bill, the man inhaled the smoke. Then he tilted the foil the other way and, as the wax seeped in the other direction, again took in a mouthful of smoke. He turned to Bristol. "You try it."

However devoted he once was to self-discipline and temperance, those days were long gone. Bristol claims he didn't know that he was about to smoke crystal meth. But he did know it wasn't rock salt. Anyway, hell, the guy *did* say that it would help him play better pool. How many professional pool players have sworn that pot helps their nerves, OxyContin and Percocet improve their reflexes, speed supposedly dilates their pupils, improving their vision and helping them to focus on the table? What could it hurt to experiment?

Bristol inhaled the line through a tightly rolled dollar bill. When he walked back into the main room, he couldn't feel his feet. He had been high before, but never anything like this, never to the extent that he felt detached from his body. A surge of energy coursed through him, leaving him feeling as though he were receiving electroshock therapy. He had no other symptoms of a cold, but his throat felt so swollen he could barely swallow. Not that he was hungry; he was too wired to think about food. Back at the table, he tried to drum up some action, and he hoped for a long set. The way he was feeling, no one was going to outlast him. While he never found an opponent, his instincts had been right. It took three days for him to fall asleep.

For the next two months, Bristol lived the life of a classic addict. The father of another pool player owned a boarding house in Sayreville, New Jersey. For $150 a week, Bristol rented a small bedroom there, though he had to share a bathroom with a dozen other vagrants. The place made the back room at Chicago Billiards look like a suite at the Four Seasons. But he had enough privacy to do as he pleased. Before long, he was having trouble making the rent. And the choice between crystal meth and a place to sleep was really no choice at all. He began spending nights in the back of his Bronco. For the first time, he had violated one of the cardinal rules of road playing: don't sleep in your vehicle.

On the road, Bristol had managed to extricate himself — and often Delicious too — from countless thorny situations. But this time he had been hustled. Some dirtbag had promised him that a hit of his crystals would improve his pool play. In a weak moment, he'd fallen into the trap. Next thing he knew, he was a junkie. And, almost as disgraceful, he was a sucker. The meth had seduced him and busted him and stripped him of dignity in a way no opponent at the table ever had.

As Bristol struggled to find a toehold, his life orbited around getting his next fix. He now played pool not to improve his mechanics or sharpen his skills, but in hopes of grinding out enough scratch to subsidize a $100 bag of crystal meth. His physical appearance, always such a point of pride, had deteriorated. In a matter of weeks, he had dropped twenty-five pounds and looked downright cadaverous. Bones protruded from his face. His once sturdy frame now looked like scaffolding. His hair was stringy and greasy. The regimented, salad-eating, fashion-conscious, self-flagellating fitness freak had officially left the building.

Calls from friends and parents went unreturned. Al Lapena saw Bristol less and less. Back from winning that $10,000 game in Florida, Delicious had heard through the pool wire that his buddy was "having some issues," but he couldn't connect with Bristol either. Bristol would have done well to go on the road with Delicious again and get away from his Jersey City dealer, who plied him with poison a few times a week. But he was too ashamed of himself to let Delicious see him like this. Besides, Delicious had shown in that arranged game in Miami that he could be successful as a solo practitioner. Maybe, Bristol thought in his fits of self-pity, Delicious was better off without him around.

Delicious was sick over Bristol's fate. But maybe because he was never able to make direct contact with Bristol, his concern was tinged with anger. For months, the contours of their relationship had been shifting: Delicious had become more savvy and responsible and appearance-conscious, sometimes at the expense of his effortless charm; Bristol had become more genial and social but lost his self-discipline and edge. Now the dynamic was flipped. They had achieved almost total role reversal.

Bristol was no longer Delicious' emotional anchor. If anything, it was the opposite. Delicious was now the one who was concerned about his buddy's self-destructive ways. "You're better than this, Bob," Delicious once yelled into Bristol's voice mail. "There's a lot of guys I can see being addicts, but you're above this, man. I want to help you get your shit together, but you gotta call me back."

Delicious also had to consider his own interests. He knew if he wanted to stave off another round of depression and continue the habits that had shaved a hundred pounds from his body, he needed to stay with his routine and get back on the road. What was it Bristol had always told him? *You need structure.* There was no structure sitting at home, waiting for Bristol to favor him with the courtesy of a return phone call.

10

WHEREVER I MAY ROAM

WHAT'S DA FIRST TING a guy in a pool hall DO when he suspects a road player has just walked in?" the I-eat-Marlboros-for-breakfast voice of 007 boomed into the phone.

"I dunno, what?" Kid Delicious answered sheepishly.

Exasperated, 007 exhaled. "He goes INNA DA parking lot and checks DA license plates of DA UTTER guy's car."

"So?" Delicious said, at once annoyed by the quiz and thrilled that 007 had resurfaced with a list of spots.

"So. I'm gonna steer you through Wisconsin and Minnesota and the Dakotas. I know a whole BUNCHA spots there. But if you take your car with them NEW JERSEY PLATES, they're gonna sniff you out right away. You come here, take my mom's car WIT DEM ILLINOIS PLATES, and if anyone asks, you're from Chicago."

"What about Bris—"

"I don't know what DA HELL'S going on with that kid. I hear bad things. But you GOTTA WORRY about yourself and get back in action."

Delicious didn't disagree. Within hours, he'd mooched a ride to Newark Airport and purchased a one-way ticket to O'Hare. This being the halcyon days before 9/11, he paid for the ticket in cash. (Since most road players either have an abysmal credit rating or don't dare disclose their incomes lest the taxman be alerted, they don't carry credit cards, complicating air travel.) An upbeat 007 met Delicious at the airport and laughed aloud when he got a load of Delicious' physique, which was veering awfully close to trim territory. "Holy shit! Looks like you suffered a skinny attack!" howled 007, himself no underwear model. "How much friggin' weight have you lost, buddy?"

They caught up on things over dinner, and 007 handed Delicious a list of spots and the keys to a dreary gray 1987 Buick LeSabre with sixty thousand miles on the odometer. He explained that in exchange for lending the car that belonged to his mother, his "detective commission" for the trip was going to be slightly higher. "Now," he said, "go make us both rich."

As he drove to Wisconsin, Delicious had to adjust to the rhythms of a solo mission. Without a wingman seated next to him, he felt somehow bereft, as though he had forgotten his wallet or pool stick somewhere. The terrain of the upper Midwest — the impossibly vast cerulean sky, the whipping wind, the roads so vacant that passing motorists would wave to each other — only amplified his sense of solitude. The patches of silence took some getting used to. Time and again Delicious would begin to speak aloud, only to realize that there was no other passenger in the car.

At the same time, there was something exhilarating about the independence. He could stop to eat wherever and whenever he felt like it. He could wake up when he felt like it. He didn't need anyone's consent if he wanted to stop at a casino. If he tossed his empty coffee cup into the back seat as he drove, no one was going to chastise him. If he wanted oldies or Cat Stevens on the radio, he didn't have to worry about someone calling it pussy music and then trolling for a classic-rock station. As a pop psychologist might phrase it, Delicious was alone, but he wasn't lonely.

His spirits were, however, soon dampened by the lack of action. Most of 007's spots weren't panning out. Delicious had a fine time at Romines High Pockets, a Milwaukee pool hall attached to a Mexican restaurant. He mainlined margaritas and watched a Green Bay Packers game on a large TV. But the player he was stalking, Larry Nevel, was nowhere to be seen. At Tips and Taps, a soulful joint near the Mississippi River in Lacrosse, Wisconsin, there was no action. Delicious took a few hundred bucks off some college kids in Madison and ripped a few hundred more off an old-timer up in Green Bay. But after nearly three weeks in Wisconsin, he was barely breaking even. A bartender in Lacrosse lamented to him that Wisconsin was a hotbed of bowling—home to more lanes per capita than any other state—and that sport had cannibalized most of the state's pool players.

Three weeks into the trip, Delicious was miserable. He felt like a recently divorced daddy who'd enjoyed a stretch of the bachelor life and, tired of spending so much time alone, was ready to enter another relationship. If that weren't incentive enough to return home, he was driving through Wisconsin when he got a call from a New Jersey friend.

"What the fuck is up with your friend Bristol Bob?"

"Huh?"

"Man, your boy is *fucked up*. He looks like a skeleton. He's all white. Owes dudes money. You gotta straighten him out, bro."

Delicious left more voice mail messages that went unreturned, Bristol being too ashamed to face his sidekick in his current state. Delicious called mutual friends, asking them to check up on his partner. He told the guys at Elite Billiards to take care of Bristol if he ever came in. Delicious decided, however, that he wasn't going to cut this trip short.

The whole situation upset him so much that, whenever he thought about Bob, he would pound the steering wheel or rifle the cue ball in anger. He had played against meth addicts and knew it was a devastating drug. But he also recalled the tough love Bristol had always dispensed. When Delicious complained to Bristol that he was tired of doing sit-ups or really craved a cheeseburger, Bristol was all about tough love: *I don't care that everyone else pampers you, Danny. I'm giving you what you really need, a swift kick in the ass.* Delicious thought, *Well, I'm not pampering your ass either, buddy.*

Even strung out on meth, Bristol managed to land a girl. A

dark-skinned cutie stopped by the pool hall one night to drop off some food, and Bristol managed to score her phone number. She was a full-time student at Fairleigh Dickinson University, and she fell hard for the good-looking pool hustler with the outlaw disposition who was so different from the guys on campus. After a progression of increasingly serious dates, Bristol came clean about his meth problem.

His new girlfriend formulated a detox plan. He would stay in her dorm room until he got the urge out of his system. He'd have a safe place to live; she'd bring him food and DVDs and check up on him between classes. As long as he didn't leave the room, he couldn't get another hit. The plan was sweet and well intentioned, but it didn't last. A few days of craving became unbearable, and he left the dorm room to find his dealer in Jersey City.

Then came his moment of clarity. Here's how Bristol describes it:

"For some reason, at around three in the afternoon I called my dealer but he couldn't meet me until eleven that night. So I parked at the pool hall and hung out in my truck. I'd been up for three days. I wanted to fall asleep, but there's like this whirring that goes on in your head, and you can't fight it. But then you crash big-time. I fell asleep and had this insane dream. Everything went totally black, and I heard chanting, like monks humming. I knew I was dreaming, but I couldn't wake up. My heart was racing and the voices got louder. I thought for sure I was going to have a heart attack.

"Finally, at about eight I wake up. I'm sweating and physically exhausted, like I've just been running for miles. I crank up the radio just to keep myself from falling back asleep. Pretty soon I do fall back asleep and have the exact same dream. Total black. Everything is spinning. The loud chanting. My heart is beating like a jackhammer. Again, I feel like I'm going to die of a heart attack. What a way to go: sitting in your truck in a pool hall parking lot waiting for my dealer.

"Somehow I wake myself up, and now I'm really determined not to fall back asleep. I go into the poolroom and see if anyone has some weed. Usually weed makes me tired, but sometimes if

I'm already tired, it gives me a jolt and wakes me up. I smoke a joint and hang out, waiting for the dealer to get there. He comes at eleven and we do our business.

"I go in the bathroom, and just as I light the foil and take a hit, I hear those chanting voices again and my heart starts racing, almost to the beat of the chants. I take one look at myself in the mirror and see what a fucking mess I am, eyes sagging, bony cheeks, my hair is messed up, my lips are chapped. I look like Skeletor. I get sick to my stomach, like I'm going to puke, and I throw the crystal in the toilet. I totally lost the desire, and I'll never touch the shit again. I know it sounds crazy, but I swear that's the way it happened."

Following a few frustrating idle weeks, Delicious' luck in the upper Midwest started to change. After grinding out a few dimes in Eau Claire, Wisconsin, Delicious drove an hour or so north to tiny Chetek, Wisconsin, where 007 promised yet another "can't miss" spot. Bobby Law, a creditable local player, owned a pool hall attached to a small bowling alley, and he was prone to playing for money.

Inside the barn-like Chetek Bowling and Billiards, Delicious took on another persona. Invoking his middle name, he introduced himself to Law, a husky type in his mid-thirties, as "Martin." He explained that he had driven up from Chicago to visit family in the area. It's the rare road hustler who passes through a somnolent town of two thousand in northwest Wisconsin, so without stopping to consider the possibility that Martin was being something other than forthright, Law assumed that this chatty guest was indeed just a bored kid eager to escape an afternoon of playing bridge with his aunt in Chippewa Falls.

Delicious made small talk and put Law at ease. Then he spotted a Ms. Pac-Man arcade game in the corner. At Chicago Billiards, Delicious was, like most of the regulars, able to play for hours on a single quarter. "See that game?" he said to Law. "I bet you twenty dollars I can play right now and get the high score." "Sure," Law said. Munching Binky, Inky, Pinky, and Sue with the rapacity he had once reserved for double cheeseburgers, Delicious soon won his twenty. He then asked Law if he wanted to play for more money at the pinball machine. That was fine with Law. The whole time he was thinking, *I'm happy to lose a little on arcade games, because I'll just win everything back playing this kid in pool,* not realizing, of course, that he was going from the frying pan into the fire.

Down around $200 after playing various arcade games, Law suggested they play nine-ball on one of the bar tables. "Oh, I don't know," Delicious said. "I used to be pretty decent at pool, but I ain't played in a long while." But he grabbed a cue off the wall and they started playing. Laying down, Delicious lost a few games, won a rack, then lost a few more. When Law had won back his $200, they quit. "If you want, Martin," Law offered, "come back tomorrow and we can play some more."

Delicious nodded and left. He checked into a shopworn motel and planned to go for a run on the banks of one of the lakes that dot the terrain around Chetek, but ended up grabbing a burger instead. Without Bristol there to play nutritionist and ration the intake of junk food, Delicious let his diet slide a bit. But he didn't much care. Finally he saw himself as others did. On that trip, alone on the prairie, he realized that he really liked who he was, personality quirks and all, and that his self-image wasn't tied to his weight. A self-satisfied grin etched on his face, he fell asleep that night eager to meet Bobby Law around noon the following day.

Playing the role of naïf to perfection, Delicious told Law that he was willing to risk $500 on a set of nine-ball. Law was ecstatic. Delicious played at full speed and quickly ran the first rack. Law knew he was being hustled and smiled with grudging admiration. Delicious ran out and, in keeping with the unwritten code of honor among pool players, Law paid without incident. "Pure and simple, you got me good," he graciously conceded. He asked Delicious about his real identity, and the two shared a laugh. Law then directed him back to the highway, wished him luck, and added, "When you make it big, Kid Delicious, don't forget about me."

• • •

Delicious decided to skip a few spots in Minnesota and instead motor across the state to Fargo, North Dakota, where 007 had instructed him to seek out a player named Rory Hendrickson, a bar table specialist. In the past, Hendrickson had beaten several road players 007 had guided to Fargo, but none, 007 was convinced, played nearly as well as Delicious. As he barreled down the highway, swigging a Coke, eating chips, and listening to Cat Stevens full blast, Delicious studied his notes from 007:

Fargo. D/T Billiards at Broadway. Easy 2 find. Rory Hendr. on br. table. Don't give me up to no one — owner mrk. is a friend. Will be pissed if he finds out I steered u.

On a night when the cold was inescapable even indoors and the snow crunched with every step, Delicious trundled into Billiards at Broadway and laid claim to a seat at the bar. He thought he felt a spasm of depression coming on — the brutally frigid weather, the short days, and the lack of companionship conspiring to get the better of him. His mood hardly improved when he asked the barmaid about Rory Hendrickson's whereabouts. She smiled and said he was out of town on business and wasn't due back in Fargo for another week.

Billiards at Broadway is a pool palace, roughly the size of an airplane hangar, that speaks to North Dakota's need for indoor activities and the inexpensive commercial real estate market. A seemingly endless array of tables — barboxes, Gold Crowns, even a twelve-footer — were scattered over two floors, amid arcade machines, dartboards, and a stage. Even on this bitterly cold Tuesday, the majority of the tables were occupied.

As he threw back shots of Johnnie Walker, Delicious took inventory of the folks on the neighboring bar stools. An outgoing gnome of a man on his left looked to have some sort of congenital condition that left him with ten thumbs for fingers. Another patron was confined to a wheelchair. A third wore a beard so thick it looked as though he was shrouded in a burka of hair. "Keeps me warm, like a ski cap," the man explained. The omnium-gatherum reminded Delicious of the bar scene from *Star Wars,* but he listened to their stories and bought them drinks. For at least an hour, Delicious, now blitzed, grew obsessed with finding a way to high-five the guy with all thumbs, just so he could touch his hands. Meanwhile, he had a hell of a time with the guys. He knew right away that none were potential marks, but they talked easily and drained their glasses.

Delicious also noted the bartender, a cheerful woman who was on a first-name basis with everyone in the room. She had long, stringy brown hair, a well-proportioned figure, and an olive complexion — Delicious mistook her for Hispanic. Recalling some lines he'd ripped off from Bristol, Delicious struck up a conversation with her. As they spoke, the menagerie at the bar seemed to fade away.

She said her name was Tanya. She'd grown up in the area and had attended a nearby college, but dropped out because she'd fallen hopelessly in love with pool. She played every chance she got and took a job at Billiards — "Everyone calls it that," she said, "just plain Billiards" — in part because of the free table time. She lived a block away in a one-bedroom apartment. Her last name was Harig, "as German as you can get." Her pigmentation, she sheepishly admitted, was the product of a tanning bed. She loved quirky, cold, close-knit Fargo but wished it were known for more than the recent floods and the noir Coen Brothers film, which took place mostly in Minnesota anyway. In all her twenty-six years she had never seen the ocean. And while she "didn't want it to sound like I'm bragging on myself," Tanya allowed that she was probably the best female pool player in the state.

Sensing that she was doing all the talking and the mystery man across the bar had revealed nothing about himself, Tanya turned inquisitor.

"What about you? How'd you end up here?"

"Oh," Delicious said, "I'm from Chicago. Just passing through town."

"Chicago?" Tanya said skeptically. "You sound like you're from back east."

"Well, I lived in New Jersey for a while."

Delicious successfully changed the subject and did some reconnaissance work. Rory, he learned from Tanya, was a stocky guy in his early thirties, an occasional roadman who played for sizable stakes and usually gave worse than he got. He was on the same pool team as Tanya and was her Scotch doubles partner in competitions. In fact, they'd recently won a mixed doubles championship in Minnesota. His specialty was indeed the barbox, the seven-foot table that is particularly popular in the Midwest. And, since Rory "did real well in business," he was beholden to no backer and gambled with his own money.

Finally Delicious asked, "Since Rory isn't here, think there's anyone else around who will play me for some money tonight?"

Tanya smiled. "I will."

By midnight, most of the patrons had left, and Delicious and Tanya played nine-ball. Pool doesn't require strength or power or cardiovascular stamina or any other trait that would seem to favor one gender over the other. Nevertheless, men tend to play better than women. Jeanette Lee, d/b/a the Black Widow, may be the most celebrated pool player today, far more popular than the best male. But she is not even the best in her own household. Her husband, George Breedlove, is a superior player, and Lee candidly admits that if both are playing their best pool, he wins. The gender gap is gradually closing — at a 2006 pro event in Orlando, Karen Corr beat the great Earl Strickland — but there's still a gap. The explanations vary. Men have more forceful breaks, so it's easier for them to dominate a rack. They execute safeties better. A prominent player even suggests that men's flat chests make it easier for them to master the proper technique.

Yet perhaps it's simply a matter of nurture trumping nature. Poolrooms have long been the province of men. As the brilliant writer Steve Rushin once put it, "Chivalry isn't dead — but a respiratory ailment prevents it from staying long in most poolrooms." While someone like Delicious had long been devoting the majority of his waking hours to the sport, Tanya had barely ventured into a pool hall until she was nineteen.

Whatever the case, Tanya's skills were immediately apparent, but she was little match for Kid Delicious — even a lovestruck, well-oiled Kid Delicious trying his best to conceal his speed. Tanya, though, was having too good a time with Danny to care.

She couldn't remember the last time she'd connected with someone like that. She closed up the pool hall at one A.M., but they kept playing and talking until four. Tanya asked Delicious where he was staying. "I'm off to find a motel room, I guess," he said. "You recommend anyplace?"

She rolled her eyes. "You can come back with me and sleep on my couch if you want." Finally this trip had brought Delicious a spasm of good luck, and he smiled as walked with her into the night, into temperatures straining to hit double digits.

At Tanya's apartment, Delicious wavered about whether to reveal his identity and the fact that he was in Fargo to snap off Rory Hendrickson. It was a pool player's equivalent of a moral quandary, and he gave in to his conscience. He came clean. When he had finished, Tanya smiled. "See," she said. "I could tell you weren't from friggin' Chicago."

They had breakfast together later that morning and kept talking as easily as they had the night before. They retreated to Billiards at Broadway, where Delicious continued to charm Fargo's pool-playing community like a modern-day Music Man. The regulars couldn't get enough of the kid who shattered their perceptions of what a hustler was like. They would sit around waiting for Delicious to come in and hit some trick shots or tell stories about life on the road.

When he went home with Tanya on the second night, the couch went unoccupied. Giddy about her role in helping out a real live road hustler, in the days that followed Tanya connived with Delicious, guiding him to local players he could drill for a few bucks without having to sweat. After a week in Fargo, Delicious hadn't made much money. But he hadn't spent much either, thanks to Tanya's hospitality.

The bankroll didn't matter anyway. He was falling in love.

For the first time in his life, he didn't just have a girl, but a dream girl. Physically, she was a class of specimen not even remotely available when Delicious weighed three hundred pounds. But never mind her looks: she was guileless and fun and carefree. That they shared a love affair with pool — and so she instantly understood his singular talent as well as the rhythms and language of the sport — was the kicker.

Among the many depressing aspects of being a road player, the chief one might be the difficulty most men have in forging meaningful relationships with women. This has always been the case. (Pool arcana: in her autobiography, the soul chanteuse Etta James claims that Minnesota Fats was her biological father, though her birth certificate suggests otherwise.) The type of dysfunctional relationship that existed between Paul Newman and Piper Laurie in *The Hustler* is not atypical today. As one pool veteran puts it: "These guys build a shell around themselves that a woman is not allowed to penetrate. They foster hot, quick relationships that wither as soon as the woman wants to crawl inside the armor. These guys get scared to death of needing someone or having to make a sacrifice or two. It is actually a sign of negative self-worth. Many do not believe they deserve the love of anyone, sometimes not even themselves."

Yet Delicious wasn't wired like those guys. He was more than happy to let the right girl inside his armor. He picked up on the irony immediately: as soon as he was starting to feel comfortable in his own skin and enjoy his own company, he met a girl who made him never want to be alone. As silly as it sounded, when Delicious called home after a few days in Fargo, he told his parents he was thinking about putting forth a marriage proposal.

Rory Hendrickson finally showed up at Billiards at Broadway. Fresh from a strong showing at the U.S. Bar Table Championships in Nevada, he was a minor celebrity in Fargo. He handled himself with quiet dignity, tersely asking for a table and, like a real craftsman, practicing methodically. Caught awkwardly between her new boyfriend and her old playing partner, Tanya introduced Delicious and Rory and then backed away, leaving them to make a game. She figured that if Rory was suspicious of the stranger with the thick accent who was so eager to play, he could find out the truth for himself.

Brimming with confidence, Rory didn't make any inquiries. He assumed Delicious was a road player, but he'd beat him the same way he beat the others. With a minimum of negotiating, they agreed to play for $100 a rack. The allegiances at Billiards were split fairly evenly between the well-liked local and the genial road player who had been charming everyone by day and romancing the popular barmaid by night.

Playing on a barbox was a risky proposition for Delicious. Nicknamed "the equalizer," the smaller, seven-foot bar table works to the advantage of lesser players. While the balls are regulation size, the table affords less room to maneuver. A player with a muscle memory developed on a big table needs to adjust his speed to keep his balls from overrunning their position. There are fewer difficult shots — none of those crazy jack-ups on the back rail or those eight-foot swatches of felt between the cue ball and the object ball — and it's easier to run out. Plus, for a player like Delicious, who'd always practiced on a big table, there was an adjustment going down in size.

Still, after only a few games, it was abundantly clear that, even on a bar table in Rory's home poolroom, Rory and Delicious were a level apart. The visitor put on a clinic, drilling shots as though the pockets were insatiable maws. With an Al Capone cigar nestled between his cheek and gums, Rory looked on impassively and, to his credit, played on. He was resilient and strategically competent, but in the end, unthreatening. By closing time, Delicious was up $1,000. Both men pleaded with Tanya to stick around and keep the place open. She fell asleep on a barstool, and they played through the night. By the time they quit eighteen hours later, Delicious was up $2,500.

It was hardly Delicious' biggest score. And he never had to play his best pool. But on balance, Fargo was as successful a tour of duty as he'd ever enjoyed. Even after Delicious wired 007 his cut, his bankroll was still in good shape. He made lasting friendships with the regulars in Billiards at Broadway, and, whether it was the people or the vast open spaces, the crisp air or the frontier mentality, there was something about the upper Midwest that resonated with him. And above all, he'd fallen hard for a girl who wasn't just cool and beautiful but could hit a massé, for Christ's sake.

There was just one problem: now that Delicious had cleaned out Rory and his cover was effectively blown, he wasn't going to get any more action in Fargo (at least not at the pool table). After a few more nights at the bar, failing to lure someone even into a game of pitching quarters, Delicious realized he had reached his sell-by date. Besides, he needed to hit a few spots in Minnesota before word got out that Kid Delicious was in the area. Sadly, he held Tanya and told her he had to go. He would come back to Fargo soon, and maybe they could travel around together. He climbed into the LeSabre. Before he reached the I-94 on ramp, tears were skidding down his face.

With the fear of God now firmly planted in him, Bristol knew instinctively that if his sobriety was going to last, he desperately needed a change of scenery. He ended up experiencing one of the more enlightened clauses of pool's unwritten honor code: players might backstab one another and hustle their own road partners, but when a colleague hits rock bottom, you have to take care of him.

Bristol was hardly a pool star, but he had enough of a name that the wire carried word that he was trying to kick a crystal meth habit. One of the first calls came from George "the Greek" Hodges, an old-timer who owned an upscale hall in leafy White Plains, New York. Hi Pockets Billiards & Café was, at the time, perhaps the finest room in the state, a sprawling pavilion filled with dozens of pool tables, backgammon tables, and a restaurant. Though the moneyed New York suburbanites who made up most of the clientele never knew it, Hi Pockets was known among road players for its basement. There were two makeshift bedrooms there, just concrete cells with futons, with a showerhead down the hall. The players knew they could crash there, and the Greek wouldn't think of charging them a dime.

The Greek permitted Bristol to stay in the basement for as long as he needed to. The catch was that he had to stay clean.

With no television, no kitchen, and only one electrical outlet in his room — a jail cell without bars — Bristol spent the spring and summer of 2000 in Hi Pockets, attempting, as he puts it, "to get my head screwed on straight again." He devoted hours to reading self-help books and spent the rest of his waking moments on the tables upstairs, trying to repair the tattered tapestry of his games. And though he was flat broke, he resisted gambling, fearful that the stress of playing for money and the erratic hours would invite back the habits that had nearly killed him.

It was a rough period, his answer to the full-moon phases that his old partner endured. But in the end the self-discipline that had defined Bristol for so much of his life helped him get through it. He worked out and ate right and soon regained his chiseled physique, which had been atrophied by the drugs. Gradually his stroke returned. Once, during some downtime, he grabbed a paintbrush that was lying around the basement and discovered that he had a real gift for painting. Like pool, it nourished something in him. There were more than a few parallels, he found, between controlling a pool cue and a wielding a brush, maneuvering six-ounce balls and applying paints. He was creating patterns on a flat surface. Before long, his room was covered with canvases. Most important, he made damn sure the poison "rock salt" stayed out of his system.

He grew sad, though, when he thought about his old road partner. An opportunity to pull off a big score is like glue: it can bond even the most mismatched personalities. When the opportunity fizzles, so, often, does the relationship. But this was different. For the better part of three years Delicious and Bristol had covered innumerable miles and grown as close as brothers. Now their relationship seemed to fray a little more each day they spent apart and out of touch. If they communicated at all, it was by voice mail and through third parties.

Delicious was back on the road, living the peripatetic life of a hustler, making some nice scores. Bristol was living in the basement of a New York pool hall, too financially strapped to pay his cell phone bill. Almost like an old girlfriend, Delicious flitted into Bristol's thoughts every day. Not an hour went by when Bristol didn't consider heading outside to the pay phone and catching up with his former partner. He never quite got around to it.

Like any enterprising businessman, 007 had the good sense to subcontract labor that others could perform better and more efficiently than he could. While he knew of some promising spots in Minnesota, he wasn't nearly as dialed into the state's poolscape as Brian McGrath, a solid player from the Twin Cities who, at the time, was working at Crown Billiards in Bloomington. McGrath would steer Delicious around Minnesota and take a percentage of the winnings, part of which he would pass on to 007. "For your jellyroll, don't commit to no percentage," 007 told McGrath. "Da kid's got a REAL GOOD heart. He's liable to give you more if you leave the amount up to him."

It turned out that McGrath had a good heart as well. He asked for nothing except a promise that Delicious would return the favor and steer him around New Jersey one day. McGrath was also aware that if he was spotted in Delicious' presence, it would kill his action in Minnesota. So he drew up intricate plans but never accompanied Delicious. When they first met, at a greasy spoon near the Mall of America, McGrath was confused. "I heard you were a big dude," he said. "You can't weigh more than a hundred seventy-five pounds." They spent an hour going over spots and creating a rough itinerary, Delicious scribbling the information on napkins.

Midway through, McGrath leaned in and pointed to his well-upholstered belly. "I ask you a personal question? How'd you lose all that weight?" Thrilled by the compliment, Delicious gave McGrath an impassioned sermon about the virtues of exercise, eating salad, and reducing carbs. "Whoever thought the day would come," he said, "when people would be asking me for weight-loss tips!"

McGrath started Delicious out at Chick's Billiards, a small room in Rochester, Minnesota, a town an hour south of the Twin Cities, best known as home to the Mayo Clinic. The target was a renowned whale in his fifties named — no kidding — Toby Dick. A computer technician for a hearing-aid company by day, Dick wore

glasses and a suit and tie, an appearance that helped him get favorable handicaps. But he was an inveterate player who could
never pass up a roadman's offer of action. His self-assessment: "I
have a lot of heart. And not always a lot of sense to go with it."

As Delicious sat at the bar awaiting Toby Dick, an employee
approached and asked if everything was okay.

"Yeah," Delicious said. "My uncle's in one of them Mayo Clin-
ics, real sick. It's been hell on the family. I'm just looking to blow
off steam and maybe get in some action. Know anyone who might
want to beat me out of a little money?"

The employee tried to stifle a smile. "Know how many times I
hear that? You're looking for Toby, ain't you? Stick around. He'll
be in soon. And if he runs out of money and offers to write you a
check, keep playing. His word is gold."

Toby Dick, as advertised, arrived looking as though he'd just
got out of his job in Cubicle Nation. He did not, however, live up
to his reputation as a big bettor. He had recently lost considerable
money playing in northern Wisconsin. His confidence wounded,
he would commit to only a few racks at $100 per. Delicious beat
him twice. Then Dick excused himself to go to the bathroom. He
returned with his tie unknotted, his sleeves rolled up, and his hair
and face dripping water. It didn't help. Delicious won the next two
games. Down $400, Dick called it quits.

Instead of sticking around Rochester, Delicious headed back to
Fargo to tryst with Tanya. The drive was more than three hundred
miles, but the payoff waiting in North Dakota was worth it. (And
besides, it wasn't his car that was getting the odometer workout.)
In Fargo, Delicious would act the part of a celebrity, buy rounds
for any interested party in Billiards at Broadway, demonstrate
trick shots for anyone who cared to learn, and, most important,
reunite with his girl. After a few days, he'd shuttle back to Minnesota and make some more money. Soon it became a ritual: after
every score — in Brainerd, St. Cloud, Bemidji, Mankato, Duluth
— he would go back to Tanya.

As winter turned to spring and the ground began to thaw, Delicious went on hustling in Minnesota. McGrath steered him to

Fat Boys, a welcoming room on the north side of Minneapolis. There Delicious was approached by an Asian woman who challenged him to nine-ball. Armed with McGrath's scouting reports, Delicious immediately identified the woman. No sooner had they made a game than she claimed to be feeling ill. "If you want action," she said, "maybe you want to play my boyfriend instead."

It was a well-choreographed hustle, but Delicious didn't mind; he was hustling himself. He agreed to play the boyfriend, a reed-thin Malaysian who introduced himself by his *nom de pool*, Moe Baker. (Delicious later heard that Baker's given name was purportedly Mohammad, perhaps not the ideal handle for building rapport and engendering trust in the heartland.) Baker suggested that they play nine-ball for $100 a rack. Delicious nodded, and they played through the night. When Delicious was up $600, Baker excused himself to make a phone call, clearly to a backer. He returned and proposed that they change the game to one-pocket. "Fine with me, Moe," Delicious said, shrugging. They played on for another marathon stretch. After they'd been spent more than thirty straight hours at the table, Delicious was up $1,800, and Baker quit.

As he drove to his next spot, Delicious was overcome by a feeling of numbness. Yes, he played pool to stave off depression. Yes, he enjoyed winning money. Yes, he relished the competition and the satisfaction that came with doing something better than most other human beings. But the more time he spent by himself, the more he realized how much of his enjoyment of road playing came from having a partnership. One plus one was more than two. Operating with a co-conspirator, sharing the experiences, working in concert, playing plug to someone else's socket . . . it was exponentially more fun than striking out alone. Delicious couldn't help thinking that he'd gladly surrender to nonstop classic rock and salads three meals a day if it meant getting Bristol Bob back in the passenger seat and in the adjacent motel bed.

But he also questioned the purpose of what he was doing. As he became more well known, he tried to make as many scores as he could, beating players and crossing their names off his list.

But pool hustling was starting to feel an awful lot like a *job*. For the first time in his years on the road he pondered the question "Where's all this leading?"

At one point, McGrath steered Delicious to Thunder Bay, Ontario, where he was instructed to find Vincent Chambers. It was somehow fitting that he was driving routes in the Iron Range that trappers once used. Even though the calendar said it was spring, the lakes of northern Minnesota were still partly frozen and snowmobiles outnumbered cars. After stopping for an hour at the Canadian border, Delicious found the pool hall in Thunder Bay. He had barely made it out of the car when he was accosted by the manager. "Aren't you Kid Sumptuous or something like that?" he said. "They called from Duluth and said you were coming up here."

Delicious played dumb. "My name's Martin. I'm up here from Chicago." But he soon realized that it was a lost cause and that there was no way in hell he would be getting a game with Vincent Chambers. The manager, though, was charmed by this genial visitor with a funny accent and funnier voice. Sensing this, Delicious tried another tack and asked if there were any other action spots nearby. The manager thought for a moment and then offered that a Cree Indian, obligatorily nicknamed "Chief," played at a hole-in-the-wall dive a half hour or so north.

Delicious crashed in Thunder Bay and late the next afternoon went in search of Chief. After ten minutes on the road, he was hopelessly lost and spent the better part of the evening driving on dirt roads, abusing the LeSabre's underbelly and tires. Finally he found an unnamed bar and, to his astonishment, inside was a hulking Cree Indian in a brown leather jacket who introduced himself as Chief. Delicious said he was "Martin from Chicago." They agreed to play nine-ball for $50 a rack—Canadian—and Delicious was as interested in talking with Chief as he was in the game at hand.

When Delicious was up $300, Chief quit. "Where are you headed now, Kid Delicious?" Chief asked.

"Kid Delicious? Where'd you pick that up?"

"Shit, they called up from the Twin Cities weeks ago and warned you were in the area," Chief said.

Delicious concluded, correctly, that if Indians in one-table rooms in suburban Thunder Bay had the wire on him, it was a good sign he'd pretty much strip-mined the region. He thought about Tanya and, briefly anyway, allowed himself to entertain a fantasy of settling down with her in sleepy Fargo. But he knew it wasn't realistic. His destiny was to be a pool player, not a husband on the prairie. Besides, as he saw it, if he settled in Fargo, he wouldn't be able to hustle anyone. Without the rush of action and competitive pool to irrigate his spirits, the depression would kick in. When that happened — when he was sleeping all day and crying and contemplating suicide — Tanya wouldn't want anything to do with him.

He made one last detour to Fargo to see her. There was no formal breakup, no valedictory for their relationship. In a sadly ironic way, it was a testament to their connection that, without ever discussing it, they both reached the same unhappy conclusion about the reality of their situation. In the morning, Delicious left Tanya's apartment and they said a tearful goodbye. "Come see me in New Jersey sometime," he said, his eyes glistening, his voice catching. "I'll show you the ocean."

Roadmen are, at their core, gamblers. And, like high rollers who sit behind mountains of chips only to leave the blackjack table empty-handed, pool players seldom cash out when they ought to. In their minds, a score of, say, $10,000 isn't a satisfying payday; it's just a toehold on the way to winning a million. More than once, the inimitable Keith McCready, a renowned player and bon vivant who scored a role in the 1986 film *The Color of Money,* has been up more than $100,000 on a Friday night. By Sunday afternoon, other players have had to lend him money to buy a hot dog and a squirt of Pepsi for lunch. Kid Delicious, too, never suffered much separation anxiety when he lost money.

And now he ruled the prairie. He may never have landed that $10,000 score, but even accounting for the gifts to Tanya, the money orders to 007, the kickbacks to McGrath, the countless rounds of drinks, the serial overtipping, and after reducing the heft of his wallet with a few jags to the casino, he was up five large for the trip. He was playing as well as he had ever played, and he hadn't lost in weeks. Then hubris took the shotgun seat.

With the cityscape of Fargo in his rearview mirror, Delicious called 007 demanding one last spot in the area before he returned to Chicago. "Nah, Danny, bring DA CAR back," said 007. "You done good. Get some rest. Relax back home in Jersey and we'll PUT YA BACK on da road soon. Maybe send you out west where no one knows ya."

"Come on," Delicious whined. "Give me one more spot. I'm playing unbelievable. It's free money."

After a theatrical sigh, 007 told him that there was a young kid named Jesse Bowman playing out of the Quad Cities. He was only seventeen but, at least on a bar table, he was perhaps the best young player since McCready. (Pool lore has it that, in the 1960s, McCready was kicked out of middle school when a gym teacher noticed that he had a $12,000 bankroll in his pocket.) 007 advised Delicious first to play Bowman's older buddy, Jamie Baraks, for a few hundred a set. "Baraks plays real good. If you're winning and playin' good, make a game with Jesse. Otherwise, get the hell outta there and come back to Chicago. And whatever you do, don't smoke no weed over there."

Delicious hightailed it to the Quad Cities, a cluster of manufacturing towns — two in Illinois, two in Iowa — on the banks of the Mississippi. The area had a certain industrial halitosis and a blue-collar vibe, which usually suggests abundant pool action. Delicious arrived in midmorning and promptly made a sizable donation at a riverboat casino. His bankroll, which had exceeded $5,000 a few days earlier, was steadily dwindling, like a balloon losing helium. After devouring a salad at a Denny's, he wiled away most of the afternoon by driving back and forth between Iowa and Illinois on a bridge, staring into the turgid Mississippi below.

Jesse Bowman's father owned Leisure Time Billiards in East Moline, but the kid played out of Miller Time Billiards in Davenport. When Delicious walked through the door, as unobtrusively as possible, Baraks was waiting. (Baraks will not reveal how he had found out Delicious was in town.)

Baraks would go on to become a world-class player, but even then, in the summer of 2000, he was the biggest shark in the Quad Cities besides Jesse Bowman. Baraks has pool in his genes. The man he refers to as his father, Mark Wilson, was an accomplished player in the seventies and eighties; his mother, Debbie Wilson, ranks among the better female players ever. With a goatee, sunken eyes, and a sinewy physique — "just six percent body fat," he proudly volunteers — Baraks cuts an imposing figure. But the menace belies a thoughtful and likable personality. He shook Delicious' hand, welcomed him to the area, offered him a bed that night, and said that he was happy to play for $100 a rack, but warned him that he needed to go home at ten P.M. to be with his wife and daughter.

Delicious had a hard time finding his stroke. And, as always, playing on a bar table neutralized some of his native gifts. Baraks played unflustered, unspectacular pool. He didn't hit any *holy shit!* shots, but he didn't dog many balls either. When the clock struck ten, Baraks was up $500. He unscrewed his cue and took the money and, though technically he was committing the sin of quitting winner, it wasn't a faux pas, since he had given fair warning. With sincerity and honor, the two men shook hands and made tentative plans to continue playing the following day.

It seemed to Delicious that his winning streak had ended. Naturally, this would have been an ideal time to leave the betting parlor. Naturally, he didn't. While he'd been playing Baraks, another player at Miller Time had called up Bowman. There's always a hope that the railbird who calls the local star to herald the arrival of a road player will get $100 or $200 as a courtesy. In any case, if a game is made the railbird can always bet on the side. By the time Bowman arrived, a dozen or so of his friends and followers had gathered.

A gangly teenager sporting a buzzcut and a cluster of peach fuzz above his upper lip, Jesse Bowman looked the part of a novice adult. But he carried himself with an authentic confidence most teenagers can't pull off. Aware that Delicious was eager to win back the $500 he had just lost to Baraks, Bowman demanded that they play on the bar table.

"Nah," said Delicious. "Let's play on the big table. I'll even give you the nine ball."

"No deal, Kid Delicious," Bowman said, stretching out "Delicious" to show that he knew who Danny was and didn't regard his nickname with much esteem. "Bar table or we don't play."

Delicious relented. "Screw it. Whatever you want, Jesse." Instead of playing at Miller Time, they would go down the street to the home of Jesse's friend "Smoky." A mountain of a man, Smoky stood around six feet five, must have weighed as much as a small car, and was an avid cue collector. At Smoky's, they could relax and play without worrying about closing time. Smoky's table, Jesse assured, was first rate, and his rec room was big enough to hold the mob of railbirds.

His judgment clouded by ego, Delicious agreed. At Smoky's they played for $100 a rack, but Delicious took plenty of side action too. From the opening break, he saw firsthand just how precocious a talent Bowman was. Game after game, he not only shot unerringly but guided the cue ball as if it were on a string. Suddenly, the weight of three straight months on the road — the vagabondage, the hours seated alone in a car, the constellation of motel rooms — crashed over Delicious like a wave. He felt stiff and sore and more exhausted than he'd ever been in his life. When it was his turn to shoot, he fired tentatively and began feeling paranoid. The table was lousy, Bowman's friends were sharking him, and it was too hot in the room. To calm his nerves, Delicious took a hit of weed from one of the railbirds.

Whether the joint was laced with PCP, as Delicious later suspected, or it was a grade of pot different from what he was accustomed to, it hit him immediately and practically incapacitated him. His head spinning, he played as though the room were shrouded in fog. By the time the early morning sun started to creep into the room, Delicious was in a massive hole. Down twenty games, he finally quit. By the time he paid Bowman his $2,000 and discharged his debts to the railbirds who'd taken him for side action, Delicious barely had enough gas money for the trip back to Chicago, where he had to return the LaSabre to 007. His bankroll, so shapely and well proportioned not long ago, had evaporated to nothing. For the first time, he experienced the bane of all road players. He'd been busted.

All the way to Chicago, Delicious rehearsed what he was going to tell his Yoda, 007. He debated whether to be defiant and pissed off ("They sharked me and drugged me, those nit motherfuckers!"), play the remorse card ("You were right, 007, and now I feel like a real ass"), or avoid the subject entirely. The last option, in turned out, was no option. When Delicious arrived at 007's modest house in Dolton, Illinois, he was immediately grilled. Clearly, 007 had caught wind of the Quad Cities Massacre not long after the last rack. "Jesus, Danny," 007 barked, "how in the DA HELL are ya gonna get back to New Jersey now that Jesse Bowman broke ya?"

Delicious didn't have much of an answer beyond admitting that he'd gambled like a fool and been played like a cheap fiddle in the Quad Cities. By this point, 007 understood the rules of engagement: there was a lovability to Kid Delicious that offset his recklessness, and, alas, a recklessness that could offset his lovability. He softened and announced his solution. He'd already put Delicious in a $1,000 game the following night in Chicago. Delicious would win the money and not spend a cent of it, even if that meant tying his hands behind his back and wiring his jaw shut. He'd go to O'Hare, buy a ticket back to Newark, and be on his way.

The plan came off as scripted, Delicious beating a high-rolling Chicago attorney out of $1,000 without having to break a sweat. The following afternoon, he was saying his goodbyes to 007.

"One more thing I gotta ask ya before ya go, Dan," 007 said. "How in the hell did you put fifteen freakin' thousand miles on my mom's car?"

11

PROS AND CONS

I T'S ONE OF THE central ironies of pool. When they're at the table, the top players are exceptionally savvy and perceptive, standing sentry over their financial interests. An assumption of treachery and deceit — or at least a reflexive skepticism — is all but an occupational requirement. Yet when it comes to assessing the bigger financial picture, these same men are stunningly short-sighted, painfully gullible around any huckster with a line of bullshit. Put another way, pool players ace microeconomics and fail macroeconomics.

Pool's popularity has fallen precipitously from the sport's peak in the 1930s, when there were more than 5,000 licensed poll halls in the Chicago area alone. Willie Mosconi was fond of recounting how in the late thirties he played in the World Championships in Chicago before 5,000 spectators. The following day he attended a Chicago Bears football game and took his place in a crowd of 3,500. Still, contrary to the pool's inherent pessimism, there's no reason to administer last rites. Today more than fifty million Americans play regularly.

Pool's great problem, though, is that, at least for the past fifty years, it hasn't been a viable professional sport. In part this is because it translates poorly to television — the slow pace is anathema to younger viewers in particular; the subtlety and strategy and spins get lost on the small screen — and TV revenue is the lifeblood of any successful pro sports league. But professional pool has also floundered because, historically, it has been a study in chaos. The players are hopelessly disorganized, prone to mutually destructive turf wars, and thoroughly incapable of aligning their interests. A string of self-serving "leaders," unfit to run a corner lemonade stand, have lined their pockets at the players' expense. As the size of the pie shrinks, the battles get ever more fierce.

Just how fractured is professional pool? AZBilliards.com, the online bible for the Republic of Pool, lists results from forty-four different tours, each with its own format and set of rules and restrictions. The failures, the alphabet soup of organizations (one as ineffectual, if not outright corrupt, as the next), the infighting, the botched alliances, and the broken promises are legion. In 1984, for instance, the Caesars Palace Billiard Classic paid in excess of $100,000 in prize money, and the winner, Earl Strickland, received $25,000. The players were to appear on ESPN but, on the purported advice of their leaders, declined to sign the television releases on the grounds that they would not receive residuals — which would have been peanuts — for repeat telecasts. The shows never aired. ESPN felt betrayed by pool; the promoter, who had recently staged several other lucrative events and had plans for more, was effectively put out of business.

For most of the nineties, the professional circuit was organized under the aegis of the Pro Billiards Tour Association (PBTA) and its controversial commissioner, Don Mackey. Blustery and hard-charging, Mackey lacked polish. But he knew how to connect with his minions and had a Svengali-like hold on many of the top players. At one point, Mark McCormack, the founder of the Cleveland-based sports-marketing behemoth IMG, expressed an interest in organizing a professional pool tour. At the time, McCormack, a Harvard-educated sports magnate worth more than $100 million, counted among his clients John McEnroe, Jack Nicklaus, and even the Pope. He supposedly wanted sixty percent of whatever revenues the pool tour generated — not unreasonable, given that IMG was going to have to foot its own television production costs, line up network partners, and cultivate its own sponsors. Mackey told the players that McCormack "was going to take sixty cents of every dollar you earn," failing to disclose the obvious upside. Mackey retained his position of power, and IMG never got into pool.

As much as golf and tennis try to shed their patrician image and cater to the mainstream, pool does the opposite, striving to attract a more upscale audience. Sports, though, are essentially what they are. And just as tennis looks clumsy trying to sell itself to the masses, not too many in the Volvo crowd are going to have their interest piqued by pro pool. After striking out with demographically desirable companies, Mackey, it seemed, justified his PBTA salary when, in 1995, R. J. Reynolds offered to sponsor a fourteen-event "Camel Tour." In Camel, the PBTA had a solid multinational company — albeit one that was a bit downmarket for Mackey — that could put muscle behind the sport. In the PBTA, Reynolds had an entrée into two of the last remaining frontiers — bars and poolrooms — where smoking was permitted.

It should have been an ideal marriage. Soon, however, Mackey and the PBTA were suing the tobacco company for breach of contract, fraud, and unfair and deceptive trade practices. Mackey claimed that the Camel folks had tried to take over the tour and then failed to follow through on financial promises. RJR asserted that it had severed ties because the tour was hopelessly mismanaged, if not worse. Mackey was left to pay tournament winners with IOUs. After a theater-of-the-absurd trial in federal court — "the Mustache" and "the Machine Gun" were called to testify — a jury awarded the PBTA a reported $886,000. The lawyers reportedly got paid. Mackey reportedly got paid and promptly retired to Florida. Nothing was left for the players. And after all the toxic publicity, other blue-chip companies wouldn't go near pro pool with a ten-foot cue.

As a result of so many missteps, even the best players have struggled to make a living. When the late Steve "the Miz" Mizerak dominated the U.S. Open in the early 1970s, he was moonlighting. His real job was teaching geography in a middle school in New Jersey — such were the wages available to the top stars. (Mizerak was best known outside pool for his appearance in a memorable Miller Lite commercial, and he told friends he made more money for that twenty-nine-second spot than he had winning international tournaments.) At pro events, even the universally well-liked emcee Scott Smith jokes about the players' financial straits. "What's the difference between a pizza and a pro pool player? The pizza can feed a family of four." Another one: "What do you call a pool player without a girlfriend? Homeless." Poverty is such a given in pool that it has lost any taboo.

In 2000, there was a new pied piper — pied pipers, actually — promising the players untold riches. A Canadian entrepreneur and his son announced that they would be starting something called the USA-Billiards Challenger, a circuit tied to a twenty-four-hour Billiards Channel and Internet venture they were in the process of launching. It was the height of the dot-com boom and a burgeoning time for cable television. The Canadians planned to sell stock in their venture. Further details were hard to come by, but shoot, if everyone and his brother were making money on the Internet, why couldn't pool players?

To seduce the top players, the Canadians hit the predictable notes. Vowing to follow the NASCAR blueprint, this tour was going to catapult a niche sport into the big time. The players would make unimaginable sums of money. Pumping up their tour at the pool trade show in Las Vegas, the Canadians predicted $500,000 qualifying events and major tournaments with $1 million purses. One player recalls the Canadians vowing to pledge $52 million — an odd figure, to be sure — to the venture. And all the exposure was going to transform anonymous pool players into rock stars. They asserted that they had a $250,000 television truck "with all the hook-ups and satellites" that would appear at each event. Soon the best players would beam into America's living rooms and enjoy the same popularity as their counterparts in football, baseball, and basketball.

If it all sounded impossibly quixotic, it hardly mattered. Players were tripping over themselves to join up. They always do. The money is part of it. As much as hustlers boast about their winnings from the road, they seldom mention the losses, the expenses, and the idle weeks. Give them a chance to earn consistent money on a tour without the uncertainties of hustling, and the option has appeal. (Bandy about numbers like $500,000 and even the most successful hustlers will show up.) But beyond that, pool players are athletes at heart, and athletes are nothing if not intensely competitive. The chance to beat the field in a legitimate, standardized format — on the level, with no weight, in front of their peers — is often an irresistible lure.

For Delicious, the announcement heralding the launch of the USA-Billiards Challenger tour led him to the crossroads that all top players eventually reach. For a hustler, playing professionally was akin to committing suicide. If Delicious played in prominent national events as a pro — especially on a tour that vowed to televise them on its own channel and splash the results over the Internet — he would become a known quantity overnight. The days of traveling incognito in Fort Wayne or Tulsa or Bethlehem and busting the locals would be over.

On the other hand, because of his scorched-earth campaigns through the Midwest and New England and Canada and the Southeast, his anonymity was already eroding. His name was popping up on Internet message boards, and, Delicious noticed, the lies he was forced to tell to conceal his true identity were getting increasingly elaborate. What's more, it was the early stages of the poker boom. The same species that played pool for money — namely, young males, dripping testosterone and eager to gamble — was gravitating to the casino, where they could always get a game and didn't have to exert themselves physically. As an occupation, pool hustler, like candle dipper and telegraph dispatcher, was becoming obsolete.

Delicious realized that if he wasn't road-weary already — as he saw it, the unpredictability and excitement gave him precious little time alone with his dark thoughts — he was certainly tired of operating in the shadows. Damn, he wanted the world to know how good he was. He left a voice mail message for Bristol. "I'm taking the plunge and seeing if I can cut it as a pro," he said. "Wish me luck, buddy."

In the weeks leading up to the first USA-Billiards Challenger event, Delicious was exhilarated to the point of sleeplessness. At the New Jersey pool halls, he talked nonstop about the new tour and its possibilities. One of his old mentors at Elite Billiards, Carlos "the Peruvian Prince" Santos, was especially interested, and soon he had anointed himself as Delicious' trainer, the Burgess Meredith figure who was going to toughen up his protégé before the big event.

Like virtually everyone in the Republic of Pool, Santos had a backstory fit for a Hollywood treatment. Born in Peru in the early 1960s, Carlos Santos grew up in abject poverty. He dropped out of school but stayed on the straight and narrow and became a pilot in the Peruvian air force. (Yes, there is such a thing.) In his late twenties, he left home intending to go to America, but he got stuck in Panama. A sketchy figure told Santos he could get him into the United States for $5,000. For more than a year, Santos accumulated the funds by hustling pool in Panamanian bars and clubs. When he had raised the necessary capital, he crossed the border late one night in 1991, sneaking into El Paso from Juarez. He eventually ended up in New Jersey, working odd jobs during the day and shooting pool at Elite Billiards at night.

Around the time Delicious left New Jersey for Chicago Billiards, Santos' fortunes began to improve dramatically. He married an American woman and gained citizenship. Several of his investments, including a cockfighting business in Panama, panned out. He made extra money driving a delivery truck for the Museum of Modern Art in Manhattan, rising at three A.M. to drop off shipments. In 1997, he bought his own pool hall, Action Billiards, a thriving sixteen-table room in Old Bridge, New Jersey. If there's still such a thing as the American Dream, Santos had achieved it.

A slightly built man then in his late thirties, with a thin mustache, a thick head of curly black hair, and a thicker Spanish accent (despite constant teasing, he would say "New YER-sey"), Santos was an unlikely mentor for Kid Delicious. But they were simpatico, perhaps united by their status as outsiders — one because of his physique, the other because of nationality — and their ability to use pool to improve their stations in life. Delicious gave

Santos the pet name "Carlito" and joked that his goal was to get Carlito to smoke weed with him. Carlito became a kind of Bristol Bob surrogate, who instantly gained Delicious' trust and loyalty.

Delicious practiced for hours at Action Billiards. If Carlito walked by and suggested that Delicious work on a new set of patterns, he would comply. If Carlito said they were going on a late-night jog, Delicious would switch into his running shoes without complaint. If Carlito told Delicious to stay out of the casinos and strip clubs and save his money, he did so. Santos recognized right away that deep down, Delicious wanted discipline. "You can work and be the best," Santos told him. "Or you can be like every other guy. It's up to you."

Doris and Dave Basavich liked Santos when they met him, but they didn't quite get it. They had scarcely heard their son mention Santos, and suddenly Danny was putting himself in the guy's hands. And what happened to Bristol Bob? In so many words, Delicious explained that pool was its own habitat with its own social mores. Relationships and alliances in pool resemble high school crushes, flaring intensely and then fizzling out just as fast. Delicious sensed something else as well: with Bristol Bob in his own wilderness, he was desperate for another traveling partner, someone who would inflate his ego, help him in his weaker moments, and share the journey. Santos could have asked for ninety percent of the winnings and Delicious would have assented, as long as it meant having someone sitting in the shotgun seat.

The inaugural USA-Billiards Challenger event was to be held in the summer of 2000 at Kelly's Billiards, in Coconut Creek, Florida, not far from Fort Lauderdale. Kelly's wasn't quite the glitzy casino venue the Canadians had promised. And the add-in purse of $25,000 seemed awfully low, given the talk of a $500,000 payday. No one who scanned the cable stations could find the Billiards Channel, and the Web site was a work in progress. But ultimately, who cared? The tour was launching, and it was only going to grow. The Canadians were supposedly finalizing plans for a public stock offering, and, the thinking went, if they could just sell, say, a million shares at, say, five bucks a share, all the pool players would be rolling in it!

Like a trainer grooming his boxer before a title fight, Carlito managed every detail of Delicious' preparation. They would practice in New Jersey and then, six weeks before the tournament, start driving to Coconut Creek. 007 would hook them up with spots, and they would thread their way through pool halls as they headed down the Eastern Seaboard. Like sparring in training camp, Delicious would get plenty of match play and arrive instroke. If they landed in Florida with some extra money, so Carlos could bet on Delicious in the tournament Calcutta — a ritual akin to a rotisserie league draft, in which backers and spectators purchase the rights to a player and cash in if their player wins — so much the better.

But first they would make a detour to Canada. Luc Salvas, the exceptionally fast player whom Delicious and Bristol had unsuccessfully stalked a few years back, agreed to play Delicious for $1,500 a set. Delicious and Carlito squeezed into the cherry-red Tiburon and headed for Quebec. After a two-day drive, they arrived at Salvas' poolroom and got down to business. Within a few hours, Delicious was down four sets, and Carlito tried his best to look nonchalant about the prospect of starting the trip $6,000 in the hole. During a break, Carlito took his friend aside and told him to disrupt Salvas' rhythm by playing more conservatively.

Frustrated by a string of safeties, muttering in his Québecois accent as he chalked his cue, Salvas missed two fairly routine balls. Delicious won a set, then another, and another. When he was up $1,000, Salvas quit. Carlito and Delicious lost money, but they left with renewed confidence. For Carlito it was further proof he was backing the right horse. "When a bankroll is on the line, you always play your best," he said, slapping Delicious on the back. "You lost weight, but you still have a big heart, you know."

They then headed south, stopping to hustle every night. They had a steady routine: Carlito would give Delicious a formal lesson on one of the tables. When they were finished, Carlito would delicately place a crappy cue in Delicious' ornate case; Delicious would unsheathe his expensive maple cue from Carlito's crappy case. Carlito would then approach the target about playing for money. The mark would decline but offer to play the pupil instead. They won this way in upstate New York, in Massachusetts, in Connecticut. At a hall outside Philadelphia, Carlos challenged the owner, who took one look at his complexion and shook his head. "I don't fuck around with no Filipinos!" he snapped.

"Come on, play with me. You like action? Well, I'm offering you action. I'll even give you the seven."

Growing increasingly incensed, the owner said, "I ain't playing you, but I'll play your buddy over there with the goofy smile."

"My buddy?" Carlos said. "Ees not my buddy. Ees my student. He can't even make three balls! If you play him, you got to give him the eight."

"Okay," the owner said.

Delicious beat the guy in the first set, keeping it close. The second set was 9–7. The third was also 9–7. Carlito had never seen anyone enjoy the acting part of hustling as much as Delicious did, never seen a player more adept at keeping the customer at the table. Here, after all, was a top-notch player on his way to a professional tournament. And after three sets, the owner, a shortstop at best, still thought he and Delicious played even.

After these sets, the owner had a deal. *If he plays me even, I'll double the money.* Delicious and Carlito feigned disagreement before consenting. They left an hour later with $3,600 in cash. To make the story twice as sweet, as they left, the owner told his tormentor, "You remind me of a young version of this big, fat guy — real good player — from up around Toms River. He goes by Kid Delicious."

Carlito did most of the driving, and, to his dismay, Delicious fired up a few joints — "fatties," he'd recently taken to calling them — while riding shotgun. But Carlito reckoned that on the continuum of vices, smoking pot paled in comparison to Delicious' old habit of gorging on food. He'd known Delicious when his weight was in the stratosphere; if the occasional spliff was helping to keep the topography of his belly flat — at least as a bluff rather than a mountain — Carlito figured it was a forgivable sin. Plus, Delicious let him fill the car with his Latin music. That was their deal. They continued hustling their way down I-95, sometimes making out like bandits, sometimes running into savvy players who recognized Delicious and refused to play him no matter how much he denied his identity.

By the time they arrived in South Florida, their bankroll had ballooned to close to $20,000. With this kind of road success — coming, as it did, with so little effort — other hustlers would have reconsidered the decision to turn pro. Delicious had no such hesitation. Sure, hustling was fun. But it had never been the goal. Weeks before, Delicious had made up his mind to go pro, to break through pool's third wall, as it were. And ever since, he'd become obsessed with matching up against the best players and beating them all.

In Coconut Creek, Carlito took his coaching duties even more seriously. When he and Delicious checked into a tournament motel, a shabby Super 8, Carlito took one look at the place and demanded they switch to a quieter, more upscale hostelry, where Delicious wouldn't be distracted by the other players in the tournament. At the new hotel, Carlito made sure they were far away from the ice machine so Delicious wouldn't be awoken. ("Jesus, Carlito, you've heard me snore," Delicious said. "You really think a few ice cubes are gonna wake me up?") He commanded Delicious to drink eight glasses of water a day and swim each morning to warm up his muscles. "If you don't win, you don't win," Carlito said. "But I didn't drive down here and leave my family for six weeks for you not to be at your peak."

Aspiring athletes in other sports dream of serving on the manicured lawns of Wimbledon, or walking to the first tee at Augusta National, or stepping onto the infield grass at Yankee Stadium. The charm-deprived, dust-shrouded venue of the pool tournament wasn't exactly a hallowed ground or the Elysian Fields. Still, it comported, more or less, with the visions Delicious had been harboring for years. As he looked around the room and saw his name on the draw sheet of a professional event that was going to be televised, he realized that this constituted his "pinch me" moment. The countless miles of interstate, the innumerable hours of practice, had all been building to this.

The Coconut Creek field of players was fairly unremarkable for a pro event, but when Delicious arrived at the hall to practice, he felt as though he had won a week at a pool fantasy camp. He looked around the room and saw A-listers the likes of Jeremy "Double J" Jones, Charlie Williams, Dee Atkins, Tang Hoa, Shannon "the Cannon" Daulton, Ronny Wiseman, José Parica, and Buddy "the Rifleman" Hall. Players had come from as far away as Japan and Europe to compete. But Delicious' confidence never wavered. He knew he belonged.

The Canadians, meanwhile, were pitching the stock offering to anyone who would listen. One renowned sweater from central California told friends that he had recently invested $50,000, a big chunk of his retirement savings, in Billiard Channel, Inc. The Canadians also announced that this event would be part of a bigger tour where the best players would compete for truly dizzying amounts of cash. In anticipation of the television coverage, the Coconut Creek competition would have a TV-friendly format.

Every incarnation of pro pool has its unique set of quirks and twists. The USA-Billiards tour took a page from professional tennis and pitted players in best-of-three sets of race-to-six games of nine-ball. Like tennis, a final score might be 6–2, 3–6, 6–4. If a set reached six games apiece, it would be decided by a sudden-death "spot-shot shootout." The cue ball would be placed eight or so inches behind the head spot, and the object ball would be placed on the foot spot. Players would have five shots to cut the nine ball into the corner pocket. Whoever made the most of his five attempts would win the set. The veterans complained that the short-race format rewarded the arrivistes, and the "spot shot" was a bit of made-for-TV nonsense, the equivalent of settling a tied baseball game with a home-run-hitting contest.

But the fans loved it. And it worked to Delicious' advantage. With a hot start, he could run out the six-game set before the opponent could get off his chair. And the spot shot was precisely the kind of trick he'd mastered during late nights while awaiting action at Chicago Billiards or while practicing alone in New Jersey.

Delicious acted the part of lesser mortal around the pros. He knew instinctively that he was the wide-eyed newcomer who should ooze deference and call the veteran opponents Mister So-and-So until instructed otherwise. He may as well have been wearing a paper trainee hat. But at the table he showed no awe and flew through the draw, working past a series of opponents to reach the semifinals. He heard that other players were complaining about his slow pace, but he wasn't about to let himself be rushed. It was immediately clear that he could execute every shot in the book — and a good many that weren't. But it was his poise that really raised eyebrows. After Delicious nailed a near-impossible three-rail kick and playfully did the "raise-the-roof" gesture for the cheering fans on the rail, one stakehorse remarked to Santos, "Your boy don't get nervous, do he?"

"Danny? He gets nervous all the time," Santos responded. "Just never playing pool."

After Delicious knocked off José Parica, the Filipino veteran quipped, "I guess he never heard of me." Next, he ran roughshod over Ismael Paez, another well-known player, 6–3, 6–1.

Delicious had arrived in Florida in dead stroke, and he remained there. It's not uncommon for hustlers to struggle making the transition to tournament pool. A high-risk, high-reward mindset is fine when there's a chance to rerack the balls, raise the bet, and play another set. But in pro events, where one careless lapse can knock a player out of the entire competition, more prudent play — "controlled aggression," Earl Strickland calls it — is vital. Delicious adjusted accordingly, playing creatively at times, but conservatively when he had no shot. After every break, his pattern became obvious. Then it was just a matter of execution. "Long as I'm seeing the table like this, I don't see how anyone can beat me," he said to Carlito. He wasn't saying it boastfully, just honestly. And he backed it up.

Delicious had been warned that pro pool wasn't nearly as much fun as hustling. But his experience was proving otherwise. There was something liberating about playing as Danny Basavich, who used his real name and played at full speed against some of the most decorated practitioners in the sport. No bullshit. No guile. May the better man win. That was the essence of sport, wasn't it? On top of that, there was prize money. Sure, it would be nice if the purse had been larger. But the money was risk-free. If he won, he won. If he lost, he wasn't going to have to dig into his pocket and pay the other guy. Without the stresses that attend road playing, Delicious could relax and play his best. "I'm loose as a mother-fucking goose!" he exulted to Carlito at one point. "I'm livin' the dream, baby!"

In an effort to "pretty up" the image of the sport, the new tour prohibited gambling — as well as smoking and drinking — at the venue. Predictably, it was ignored. (It always is.) Delicious was still enough of an unknown that, in after-hours play, he could find action with the "name" players. And Carlito was getting plenty of action on the rail. After a few nights, they were up more than $10,000, and Delicious was already guaranteed at least another $2,500 in prize money. By the time he outlasted Ron Wiseman to reach the finals, he was the toast of the tournament.

After hours, Delicious had managed to make friends with eve-ryone, buying drinks for any player within shouting distance of the bar and volunteering his various spots around the country to anyone who needed action. In a workforce notorious for backbit-ing and fragile alliances — like the famous line about academia, in professional pool the battles can be so fierce because the stakes are so low — Delicious brought a sense of collegiality. "Even when he was a fifteen-year-old he wanted to be popular," says Carlito. "You know why he was wanting to kill himself when he was a teenager? It was because he was wanting more friends. So here he is with the best pool players, guys he looked up to as a kid. He's buying everyone drinks, they love him, he's just beaten Parica and Ron Wiseman, and everyone's complimenting him. If that had been his last night on earth, he woulda died happy."

With Carlito monitoring the alcohol consumption, Delicious left the bar around midnight and got a good night's sleep before the final. His opponent was Buddy Hall, a recent Hall of Fame inductee who would make most lists of the five best pool players ever to draw breath. Whether he was inoculated against the pres-sure or simply too naïve to appreciate the weight of the occasion, Delicious played brilliant pool.

Crouching over the table, Delicious stroked his chin pensively and took dozens of practice strokes, all the while looking up at his target. Then, with classic form, his body made a series of isosceles triangles. He placed one leg behind the other, bent his elbows, formed a perfect bridge with his left hand while his right acted as a piston. Then, with a crisply calibrated stroke, he accelerated through every ball. Most of the time he connected with the cue ball in the center, sometimes with force, other times with a painterly brush. Occasionally he laced the cue ball with a dollop of spin or English. Mostly it was straight firing. It was virtually a given that the object ball would descend into the pocket. Delicious' eyes followed the cue ball instead, assuring that it came to rest at the desired location. For rack after rack, he guided the cue ball with such accuracy that any hack could have made the next shot. The genius, of course, was in the setup.

Delicious potted every ball until late in the sixth game. Hall had been unnerved by his opponent's glacially slow play, but he made the most of his chance and forced a spot-shot tie-breaker. All the while smiling and engaging the crowd, Delicious nailed four straight cut shots of the nine. When Hall missed two, the first set went to Delicious. "Yyyyyeeaaaaaaaaaaahhhhhhhhh," he roared to the crowd, a silly but authentic display that even drew a smile from Hall.

In the second set, Hall found his rhythm and his radar and won 6–4. In the third and decisive set, he played tactical pool, making balls or else declining to give Delicious a shot. He jumped to a 4–2 lead and was in firm control of the match. Then he made a few uncharacteristic misfires, and Delicious told himself he could no longer afford to miss another ball.

As if it were as simple as that, he rallied to run off five of the last six games. Through it all he kept up a playful monologue and slapped five with the railbirds. After a particularly sensational piece of shotmaking, Delicious caressed his cue and said, "Oh, baby, we're gonna get down tonight." The crowd ate it up, accustomed as they were to stone-faced players who behaved as though their very salvation rested on the outcome of the matches. Delicious closed Hall out with a spectacular run in the final game, putting an unholy amount of English on the eight to set up the nine.

Here's how *Pool & Billiard* magazine put it, in a tournament account titled "Danny Basavitch [*sic*] Takes First Title":

> Youth exploded. With a I've-got-nothing-to-lose attitude, Danny began an impossible journey that saw his most incredible shot-making of the tournament. His confidence grew and grew with each ball that fell. When we spoke with him afterward he said, "It's unbelievable. A dream come true. I played my idols and I beat 'em! I just want to thank my parents Dave and Doris. I owe them everything and I hope they realize that." Hmmm, quite a step back from the usual overpowering egos that blast off to new heights after a win. Here was a new face with a new attitude. But don't let the smile and eager handshake fool you. Put this kid near felt and he's a killer.

The winner of the inaugural Billiards Challenger tour event gripped his check of $6,360 as if it were a long-lost relative. He held the shiny trophy aloft, admiring his giddy reflection in it. He posed for pictures, accepted rounds of backslaps, and wore a smile that didn't desert him for hours. When he called Doris and Dave, he could barely choke back the tears. He phoned Bristol Bob to share the news — predictably, his call went straight to voice mail — sure that his old sidekick would be proud of him.

After the awards ceremony, Delicious, Carlito, and the clutch of friends he had recruited during the week repaired to a bar, where everyone drank on the champion's tab. Kid Delicious had *arrived*. So much for agonizing over his decision to come off the road and reveal his identity. He was too besotted with happiness (and Cuervo shots) to notice that the $250,000 satellite truck was nowhere to be seen.

While Carlito's bankroll had grown, his domestic capital had dwindled since he left his wife and their infant daughter to spend six weeks on the road. So the day after the tournament, he flew home to do some heavy-duty family damage control, leaving Delicious to drive himself home in the Tiburon.

With the gleaming trophy from Coconut Creek riding shotgun, Delicious zipped up I-95, a smile still carved onto his face. A few years earlier he had been an overweight kid with depression, a piñata for the bullies at his high school. Now here he was, having just played in his first professional tournament, an achievement in itself. Not only that, but he had won the damn thing. And not only that, but he had beaten Buddy Hall — Buddy friggin' Hall! — in a spellbinding final match. In his mind, anyway, he had done it: he had scaled the summit of Mount Pool. And this confirmed to the world what he had known for years, that pool had delivered him.

Driving through the folds of Georgia and the Carolinas, he sang to himself at the top of his lungs, looking over at the trophy and laughing, banging out rhythms on the steering wheel. Happier than he had ever been, he leaked tears of joy. He was playing the best pool of his life; his confidence was soaring; he weight was nearing an all-time low. It had been more months than he could recall since depression paid him a visit. Life, in short, was good. He'd stop and get lunch and leave a $50 tip. He'd go to a strip club and spend money like a millionaire. He didn't care. "My attitude was: Kid Delicious has arrived! I have another tournament coming up in a few weeks, and I'm gonna win that. Another a few weeks later. Then another. I have it made, brother."

He may have been living large, but he was also taking his new job as a professional pool player seriously. Galvanized by his win in Coconut Creek, upon returning home he practiced as much as fourteen hours a day. At Carlito's suggestion, Delicious worked on those spot-shot formations that decided sets at six-all. Since he intended to go back to trolling for late-night action after the tournaments ended, stamina would be crucial, so he kept up his fitness regimen and his salad diet. He had proven that he was an elite player. Now he wanted to show his new fans and new colleagues that his success in Coconut Creek wasn't beginner's luck.

Delicious was disappointed to learn that events scheduled for

Tulsa and Atlanta had been canceled. "Low turnout" was the explanation given, though it was unclear whether that referred to fans or players or sponsors. Still, the next USA-Billiards event, outside Baltimore, had a full field. Delicious and Carlito headed to Maryland together and spent the bulk of the drive talking pool tactics.

In Baltimore, the energy and anticipation of the Florida event was lacking, the crowds were negligible, and there was no corporate sponsorship in evidence. Delicious played creditably in the early rounds and, with Carlito taking side action, was soon up $5,000. But he lost to a German player, Christian Reimering, in a third-set spot-shot shootout. Delicious made all five of his shots, and, remarkably, Reimering calmly pocketed his five. Finally, after making seven in a row, Delicious missed a shot by a fraction of an inch. Reimering made his to win the match. The loss stung, but Delicious still finished tied for ninth in the sixty-four-man field. Not bad.

A few weeks later, at the next event, held at J.O.B. Billiards, a classic, throwback pool hall outside Nashville, Delicious again finished tied for ninth. He wasn't particularly distraught: he was clearly on the same plane as the other pros, and he was getting paid to play pool. On the last day of the tournament, the tour posted its cumulative rankings after three events. Delicious was first. Efren Reyes, arguably the most accomplished player, was second.

Still, it didn't take a financial analyst to deduce that the tour was in trouble. The Nashville event was conspicuously lacking in sponsor banners, television cameras, and media coverage — the usual trappings of a legitimate pro sporting event. As for the fans, the running joke was that large crowds came to the event dressed as empty seats.

When players and backers asked the Canadians what was going on, answers were hard to come by. In fact, the Billiards Channel circuit was hemorrhaging money. Shares in the company were worthless. The Canadians weren't returning phone calls. Later an announcement appeared on AZBilliards.com: the tour was shutting down operations. "It was run by con men who never had a great talent for conning," says Jerry Forsyth, a *Pool & Billiard* editor who covered the downfall of the tour. "It was just another sad chapter in professional pool."

As far as Delicious was concerned, whether the Billiards Channel was a scam or just a poorly run business didn't much matter. He had entered the Celestial City of tournament pool only to find that it was just another Oz. It was finished, yet another venture added to the pyre of failed pool tours. And now he was finished too. Impaled by his own success, surely he could no longer walk into a pool hall and rely on his charm and anonymity to hustle action. In the past month alone, his picture had been printed in two pool magazines. His walking into a pool hall would be like someone on the Most Wanted list strolling into a police precinct wearing a nametag. As Delicious saw it, the rest of his life was going to feel posthumous.

Doris and Dave had recently sold the family house, downsized their life, and moved to an exclusive, sanitized retirement community in Manchester, New Jersey. Delicious was marooned in this strange new home. His dream of becoming a pro player would have to be, at the very least, deferred. He presumed that his hustling days were over as well. His road partner and best friend was still trying to reclaim his life. As ever, when Delicious stopped moving laterally—navigating the country with a pool cue in his trunk—he started moving downward. Without pool to nourish his spirit, he was soon in the vise grip of depression.

He was used to the crying jags and low energy. But during this episode he couldn't shake visions of suicide. Alone with his thoughts, he often asked himself, "Without pool, what do I have to live for?" The answers were slow in coming. He even settled on a method for ending it all. Because of his intense fear of pain, he couldn't imagine driving his car off a cliff, say, or jumping off a bridge. *Even for a split second, that's gotta hurt like a motherfucker,* he thought. No, he would OD on pills and fade into an irreversible sleep.

In a perverse way, though, the depth of this depression actually saved his life, because he couldn't muster the energy to do anything so dramatic as follow through on his suicidal thoughts. The conventional wisdom is that the antithesis of depression is happiness. But for Delicious, the opposite of depression was *vitality*. When depression kicked in, he didn't think about trying to find joy and pleasure; he thought about rationing his energy in order to function. Normal activities — getting out of bed, going to the store, picking up a movie — just felt like so much *work*. There were times when he would slink to the refrigerator to get a Coke. If the two-liter bottle was sitting on a high shelf, not the middle shelf where he was looking, he would retreat to his bedroom, unable to exert the extra effort to reach for it.

By late 2000, Delicious was sleeping sixteen, eighteen, sometimes twenty hours a day. When he was awake, he seldom left his room; he'd watch movies in bed or comfort himself with food. When healthy, he played pool and gambled compulsively; when depressed, he ate compulsively. His weight was rapidly rising, and he didn't give a damn. He was going to die soon anyway, he reckoned, so why watch his diet? The salads were supplanted again by cheeseburgers and fries. The push-ups and sit-ups and jogs were grainy memories. Delicious turned flaccid and then, as Carlito puts it, "his belly started to grow like a pregnant woman."

The rest of his physical appearance was in a state of neglect too, his fatalism and bone-deep malaise overwhelming any impulse to shave or bathe or brush his teeth. His hypochondria and his mortal fear of doctors were stronger than ever. He felt a pimple on his neck and was certain it was a cancerous tumor, but he wouldn't go to a hospital to have it checked out. He came down with a cold and was sure it was pneumonia.

His phone messages went unreturned. Innocuous questions from Doris and Dave were answered with monosyllabic grunts. The demarcation between days ceased to exist, as everything melted into one blue period. When the crew at Elite Billiards didn't see Delicious for a few weeks and they knew he wasn't on the road hustling, they figured it could mean only one thing. Carlito and Neptune Joe and the boys took it as an article of faith that Delicious was in one of his full-moon phases. They left messages encouraging him to stop by and hit some balls, knowing that the odds of seeing him anytime soon were minimal.

Instinctively — almost telepathically — Bristol was sure that his old partner was in trouble. He could appreciate how big a risk Delicious had taken when he'd decided to "go legit" and enter those professional events. He knew that Delicious was in ecstasy when he won the Coconut Creek event. And he knew Delicious was crushed when the circuit folded, leaving him exposed and with nowhere to play. Now it was his turn: he left messages on Delicious' voice mail, urging him not to give in to his demons, to use pool to pull himself out of his prison. "Don't let that depression shit get you," he pleaded.

But by then the demons were kicking his ass, and Delicious couldn't locate either the energy or the interest to get back to the pool table. Like many who suffered from mental illness, Delicious had always struggled to explain his condition to other people. They just didn't get it. Then again, neither did he. Activities he knew he enjoyed were bringing him no pleasure. No matter how hard he tried to convince himself that life wasn't so bad, he couldn't stop feeling "like total shit." As for pool, rationally he knew it was the one thing that made him happiest, the one thing he was put on this earth to do. But he felt indifferent to it all.

Doris and Dave had grown accustomed to watching their son descend to some dark places. They had almost come to expect it. As Dave reasoned, if Delicious was home, it probably meant he wasn't playing much pool. And if he wasn't playing much pool, it probably meant he wasn't happy. But this time, Doris and Dave grew more concerned. Dave, in particular, nagged Delicious to get help and visit a psychotherapist. Delicious resisted at first, then relented, mostly, he says, to show his dad that he was really nuts, that nothing would help, so he should just leave him alone.

Filled with skepticism, Delicious allowed Dave to drive him to a mental health clinic in Freehold. For $20, he spent an hour talking to a solemn clinical psychologist who looked like a nerdy kid eagerly awaiting the onset of puberty. The young shrink peppered Delicious with questions. He betrayed no empathy or charisma and rarely looked up from his notepad. Delicious would tell the guy everything — about his depression, his weight problem, his gambling, his pot smoking, his pool, his persistent thoughts of suicide. The shrink would sit silently. Finally he would look up and say something on the order of, "Your lifestyle isn't healthy." *Well, no shit*, Delicious thought.

Still, with nothing better to do, Delicious went to the clinic three times a week for a month or so. The psychologist diagnosed him with bipolar disorder. Delicious' depression was obvious. His mania was less apparent — hypomania, he called it — but, the doctor speculated, it manifested itself in impaired judgment, particularly when it came to eating and gambling. He also thought Delicious might be suffering from obsessive-compulsive disorder. That made sense to Delicious, furnishing an explanation for all that repetition at the pool table. Provided that Delicious promised to stop smoking marijuana, the doctor put him on Paxil, the popular drug used to treat depression and anxiety disorder. Armed with a prescription, Delicious quit the psychotherapy, either not realizing or not caring that one often fails to work without the other.

After months of doing little other than eating and sleeping, Delicious felt a bit better. He noticed that he was dreaming about pool feats — envisioning patterns and making pressure-packed shots to win tournaments. He took the dreams as a sign that his playing days somehow weren't over. Eventually he was able to summon the energy to go out in public.

He started with trips to a strip club, beginning with a low-rent joint called Bourbon Street, in nearby Sayreville. But every time he walked in, it seemed that someone recognized him — "Hey, aren't you that pool guy?" — and tried to strike up a conversation. The last thing he wanted to do was make small talk. Plus, the recognition reminded him how hard it was going to be to hustle action. He switched to the Marley Bone, a cross between a no-frills biker bar and a strip bar. The Algonquin it wasn't. But the drinks were cheap, the exotic dancers were friendly, if not especially attractive, and best of all, no one bothered him. He would sit in the corner against the wall, alternating between beer and shots of Jägermeister, nursing his sorrows. He'd drive home — sometimes drunk, he ashamedly admits—fall asleep, and return the next night. On an administrative leave of sorts from his job, his cash flow slowed to a trickle.

Soon he added to his itinerary off-hours trips to Atlantic City. In a departure from his usual freewheeling MO—playing the role of the lovable loudmouth, tipping extravagantly, and concealing any sign of desperation—he approached these trips with a sense of fatalism. On a typical night he would arrive after midnight and gamble alone at the craps (or blackjack or pai gow or poker) table, all the while drinking liberally. When his stack of chips had diminished, he'd leave quietly and pass out in the front seat of the Tiburon. A few hours later he'd wake up, inhale a cheap and greasy breakfast to sober up, and beat a shamefaced retreat back home, more depleted emotionally and financially than when he'd left.

By the spring of 2001, Kid Delicious wasn't just broke. He was broken.

12

ROLL TIDE

I T TOOK MONTHS, but gradually life started to feel less hopeless, death less imminent. Delicious started to regain his old
energy level, and while he never lost his heroic appetite, he was
sleeping a little less, drinking a little less. Once a mere flicker, his
flame for playing pool was burning again. He began to practice
and was soon spending up to eighteen hours at the table, trying
like hell to get back in dead stroke.

In the interim, Carlos Santos — Carlito, the Peruvian Prince —
had opened a pool hall, Prime Time Sports Bar & Billiards Café, in
South Amboy. As Delicious hit balls one night, he and Carlos discussed options. While Carlos offered to stake him and send him
back on the road, they both knew that his cover had been blown
and it might be hard to shore up action, at least on the East Coast.
On the other hand, Delicious hadn't picked up a cue in months
and was in no shape to try his luck at pro events. This frustrating
impasse would soon trigger another depression.

A few weeks later, in the summer of 2001, Delicious got a
phone call that, in retrospect, may have saved his life. He saw the
708 area code on caller ID and picked up. Like a guardian angel — albeit one working on commission — Greg Smith, the great

pool detective, emerged from the ether to announce that he had a killer spot: "Two words, BIG FELLA: Bessemer, Alabama."

If Smith's voice sounded as if he had just gargled with cue chalk, it was pure honey to Delicious' ears. "Double-Oh Seven!" Delicious screeched into the phone. "How you been?"

"TWO WORDS: Bessemer. Alabama."

"What about it?"

"You'll win a ton of money there. Five grand a week."

"Won't they know who I am?"

"Jeez, Delicious, listen to me, WOULD YA," 007 said. "It's Bessemer, Alabama. They don't know shit about nuthin' there."

Smith explained the setup. One of his many "best friends," a guy called Big City Smitty, was based in Bessemer, a rural community outside Birmingham. (Only in the funhouse mirror of pool would someone from Bessemer, Alabama, assume the handle "Big City" without a trace of irony.) Once a high roller operating out of La Porte, Indiana, Big City Smitty ran a successful car lot and was a big stakehorse for pool players. Alas, according to Big City Smitty, he "got into some trouble with the attorney general over there" and abruptly relocated to Alabama, where he opened an X-rated video store and lived on two hundred acres with his son, Jimi, a former road partner of Bucky Bell — the same Bucky Bell whom Delicious had beaten in Warsaw, Indiana.

The plan for backing Delicious was simple: Smitty and Jimi would start him out in the area and then expand the operation to the entire Southeast. As 007 warned Delicious: "Smitty ain't looking to gamble with you playing on the level. He's looking to steal. He'll only be backing you in games he knows you'll win. And he's gonna ride you like a racehorse. It's gonna be like pool prison."

By then, Delicious was barely listening. He'd already begun throwing clothes into a duffel bag.

Stopping only to take in food and fuel, Delicious drove through the night, making it to Bessemer the next day. When he arrived, Big City Smitty greeted him by saying, "Welcome to Alabama. Set your clock back thirty years."

But to Delicious it was hardly a joke. Perched in the foothills of the Appalachians on the fringes of Birmingham, Bessemer seemed like a foreign country. The people dressed differently. The food was like nothing he had ever tasted — although, originating as it did in a deep fryer, Delicious liked it plenty. He often struggled to decipher the local dialect. ("Who's Barbecue Pete? . . . Oh! *Pit*. Barbecue pit. Got it, brother!")

Delicious' living quarters were alien as well. Big City Smitty, a funny, outgoing soul, generously allowed his guest to stay in a thirty-foot camper that sat vacant in the yard. It had all the amenities of a small apartment — bedroom, shower, television, and card table — but Delicious grew claustrophobic in this corrugated steel bubble and often went to bed frozen with fear over the yelping dogs and shotgun blasts resounding outside. His first night, he used his cell phone to call Jimi, who was a few hundred yards away in the family house.

"What's that shooting, Jimi?"

Unaware that Delicious was in a fragile mental state, Jimi said flatly, "Oh, didn't you hear? It's the Iraqi army. Saddam Hussein declared war on Alabama."

Not long thereafter, Jimi's phone rang again. This time it was Dave Basavich. "What are you guys telling Danny? You've got him scared shitless!" said Dave. "I can't calm him down. Can you go over there? Or at least call him back and tell him you were kidding." Jimi called Delicious and explained that the gunfire came from the local SWAT team, who sometimes took target practice on the property.

"Thanks, Jim," said Delicious, "but that don't make me feel much better."

If Delicious never fully cottoned to southern living — "You know they still call the Civil War 'the War of Northern Aggression' down there?" he says — at least he was back to hustling pool. And that buoyed his spirits, even if his game was coated in the pool equivalent of ring rust.

His first night in town, he and Smitty played a partners game against two local kids and lost $300. A few nights later, Jimi drove Delicious to Cullman, Alabama, and backed him against a player known only as Justin the Roadman. Delicious missed balls that, months earlier, he would have drilled in his sleep. They lost $300 and returned the day after to lose another $400. Smitty called Greg Smith, wondering what the hell was going on with "the unbelievable Kid Delicious" he had sent to Alabama. "Just wait till he GETS IN DEAD stroke," 007 responded. "JUST YOU WAIT."

Like riding a bike or playing a musical instrument, shooting lights-out pool is one of those skills that never totally deserts the skilled practitioner. Delicious spent a few days knocking balls around alone and got his groove back. The state of his game and the state of his mental health moved in lockstep. By the end of his second week, his stroke had returned and his spirits were soaring. According to Jimi, once Delicious took a few losses and got out of his funk, there was little doubt he was the best player in the state of Alabama. With Smitty and Jimi leading him around and acting as his backers, Delicious was soon winning money at every pool hall in the area.

Delicious was in Bessemer for only a week when he got wind of a player one state over, in Mississippi, gambling for astronomical sums of money and, more often than not, losing those astronomical sums of money. There's a misconception in pool hustling that the microeconomy is greased by the winners. In fact, it's greased by the losers, the so-called rainmakers, who gamble unwisely and lose big. And at the time, Little John Macias was a rainmaker, a human money spigot.

Little John was in his early twenties, roughly the same age as Delicious, but at odds with him in every other way. Estranged from his parents, Little John says he was raised by his grandparents in a small town outside Hattiesburg. As a kid, he was a promising baseball player, but it became an afterthought the day he walked into a poolroom. After learning a few slick shots he was hopelessly hooked. He dropped out of school and spent innumerable hours practicing at Snake's Palace, a bare-bones room nestled in a strip mall near the Southern Miss football stadium.

Cocky and aggressive — and, at six feet one, not particularly little — Little John burst on the scene as a gambler, not a hustler. He didn't, as he puts it, "mess around with grinding out chump change." Though he wasn't much better than your average short-stop, he gambled high. With a network of local backers, including Snake himself — the pool hall owner, a soft-spoken African American with an impossibly round head — Little John thought little of putting $10,000 atop the light for a set of nine-ball. "Don't matter how good you are," Little John reasons. "You don't make real money playing for twenty bucks."

To the dismay of his backers, he took his lumps in the beginning and concedes that he may well have lost a six-figure sum in those first few years when he was starting out. Soon, Snake's Palace in Hattiesburg received a double asterisk on every road player's atlas. "I'm not like most guys. I don't lie about my losses," Little John says. "Hell, I advertise them. I took my beatings. Hell yeah, I did. But no one is going to want to play someone who wins every game. I got a lotta gamble in me, and everyone knows it."

When Delicious informed Smitty and Jimi that he wanted to make a foray to Hattiesburg and bust Little John, it drew laughs. "He's gonna want to play two large a set for a minimum of five sets," Smitty retorted. "If you don't have five figures, he won't mess with you. We gotta build up a bankroll. Then go there and stick him."

The whale that was Little John became Danny's Ahab-like obsession. Virtually everything he did was in single-minded pursuit of a big score in Hattiesburg. To conceal his identity, Delicious dyed his hair and again reverted to using his middle name, Martin. He concocted an elaborate story about being Smitty's nephew from Chicago, who had gotten into some trouble with the law up north and had to relocate to Alabama. When he found no action in Bessemer or Birmingham, Delicious practiced his bank pool and his eight-ball, in case Little John didn't want to play nine-ball. One night, Delicious heard that Little John was playing at a hall in Starkville, Mississippi. Delicious drove for two hours, hoping to go incognito and get a read on Little John's game and mannerisms. When his quarry failed to show, Delicious turned around and drove home.

A month into his Alabama stint, Delicious was feeling increasingly comfortable. Having grown fond of his hosts, he took to calling Smitty "Uncle Smitty." And away from the poolrooms, Jimi became something of a big-brother figure to Delicious, teaching him how to shoot an AK-47 and maneuver a Polaris ATV. Delicious soon realized that he'd get nowhere unless he converted to the local religion. So he did, buying all manner of University of Alabama football paraphernalia and, with his best southern elocution, interjecting a robust "Roll Tide!" when the conversation hit a dead spot.

His depression seemed to have vanished, and he was thrilled that no one seemed to recognize him from his time on the Billiards Channel tour, which never did make it to television. He was no longer afraid to go to sleep to the lullaby of shotgun blasts. Not least because he tended to leave a tip as big as the check, he was a welcome regular at the Crossroads Diner, the greasy spoon near Smitty's property. Without Bristol Bob to play nutritionist, he would inhale industrial-sized plates of biscuits and gravy, chicken-fried steak, baked beans, and other sclerotic southern delicacies. ("I swear, Martin, you eat more than any three people," an awed waitress once said.) Back to eating mountainous portions, he was gaining weight by the week. He was unbothered by it all. "I was meant to be fat," he told himself. "This is who I am."

The typical road hustler has a fluid notion of time. With no school semesters, fiscal quarters, kids' birthdays, or anniversaries to help mark time, the seasons bleed together, one year slipping into the next. Ask Kid Delicious about a set he played years ago, and he can summon the details with stunning precision, even recalling configurations of balls. Ask him what year it was when that game took place, and he can venture only a wild guess.

Nevertheless, he could later recall that on a clear September morning, Smitty and he sat on the porch plotting a trip to Meridian, Mississippi, to take down a local player named Ricky Simpson. Their conversation was interrupted when Jimi's thirteen-year-old stepsister came running out of the house. "You gotta see what's on TV," she said. "You're from near New York, right? They're flying planes into buildings there!"

When Delicious went inside, his mouth made an O as he stared at the World Trade Center, dense smoke billowing into the sky. "Holy shit," he said, again and again, before picking up the phone and calling home. He was relieved to hear that his mother's sister, Aunt Karen, hadn't gone to her job in one of the towers that day.

Afraid that the events of 9/11 would trigger an all-out Kid Delicious panic attack — and put their thoroughbred hustler out of action — Smitty and Jimi were especially solicitous. There would be no pool that day, and as Delicious watched the news reports, Jimi and Smitty made sure to keep the food coming. Hearing gunfire behind his trailer may have freaked out Delicious, but a terrorist attack about forty air miles from where he'd grown up didn't much register. He was back at the pool table on September 12.

A few nights later, Delicious was roused from sleep by someone rapping on the side of the camper. Smitty, Jimi, and an African American with the build of a linebacker were at the door. *Get up. We got action.* The game was at On Cue, a pool hall with an exclusively black clientele, square in the middle of Five Points West, one of Birmingham's dodgier neighborhoods. The linebacker, a friend of Smitty's who was a member of the Birmingham police force, was serving as security detail in exchange for a cut of the winnings.

On Cue resembled a modern-day speakeasy. It was a small, nondescript building without so much as a sign out front. Once the visitor passed the threshold, he — the patrons were exclusively male — entered a large room with five pool tables, overstuffed couches, and a television with a sixty-inch screen. It had the vibe of a soulful lounge. The three pasty-faced visitors were more than a little conspicuous. Mike, the owner, offered each of them a Styrofoam coffee cup. Delicious got one whiff and recognized the contents: cognac.

The game of choice was, not surprisingly, one-pocket. For whatever reason, one-pocket and its cognate, bank pool, are particularly popular among African Americans. One possible — and borderline racist — explanation: for decades pool players paid by the rack and never racked the balls themselves. Instead, they paid the "house man" a fixed amount to rack each set. Blacks preferred bank pool because the individual racks lasted longer, hence the hourly rate was effectively lower.

Shattering any tension in the room, Delicious looked at the regulars and asked, "How come we gotta play one-pocket? You know what they say: white men can't bank. I swear, some of you brothers, I could put a ball in front of a pocket and you'd blow it. Then it's time to bank a shot and you do some beautiful things. What's that all about?"

Coming as it did from an overweight interloper with dyed hair, who wore a goofy, unimposing grin, the soliloquy drew laughs from the clientele — a mix of older men, an avowed drug dealer and pimp, and assorted heavily bejeweled kids whose money was assumed by everyone to be of dubious provenance.

A cocky kid wearing tubes of gold chains, who introduced himself as Lamont, was the first to take the bait. The police escort explained that he could have his choice of opponent: Smitty, Jimi, or Delicious. Naturally, Lamont chose "the fat kid." The bet was $400, but Lamont turned to Smitty and Jimi. "For looking silly over there, I'll let you bet a hundred on the side." Fair enough. Delicious closed out the game with relative ease but made enough intentional mistakes, in tactics and execution, to inflate the rest of the room with hope.

All the while, he deployed his singular gift for seducing players as he took their money. Early in the game, he strolled over to the jukebox and announced he was putting on "honky music." The place went silent, and when Marvin Gaye's sultry voice filled the air, there were smiles all around. "He was like Bob Hope the way he worked that room," Uncle Smitty recalled.

At one point, Lamont grew agitated with Delicious' glacially slow play, the practice strokes and rechalking and other tics that made every routine shot a three-act drama. "Chill out, young blood," Delicious said, remembering the expression he had picked up from One-Pocket Harry in Akron. Then he turned serious. Paraphrasing the famous Wyatt Earp line "Fast is fine, but accuracy is everything," he said sternly: "I play best when I take my time. Don't you want my best game?" Lamont could only shake his head.

For the next few months, Delicious returned many times to On Cue. He played them all: Monster John, Sow's Meat, and Larry. Early on, he deduced that the players had too much ego to ask for a spot from a fat white kid. And he was sure to lose every now and then — sometimes on the square, sometimes not — so the regulars held out hope. He never felt heat there. It may have been in a bad part of town, and he and Smitty may have been the only white guys in there, but it wasn't really a problem. He respected the regulars, and they respected his coming to their place to play their game, giving everyone action — and still winning almost every night.

The sense of comfort ended abruptly. On a slow Sunday night, Delicious made a one-pocket game with a player he hadn't seen before. When the opponent fanned a stack of hundreds and demanded they play for $3,000, Delicious shrugged and consented. The game was genial and unremarkable, and the opponent, while not untalented, was nowhere near Delicious' skill level. Delicious later could not recall so much as a curse word after the opponent missed a shot. When Delicious potted his final ball, he shook the man's hand and took his winnings. Wearing a crooked smile, the man leaned in and said, "If I ever see you here again, I'm gonna spray the place up. Got it?" Thus concluded Delicious' run at On Cue.

By then it was late October, and Delicious had amassed a thick bankroll in Bessemer. Even accounting for his hefty daily tab at the Crossroads Diner and a few ill-conceived trips to the casinos in Mississippi, more than $10,000 had managed to adhere to his pockets. It was time to stick Little John.

With Jimi driving and Delicious riding shotgun, the pair bounded through the heart of Dixie. The plan was to play a "tune-up" match at a pool hall in Philadelphia, Mississippi, before moving on to Hattiesburg. As the countryside whipped by — the Tara-like mansions, the roadside stands selling boiled peanuts, the stately magnolias, the trains headed east to Savannah or south to the gulf, and "all that friggin' mud" — Delicious took it all in.

Somewhere in the innards of Mississippi, he saw a sign for a state sanatorium. "What's that?" he asked Jimi. "A place to get clean?"

"Nah," Jimi said, laughing. "That's a place for crazy folk."

"Man," Delicious said, barely above a whisper. "I gotta keep playing pool so I stay out of there."

At Freddie's, a pool hall near the Silver Star Casino in Philadelphia, Jimi floated the proposition that Delicious would play anyone even for any amount of money. The owner made a few calls. Within an hour, Barry Emerson, a pro player of some distinction south of the Mason-Dixon Line, arrived.

Delicious felt sick to his stomach when he saw Emerson's backer follow behind him. "I'm Barry," Emerson said by way of introduction. "This is my buddy, Little John."

Thinking that any hope of slinking into Hattiesburg and hustling Little John was shot to hell, Delicious tried to goad Emerson into playing big. (Little John later said that he had known all about Kid Delicious by then anyway.) They agreed to play two sets for $300 apiece. Jimi bet Little John another $400 on the side. In dead stroke, Delicious polished off Emerson handily, running out the last four racks in both sets. It was a solid score, $1,000 was. But there was no joy in Mudville. As he often did when he felt the first signs of depression, Delicious headed to the casino that night and made a sizable involuntary contribution at the poker table.

The next morning, figuring he had nothing to lose, Delicious placed a call to Little John, trying to make a game. Little John had seen Delicious at full speed and had no interest in playing him even. But since he was an incorrigible gambler with a reputation to uphold, that didn't mean they couldn't make a game. "Why don't you and your backer come down to Snake's and let's see if we can't get it on," he said breezily. "Give me the right weight and you can step in the box."

It would be hard to imagine a less likely big-action venue than Snake's Palace. As pool halls go, it's a fairly typical small-town joint filled with bored college kids and local bangers playing on one of the thirteen barboxes or in the de facto pit, a large table adjacent to the counter. (For obvious reasons, the best table in

the house is almost always near the cash register.) Table time at
Snake's goes for $4 an hour per person, more than reasonable.
Cold beer costs a buck a bottle. A bag of potato chips will set you
back fifty cents. Even on a busy night, it's difficult to imagine the
place grossing more than a few hundred bucks. Yet in the course
of an average week, $50,000 might change hands over a few sets
of nine-ball. Go figure.

When players gamble instead of hustle, they waste little time
with niceties. No sooner were Delicious and Jimi in the door than
they began to negotiate with Little John and Snake. Delicious
suggested that Little John take the eight ball. Then the seven. "No
way," Little John said, running a hand through his close-cropped
hair. "If you're running racks, it does me no good to get balls. I
want games on the wire." With the prototypical southern rockers
Lynyrd Skynyrd squawking in the background, the two parties finally reached an agreement. Delicious would spot his opponent
three games in a race to ten for $2,000. He handed the money to
Snake, who deposited it in a vault behind the counter. While Delicious was happy to be in action, it was hardly the match he had
been fervently anticipating for months. Three games was a hell of
a spot, roughly equivalent to giving up the six ball. And it was Little John's home table.

From drug dealers who packed heat to drunken frat boys who
mercilessly mocked his weight, Delicious had played hundreds of
opponents without letting a single one pierce his calm. He may
have lost a few games here and there, but it was never because an
opponent had gotten under his skin or into his head. This opponent, however, came close. Handsome and well dressed, dripping
attitude and hair gel, Little John struck Delicious as an older version of the kind of kid who'd bullied him in high school. Before
they lagged to break, Little John got a laugh out of the railbirds
by saying, "Big boy, when we're done, they're gonna call me Little John Delicious." The head games continued. Little John complained so much about Delicious' rack that they agreed to play
rack-your-own.

Decidedly off his game, Delicious was both rattled and frustrated as the bet went back and forth a few times. After three

hours of play, they had each won two sets. Delicious took his break and marched to the bathroom. As he splashed cold water on his face and tried to energize himself, inspiration struck. Realizing that he needed to lengthen the games in order to neutralize the generous spot he'd conceded, he came up with an idea: he would offer Little John six games on the wire in a race to twenty.

Little John agreed to this, thinking that the longer his overweight opponent had to spend on his feet, the faster he would run out of steam. Little John then added a condition: they would raise the bet to $4,000. Fine. Fine. For good measure, Jimi took $500 on the side with one of the railbirds.

Athletes in all sports talk about entering "the zone," that blissful, mystical state in which the mind is cleansed, time is elastic, and peak performance is attainable. Having entered a sort of cocoon of unshakable calm, the athlete's target — be it a basketball hoop, a golf hole, a pocket of a pool table — becomes enormous. That fastball appears to be tossed underhanded. That impossible running forehand seems routine. A thirty-foot jump shot is no more difficult than a lay-up. Brilliance is elevated to perfection. "In the case of archery, the hitter and the hit are no longer two opposing objects, but are one reality," D. T. Suzuki says in his introduction to an unsurpassed sports psychology book, Eugen Herrigel's *Zen in the Art of Archery*. "The archer ceases to be conscious of himself as the one who is engaged in hitting the bull's-eye which confronts him. This state of unconsciousness is realized only when, completely empty and rid of the self, he becomes one with the perfecting of his technical skill."

At the big table at dowdy Snake's Palace, playing high-stakes nine-ball against a loudmouth gambler, Delicious entered "the zone" and achieved that unconscious state. To this day, he recognizes it as the best pool he's ever played. Not surprisingly, he can't remember much about that night, but others — including his opponent and his backer — call it the most awesome performance they've ever seen. For an hour, Delicious essentially played solitaire, stroking the ball as if it were a guided missile, letting muscle memory do the heavy lifting. The six pockets became ravenous maws, gobbling up every ball.

As his opponent ran rack after rack, Little John grew numb. "Wake me when it's my turn, Snake," he told his backer. With that, he dozed off in his chair.

When Snake finally tapped him on the shoulder, Little John asked him the score. "It's eleven to nothing. Well, eleven to six." Delicious had played a safety, and after Little John missed a difficult shot, Delicious picked up where he'd left off, running out two more racks. Not counting the safety, he had reeled thirteen — *thirteen!* — straight racks. That he had done so with $5,000 hanging in the balance, playing in a game he'd been anticipating for months, was more remarkable still. In barely an hour, he won 20–9.

In keeping with his reputation as an honorable player, Little John opened the money spigot and paid off his debt without a trace of bitterness. Desperate to recoup some of the king's ransom, Little John, ever the gambling addict, summoned Barry Emerson to the pool hall and stubbornly insisted that Delicious give him the eight ball and play him for $2,000.

Jimi briefly tried to usher his protégé out the front door. But Delicious, by this point floating on a cloud of confidence, agreed on the spot. His visit to "the zone" was an extended one, and he continued his otherworldly playing, beating Emerson for the second time in a week. Little John delivered another two grand, saying, "Unbelievable playing. Now get the fuck outta here."

Delicious knew that he was not only finished in Hattiesburg, but, having busted Little John, the biggest rainmaker in the area, it was going to be tough for him to hustle incognito anywhere in the Southeast. Besides, Delicious had been in Alabama for six months, and it was time get home to New Jersey. Still, as he fanned the $7,000 he'd won, he couldn't resist a parting shot. "You were right about what you said before, Little John," he said theatrically. "You *are* delicious."

13

BACK IN FORM

B RISTOL BOB'S STINT in the dank basement of Hi Pockets
Billiards was cathartic in its way, a cross between a prison
sentence and a stay in a minimalist rehab center. With no
television, no phone, no Internet access, and no disposable income to dispose of, Bristol had plenty of time for deep thinking
and self-discovery. He devoured self-help books. He painted large
canvases and experimented with his art. He punished himself doing sets of push-ups and sit-ups and crunches, rebuilding a body
that had, over the past year, lost much of its architecture. Most
important, he stayed clean and sober.

By the spring of 2001, rudderless no more, Bristol was ready to
get on with his life. He learned quickly that, as a twenty-six-year-
old without a college degree, it wasn't going to be easy to find a
job, at least one that would allow him to sustain the lifestyle and
income he'd been accorded as a road player. When you're accustomed to bringing in a fistful of large bills (untaxed) a week, setting your own hours, and authoring your own adventures, it's
tough to abide a numbingly monotonous $6-an-hour job making
specialized lattes or stocking shelves at Home Depot.

If Bristol had gotten the taste for meth out of his system, he
was having less success fighting another nasty addiction. Pool.

The sport is all about repetition, and Bristol paid a big price for his wretched decision to try to change his style. But, in a perverse way — albeit one even recreational bangers can understand — his erratic playing only made pool *more* seductive. On the good days he thought, foolishly perhaps, that he was on the verge of solving the riddle of it all. On the bad days he felt a compulsion to return to the table and seek redemption. He'd play like crap and then wouldn't be able to sleep, envisioning his misses and lost chances all night long. As he put it: "It's like I need to get validated — *Yes, Bob, you really do know what the fuck you're doing at the table* — before I have any peace."

Practicing on the Gold Crowns of Hi Pockets, he slowly found his stroke again and tried to unlearn some of the Filipino techniques that had splintered his game — and prompted him to smoke up those poisonous white crystals. Unable to bring himself to take a low-wage job with conventional hours, Bristol found work at Action Billiards, in Old Bridge, New Jersey, giving lessons at $40 an hour, specializing in helping novices improve their break. It made for a strange existence: he worked at one pool hall and lived at another, more than an hour away. But, as he saw it, this beat the other limited options. And it kept him in the pool world.

One of Bristol's regular pool acquaintances at the time was a man we'll call Yosemite Sam, a ball of fire with a shock of fading reddish hair who was generally calm but had a volcanic temper. Sam had been an educator before discovering a more lucrative career as a sports bookie. Based off the turnpike in central Jersey, Yosemite Sam ran a fairly elaborate operation. His computer was wired directly to a Las Vegas sports book, and he made a healthy living processing bets on football, basketball, baseball, hockey, and horseracing. On a good weekend during football season, Sam could take hundreds of tickets, usually making $20 or so per ticket. Business was so robust that he needed help, a runner to take calls and enter all the bets into the computer. Might Bristol be interested?

Bristol was hoping for more legitimate employment, but then he heard the terms of the job. The pay was $600 a week. In cash.

In addition to an apartment where he conducted his business, Sam owned a two-bedroom condo nearby, on the Pennsylvania side of the Delaware River. As part of the compensation package, he told Bristol that he could live there rent-free. The best part of the job was that it entailed just a few hours of work a day. The rest of the time, Bristol could do as he pleased.

He had his reservations, but the pool hustler's situational ethics kicked in. He rationalized that working for Sam would be a good way to get back on his feet and replenish his cash reserves. And if running a sports book was technically illegal, it was essentially a victimless crime, wasn't it? No one was getting robbed or injured. (In fact, all the phone calls from the bettors were recorded, so discrepancies were easily resolved.) Sam extended his clients a line of credit, and if they exceeded it, he simply wouldn't take their bets. In other words, Bristol wasn't going to be breaking anybody's kneecaps.

For more than a year, Bristol repaired the fabric of his life. In a matter of months, he'd made enough money to put down $8,000 in cash to buy a silver Volkswagen Jetta. He was "slating" (his new euphemism) as many as three women at a time. He was working out for three hours a day, bench-pressing 225 pounds, pumping up his physique until it was bigger than before. He kept up his painting. And he was back to playing at least B-level pool, hustling all over the Philadelphia area, supplementing his income from Yosemite Sam with a few grand a month in table winnings. It wasn't only that he had money in his pocket or that he was back to playing pool. His life had some semblance of structure and purpose again. To his parents' delight, he even enrolled in a few courses at Bucks County Community College.

Playing late one night at Pete Fusco's poolroom in Feasterville, Pennsylvania, Bristol noticed an attractive, sylph-like blonde behind the counter. He checked himself in the mirror and then worked his rap. The more they talked, the more he liked.

The blonde's name was Janelle. In a thick Philadelphia accent she explained that she was a recent graduate of St. Joseph's University and had paid her way through school by working at the pool hall. She had stumbled on the job by accident, but the regulars fell in love with her, and soon she was running the two A.M. poker games, making far more than she would have by shoveling mashed potatoes and beef stroganoff in the campus dining halls.

She'd recently graduated and now, at age twenty-three, was working as an elementary school teacher. But she was still moonlighting at the poolroom — named, incongruously, Family Recreation Center — hanging out with the guys. She never really took up the sport herself, but something about the atmosphere was irresistible. As an aspiring writer with an eye for detail and an appreciation for a rich plot, she found all the intrigue at the pool hall, with its diverse cast of characters, endearing in its way.

Janelle told Bristol that she'd just gotten out of a relationship with a Philadelphia pool player. He had treated her well, and she understood the wildly erratic hours and even more wildly irregular paydays. But she didn't want to go through that again. She told Bristol that her next boyfriend wouldn't be the kind who slipped out of town for indeterminate periods of time and gambled at the poolroom until sunrise.

Bristol said he could abide by this, telling Janelle that as much as he still loved the sport, the prospect of road playing had lost its appeal, and he realized that he wasn't good enough to become a professional. Pool, he figured, would always be a big part of his identity, but it would no longer define him.

Though you'd never have known it by looking at her, Janelle was fighting a variety of ailments, some life-threatening. Hardly a season went by without her spending time in the hospital, and her diet was heavily restricted. But she was one of those people who were blessed with a deep reservoir of inner strength, refusing to accept the possibility that she'd been dealt a lousy hand.

As Janelle and Bristol got more and more serious, she became as much a life coach as a girlfriend. It was Janelle who encouraged him to take more college-level courses and helped edit his papers. Always an underachieving student, Bristol not only attended his classes but actually enjoyed them. He aced psychology and nutrition. It was Janelle who encouraged him to continue experimenting with his painting. She persuaded him to quit his lucrative but shadowy work for Yosemite Sam — "You're better than that," she told him — and it was she who made sure he stayed away from the meth.

Speaking on the phone with his mother one night, Bristol learned about a younger cousin back home in Connecticut who was having a rough go of it, working the graveyard shift at a dead-end job at a CVS drugstore and wrestling with some personal problems. Bristol had always liked the kid, and, having extricated himself from his own dark place, he was happy to help. He invited the cousin to live with him in Pennsylvania and got him a job working for Yosemite Sam. Thinking back to his time with Delicious, Bristol remembered how good it felt to be in a position to help someone improve his station in life.

Soon he and Janelle moved into her apartment in northeast Philadelphia. She was busy helping Pete Fusco design a new pool hall, a cavernous converted warehouse that would feature dozens of tables, a Ping-Pong area cordoned off by nets, and a "lunar-themed" room. Bristol was taking courses at the community college and online, devouring knowledge, and contemplating a career as a teacher. He was physically fit and actually going to sleep before the sun came up. He spent his downtime with a paintbrush, not a cue stick, in his hand. His parents figured that at long last he was on the right path. Surely he would marry Janelle, they'd have a few rug rats, he'd get a steady teaching job, buy a minivan, and live a happy, perfectly conventional life. In pool terms, it was an ideal configuration for running out the rack.

There was, of course, one problem. Like a cue ball laced with backspin, his passion for life on the road had returned in full force.

14

A NEW WINGMAN

THE LEGENDARY BOXER Floyd Patterson was so afraid of showing his face after a defeat that he traveled with a bag of elaborate disguises. After one loss to Sonny Liston, Patterson spent the next few months wearing a dark beard and thick glasses. In pool hustling, it is the *winners* who disguise themselves. And often with no luck. In a 1977 profile in *Sports Illustrated*, the renowned hustler Danny DiLiberto remarked, "I've grown a beard, smeared grease on my face, driven up to a place that is nowhere, limped in the door and the first thing a guy says to me is, 'Aren't you Danny DiLiberto?'"

Delicious could relate. Desperate to prolong the ride, he took to dying his hair orange and platinum, shaving his goatee, and wearing a pair of overalls that he'd once impulsively purchased in Alabama. He called himself Martin. But his efforts fooled few. That gut, that magnificent, ever-swelling belly of his, undercut the black-ops treatment and the stealth maneuvers. No matter what shade the hair or what style the outfit, there were precious few obese men with such lavish pool talent. As for players who knew Kid Delicious from his days of weighing 180 pounds, his bloated body might buy him a few extra months of hustling. Still, they would soon recognize his distinct voice and observe his trademark slow play and easy manner and wouldn't be fooled for long.

At least east of the Mississippi, Delicious was a known commodity in pool circles, easily researched on the Internet and discussed on the pool wire. He would amble into a room looking for action and be besieged by locals, who would congratulate him on his latest scores and sometimes even tell him how happy they were that he seemed to be licking his depression. He was playing as well as ever, but no one would go near him. Someone once remarked that the saddest thing in the world is a good player without a game. That was Kid Delicious. Deep down in that gut, he knew that he had a dwindling number of hustles left in him, knew that his notoriety would soon bring about his expulsion from the hustling kingdom.

After a few idle weeks, Delicious determined that the Deep South was essentially fished out. In late November of 2001, he thanked Smitty and Jimi for their hospitality in Alabama and headed back to New Jersey. Jimi mentioned that on the drive home Delicious ought to stop at a Viking Cue Tour nine-ball pro event in Lexington, Kentucky. The tournament was paying only $5,000 for first place, but there would be some good gambling opportunities. Most of the players entered in the field already knew Delicious, so it wasn't as though he'd be blowing what little cover he had left.

So it was that Delicious changed his route and piloted his Tiburon due north. During the six-hour drive through the guts of the South, he again contemplated how much he missed the camaraderie and security of a road partner. Best he could tell from their exchanges of voice mail and their third-party contacts, Bristol Bob was doing better, living in Philly with a girlfriend, but he was still untangling his life. As for Carlito Santos, he was busy providing for his immediate family in Jersey and his extended family in Peru. Delicious had to go it alone.

The Lexington event was held at the Continental Inn, and in a stroke of good fortune, one of the first players Delicious encountered in the lobby was Chris Bartram, the deceptively strong player he and Bristol Bob had battled in Columbus, Ohio. Delicious had fond recollections of gambling with Bartram. The kid had played with quiet dignity, hardly uttering a sound during the sets, happy to let his pool speak for itself. Bartram didn't gloat when he won. He paid up when he lost, which was not often.

In the five or so years since he had played sets with Delicious in Columbus, Bartram had improved steadily to become a high-level player, able to execute any shot in the book. Like Delicious, Bartram was blessed with the ability to play his best when the stakes were highest. But beyond that, Bartram was a slick gambler, a hustler's hustler whose natural habitat was hunkering down in the weeds. Some hustlers project badass, some project mental instability. Bartram never revealed enough about himself to create any impression. Pointedly, he had no pool nickname. As he saw it, a moniker was just a way to publicize his identity, the last thing he wanted to do. Even his voice had an elusive quality to it.

Bartram, unlike many of his colleagues, also understood the virtue of patience. He would happily lose $500 today if it might help him win $5,000 in the future. He also made a habit of betting big with the rail, so a $100 set might be worth ten or twenty times that to him. He took pains to stay undercover, even assuming an alias on his own voice mail, and this combination of skill and savvy took him far. If Delicious was, as the anecdotal evidence seems to suggest, the premier road hustler at the time, Bartram sure wasn't far behind.

After giving Delicious grief for his hefty appearance, Bartram suggested they team up that night and try to make a Scotch doubles game against another pair of players. Hungry for any action, Delicious agreed. Later that night, he and Bartram took on Sam Monday and Keith Bennett, two strong young players from North Carolina, for $2,000 a set. In Scotch doubles, the usual rules of nine-ball apply, but the players on each team alternate shots. Like any kind of doubles event, the two teammates may be terrific individual players, but if they don't click or never get in rhythm, they can make a lousy team. In the case of Bartram and Delicious, there was instant synchronicity. Delicious would bury his ball and leave his partner in perfect position. Then Bartram would return the favor.

Bartram played pool the way he gambled, methodically and conservatively, free of any look-at-me flourishes. His balls often trickled as slowly as syrup before finding a home in the bottom of the pocket. Without much resistance, Bartram and Delicious won two sets. And they both had a hell of a lot of fun. They made tentative plans to go on the road together. The way they left it, Bartram would call Delicious when he came across a promising spot.

Meanwhile, Delicious laughed when the saw the Lexington tournament pairings. His first match was against Larry Nevel, a well-respected pro Delicious had once unsuccessfully stalked during a run through Wisconsin. Already in gambling mode, Delicious found a sweater willing to bet on Nevel. Delicious put $500 on himself in the race-to-nine set. He found himself down 6–1 to Nevel, a serious, inexpressive blond with the build of an NBA forward. Delicious then did what he did best, taking advantage of an opponent's error and catching a gear. From 6–1, he evened the set at 6–6 and soon ran out, 9–6. Between the Scotch doubles and the side action against Nevel, after one night Delicious was up $2,500, more money than the tournament's second-place finisher would make.

Delicious gave a respectable account of himself in the tournament. He lost to Tony Watson — a well-regarded player whom Delicious had purposely avoided at the Sports Palace in South Carolina — but slithered through the back draw to finish tied for seventh place, good for $1,000 and, more important, a surge of self-confidence. All in all, it had been a riotously successfully weekend.

Delicious' detour to Lexington had birthed a completely new itinerary. During the Viking tournament, Delicious got into a late-night conversation with Gary Abood, a talented player from New Hampshire who had come to troll for off-hours action. Abood's partner had left him, and he needed to get to Shreveport, Louisiana. Delicious offered Abood a lift in the Tiburon and said he would steer the kid around Alabama and Mississippi. Having just spent six months in the South, Delicious knew the landscape and was confident he could win big by staking Abood. After that, Delicious, with his newfound surge of self-worth, thought he would then drive on alone to Reno and enter another pro tournament.

The spots Delicious provided Abood weren't as fruitful as either had hoped. Still, with Delicious often waiting in the car lest he tip anyone off, Abood did his part and scrounged up $1,000 or so for the week. Delicious enjoyed the company but got no vicarious thrill backing Abood. He wished that he were the one in action — not the one with the ridiculously dyed hair, lying in wait in his car.

When they got to Shreveport, Delicious dropped off Abood at a frumpy pool hall, Tournament Billiards. Then he made the mistake of getting a room at Harrah's Casino, outside of town. His bankroll at the time was $7,500. Within two days he was broke. Not unlike a Scotch doubles team, Delicious' depression and gambling addiction worked in devastating tandem. Feeling like hell, he tried to cheer himself up at the craps and blackjack tables. The more he lost, the more he played. As low as he'd already been, he only felt worse after frittering away so much. The following morning, he would seek to self-medicate by gambling again with what little of his money remained. The casino did its part too, plying him with free screwdrivers and keeping him at the table with vague promises of a comp room or a free bottle of champagne. *Hey, here's the guy with the weight problem and the depression. No way is he getting out alive.*

His pockets empty, Delicious had to track down Abood for an emergency "gapper." Abood knew about his depression and sensed that Delicious was in a bad way. He gave Delicious $300, figuring he would never see it again, but it seemed a fair exchange for the ride from Lexington. He also suggested that Delicious drive three hours west, to Mr. Kim's poolroom in Dallas, and try to rustle up some action there.

With no plan of action other than getting out of Shreveport, Delicious hightailed it to Dallas. In a grim poolroom he played a set for fun against a paunchy man wearing (or course) a leather vest and cowboy hat, known to all as the Plumber. With no money on the table and a burning desire to get back in dead stroke, Delicious did nothing to conceal his speed. "You play like burning hell!" the Plumber said, dumbfounded. "Can I back you?"

The Plumber made a few calls, and by midnight Delicious was matching up against a local ringer, Javier Franco. There's a proportional relationship between a player's financial desperation and his willingness to part with the nuts. Without having seen Franco hit a ball — and the kid could play jam-up pool — Delicious gave up the six ball and a game on the wire in a $2,000 race to seven the next night. Meanwhile, Gary Abood, concerned about Delicious' state of mind, called to check in.

On the phone Delicious sounded far more upbeat than he had been a few days before. As usual, the chance to match up at the pool table had a restorative effect on his mental health. He then told Abood about the set he was about to play against Franco.

"Are you crazy?" Abood yelled. "That guy's a good fucking player. He's robbing you, making you give him a ball and a game on the wire!"

"It's cool, Gary," Delicious said calmly. "I'm feeling good again. And I'm getting backed by the Plumber guy."

Calling forth yet again his preternatural gift for playing his best when there was money on the line, Delicious managed to win four sets. Even after splitting the spoils with the Plumber, he'd made $4,000. His first stop was the post office, where he filled out a money order and wired Abood back his $300. Abood figured it marked a record for the shortest time it ever took a pool player to repay a loan.

Delicious was suddenly swollen with both confidence and cash, but he hadn't forgotten that pro event in Reno. If he started driving soon, he could be in Albuquerque by —

His calculation was interrupted by a phone call. It was Chris Bartram.

"Where are you?"

"Shreveport. But I'm heading to Reno."

"Turn the car ninety degrees and drive to Kansas City. I got us real strong action."

"Thanks, Chris, but I'm playing like a god. I can win that thing in Reno."

"Let me ask you a question: how much would you get for winning?"

"I dunno. Ten grand?"

"Danny, we can make that in one night in Kansas City."

Were it anyone else, Delicious would have rolled his eyes. He had been in the pool world long enough to know that "guaranteed money" and "sure things" were usually anything but. Yet he also knew that Bartram wasn't one to go prospecting for fool's gold.

Bartram assumed from the pause in the conversation that he had made a sale. "I'm flying tomorrow. Pick me up at the Kansas City Airport at four."

If Bristol resided at one end of the personality spectrum and Kid Delicious at the other, Bartram was roughly in the middle. He wasn't particularly intense, but neither was he a slacker. At five feet seven, 220 pounds, Bartram didn't exactly have a sculpted physique to rival Bristol Bob's. But he tried to watch his diet. He didn't drink, didn't smoke, didn't pop pills. He did, however, patronize his share of casinos. He wasn't a neat freak, but he did have a certain sense of tidiness.

His initial delight at meeting up with Delicious at the Kansas City Airport was tempered when he leaned into the Tiburon. The car smelled like a farm, and the upholstery was barely visible under a sea of fast-food bags, newspapers, and empty coffee cups. Before sitting in the shotgun seat, Bartram scooped up piles of trash and deposited them in a nearby garbage can. Not a mile outside the airport, Delicious realized that, along with all the junk, Bartram had inadvertently thrown away his road atlas containing spots, phone numbers, and notes.

"Chris, that was like throwing out a stack of hundreds!" Delicious screamed.

"Well," Bartram shouted back, "if your car wasn't so disgusting, I wouldn't be throwing anything out!"

An auspicious start to the partnership, it wasn't.

As usual, Bartram's prep work was excellent. He had received a spot that a new poolroom, Side Pockets, had opened in Kansas City — always a good action town to begin with — and the owner, an affable man named Duff, wasn't afraid to bet high. Better still, Duff was backing a local kid named Shane, who had some skills but was no threat to a player of Delicious' caliber.

Located in the quiet suburb of Lee's Summit, Missouri, Side Pockets was one of those glistening, palatial, upmarket sports bars that have accelerated the death of the smoke-filled poolroom. The place was stuffed with dozens of pool tables, electric dartboards, eight-foot projection televisions, a full bar, and a trendy menu. Purists might lament that the proliferation of nouvelle rooms like Side Pockets was bleaching the color out of pool, but how can those dank, subterranean rooms have any hope of competing with fajitas?

Bartram and Delicious had no problem finding action and were soon in the pit, locked into $1,000 races against decent locals. Sniffing a pair of young, unimposing road players, Duff came over and made a point of introducing himself. He suggested calling his buddy Shane so the four of them could "jack around a bit" and maybe play for some money.

After a long negotiation, Bartram and Shane agreed to play on the bar table, Bartram giving Shane the eight and the last three in a $2,000 race to ten. Simultaneously, on the adjacent table, Delicious played Duff for the same amount, Delicious giving up the six, the eight, and the last four. Slapping five and grinning at each other as they played, Bartram and Delicious each won his set. Mistakenly thinking that Bartram was the superior player, Duff and Shane suggested they keep the bet and the spot but switch opponents. This time Delicious played Shane and Bartram played Duff. The result was the same. They were now up $8,000, this on top of the $3,000 they made earlier in the evening.

Duff and Shane may have been relieved of some significant wallet heft, but otherwise they had nothing against the two road players. In fact, they liked the guys. "Total gentlemen gamblers," Duff later recalled. "No one likes losing money, but if you're going to do it, it might as well be to guys like that."

After getting beaten out of eight grand, Shane and Duff invited

Bartram and Delicious to stick around and regale them with stories from the road. The four of them hung out until the morning. Delicious and Bartram stayed in a nearby Holiday Inn Express and returned to Side Pockets night after night. They played everyone they could and concocted more games with Duff and Shane, giving away plenty of weight. After a week, they had played out Kansas City, but not before netting $15,000. "I told you," Bartram said to his partner. "You'll do better with me than you would playing those pro events."

Bartram wasn't done. After Kansas City, they doubled back across Missouri to Wright City, a blink-and-you-miss-it town off I-70, about an hour west of St. Louis. As they drove, Bartram explained that the previous year, he had been tipped off to Carl Bolm, a high-rolling St. Louis entrepreneur and a pioneer in the riverboat casino business.

Mr. Carl, as he was known, lived in St. Louis but also had a home in Wright City and repaired there to gamble on one of the two tables in a honky-tonk outpost named, appropriately enough, Hillbilly Heaven. As a player Mr. Carl was still a work in progress, but he loved action and would play anyone, provided he was spotted enough weight. He could lose $25,000 and seem none the worse for it. As a result, plenty of players — including Jeanette "the Black Widow" Lee — detoured to Wright City. There was one catch: Mr. Carl didn't like betting conventional dollar amounts. For reasons unclear, instead of playing for $1,000 a set, he'd play for, say, $977.42. And he demanded that his opponent put up the exact amount, down to the penny.

Bartram saw Carl play. He saw Carl gamble. He saw Carl giggling as he paid off an eccentric wager of $1,001.84. He knew this could be a whale. He called an Indianapolis backer, "Big Arm John," and told him to get in his car and meet him in Wright City. Big Arm John picked up Bartram in his Mercedes, and when they got to Hillbilly Heaven he parked it conspicuously near the front door. Bartram then sought out Carl. They made a game, and Bartram purposely lost nearly $2,000. Bartram and Big Arm John left the place as if the loss were mere pocket change.

That was the previous year. Bartram had made his investment, and now it was payoff time. Flanked by Delicious and Big Arm John, Bartram walked into Hillbilly Heaven. Within an hour, Carl arrived, no doubt tipped off by one of the railbirds who'd recalled Bartram peeling out of the parking lot in a Mercedes. Giving up enough weight to satisfy Carl, Bartram broke in a race to ten for $747. Meanwhile, Delicious and Big Arm John trolled the rails for more action. Bartram won, and he and Carl agreed to raise the bet to $1,496.

As Bartram took Carl to the woodshed, Delicious saw Andy Quinn, the St. Louis hotshot he had battled years back. Delicious nodded amiably in Quinn's direction, but Quinn looked through him as if he were a pane of glass. Delicious was affronted until he remembered that he'd put on more than a hundred pounds since the last time he was in the area. Silently, he forgave Quinn. Then he seized on an idea. "Hey," he said to Quinn, trying his best to disguise his accent, "you know anyone else here who likes to play for some money?"

Within minutes, Quinn had Carl backing him against Delicious in a $5,000 eight-ahead set on the bar table. When they had played several years before, Delicious had to pull a rabbit out of his case just to end up even. This time he blitzed Quinn and won the set within two hours. The score wasn't huge, not so long as Bartram and Carl had $10,000 (or more like $10,231.23) above the light. But Delicious was happy that he was contributing.

If Carl was losing a small fortune, he didn't seem to mind. In between racks, he would cackle and challenge Bartram to flip a coin for, say, $897.13. Just to make sure Carl stayed in gambling mode, Bartram played along. There were thousands of dollars above the light, but watching Bartram count off the last pennies seemed to mollify Carl. They played until three in the morning, when Carl flew the white flag of surrender. Bartram had stuck him for more than $15,000.

Including the side action and Delicious' $5,000 set, the haul was roughly $20,000. Split three ways, Delicious was still up $6,666.67, a figure Carl would have appreciated. And that didn't include the ten dimes they had made in Kansas City. "That's my partner," Delicious said, his arm slung around Bartram as they ate celebratory steaks at a TA truck stop, polishing off their meal just before sunup.

Broke just a few weeks prior, Delicious now sported a massive bankroll. But Bartram's value went beyond his earning power. Delicious would view any road partner through the prism of Bristol Bob, the way a new girlfriend is invariably compared to the previous one. Delicious and Bristol had always fed off their contrasts. Nevertheless, Bartram stacked up pretty well against his predecessor. His willingness to lose a little now for the chance to earn a lot later was a good influence on Kid Delicious, who too often played impetuously. Leading by example, he showed Delicious the virtue of meticulous planning. Even in the Darwinian pool world, Bartram's street smarts were extraordinary. Once, in Kansas City, he was playing $50 racks but betting multiples of that on the rail. He lost one game and "accidentally" overpaid his opponent by $50. Just as Delicious was about to correct his partner's error, he realized Bartram had slyly overpaid just to keep the action going.

Bartram wasn't about to take a page from Bristol Bob's book and demand that Delicious adopt an exercise program. But he didn't drink or do drugs — "I don't play my best unless I'm sober," he says — and he was sympathetic to Delicious' mental fragility. Early in the trip, when they were flush, Delicious warned him that when their fortunes reversed, as they surely would, he'd sink into depression and have wild mood swings. No problem, Bartram said, adding that if Delicious ever felt like taking a night off, he should always feel free, no questions asked.

Bartram did have one vice. Like most pool players, his fondness for gambling didn't begin and end at the pool table. He was hopeless to resist the magnetic pull of casinos. He was so conscious of money that he clipped coupons from the back of an AAA atlas to save a few bucks at a motel. But all financial prudence disappeared when there was a craps or blackjack table nearby. The day after the Wright City Robbery, as they called it, Big Arm John headed back to Indianapolis, and Bartram and Delicious drove to a riverboat casino. In a few hours they had burned through much of their bankroll, indirectly enriching Carl, the shortstop they'd just busted. When they finally had the good sense to leave, Bartram smiled wryly. "Look at it this way: we just paid our taxes." It was with significantly lighter wallets that they moved on to Oklahoma City.

For a modestly populated state, Oklahoma had always furnished the pool world with a disproportionately large number of big-time players and action spots. The armchair sociologist might attribute this to the state's boom-or-bust spirit, coupled with limited entertainment options. Surely the state's central location plays a role as well: hustlers from anywhere in the country can converge on Oklahoma on a day's notice. If a player from New York wants to match up with a player from California, for example, chances are they'll do it in Tulsa.

But in 2002 there was another reason why Oklahoma was a center of action. The epidemic of meth — "hillbilly heroin," the same drug that ensnared Bristol Bob — was quietly cutting a swath of destruction through the heartland, and the Sooner State was particularly hard-hit. That year, more than half of Oklahoma's citizens sentenced to prison were there for meth-related offenses. Meth users experience a euphoric rush that can last for three or four days, followed by a crash that can last just as long. While everyone else is asleep, the speed freaks are jacked. It's two A.M., you've never felt more awake, you're feeling hyperconfident, your judgment is clouded, and in all likelihood you could use some easy money. Where do you go? The pool hall, of course.

While Oklahoma was chock-full of spots, the biggest action clustered at Mikey's 24-7, a spirited joint on the north side of Oklahoma City that, as the name implied, never closed. At four in the afternoon, the place was quiet. At four in the morning, it was blazing with life. The two dozen tables, most of them barboxes, were all occupied. There was poker in the back, gambling arcade games on the side, and plenty of spillover in the parking lot. Delicious and Bartram took in the tableau for the first time and reached the same conclusion. They knew it wasn't going to last, but there was huge action, so they needed to get to work and do as much damage as they could.

On their first night at Mikey's, Bartram beat a shady-looking character out of $10,000. Delicious beat one of the room's part owners out of $2,000. Like contenders on *Supermarket Sweepstakes* who knew they had to grab the expensive cuts of meat before time ran out, Bartram and Delicious set out to win big night after night. With the abundance of meth addicts in the place, they were both concerned for their safety, particularly as word of their winnings got out. After they woke up in their $45-a-night room at the La Quinta, their first play was to find the post office and wire some of their cash home.

The two "Big Yankees," as they were nicknamed—one merely plump, the other immense—became cultural curiosities at Mikey's. After getting beaten out of $10,000, one shortstop was so enchanted with Delicious that he invited him back to his place for dinner and to spend a few nights. Delicious happily accepted. Bartram could only shake his head in disapproval. "To me, you don't want to get that close to guys you gamble with," he told his partner. But so long as they were winning big money, he wasn't going to argue.

As both of them had predicted, their gold rush at Mikey's came to an abrupt end. During his weeks at the poolroom, Delicious had become friendly with the girlfriend of one of the players. The girl was a slender blond stripper, but Delicious' physical appearance likely put the boyfriend at ease and failed to trigger any jealousy. One night, the girl pulled Delicious aside and looked at him earnestly. "I overheard my boyfriend talking, and a bunch of guys is planning to rob y'all. They say y'all been winning too much." That was all Delicious and Bartram needed to hear. A current of danger had always coursed through Mikey's. Now, with this warning, they weren't about to press their luck.

They had one last hurrah there. Delicious had spoken several times with Greg Hogue, a regular who lived in Tulsa and made the ninety-minute drive to Oklahoma City almost every day. Hogue claimed he got his nickname, "Spanky," because, as a kid, "I played a ring game against adults and they complained to Grandpa that I spanked 'em all." But he might have picked up the name because he resembled the Spanky character from the *Our Gang* comedies. Hogue was in his mid-twenties but had a boyish face and was missing an upper tooth, the result of an accident that occurred, he says, when he was changing an oil filter on a tractor.

Delicious could tell right away that Hogue had serious talent. But owing to his physical appearance, Spanky was the resident whipping boy at Mikey's. Other players needled and bullied him and belittled his pool skills. A former backer called him a "dog" — a player who chokes when there's money above the light — and mockingly barked whenever he passed the kid. All too familiar with being targeted by bullies, how it could erode the victim's sense of self, Delicious made a point of being nice to Spanky. On his last day at Mikey's, Delicious pulled him aside. "They call you a dog?" he said. "Well, I'm going to turn you into friggin' Cujo."

First, Delicious brokered a Scotch doubles game pitting Bartram and Spanky against Justin Whitehead and Gabe Owen, two pro-level players who were based in the area. (Owen, at age twenty-seven, would win the 2004 U.S. Open.) With Delicious making himself hoarse cheering on Spanky — "That's my friggin' Cujo!" he yelled whenever Spanky made a ball — they won the $3,500 set.

Figuring that Spanky's self-esteem was now fully inflated, Delicious backed him in a set against one of Mikey's co-owners. In a race to ten, Spanky took a commanding lead. Then he got a phone call. He retreated to the counter and made a sour look as he listened. He returned to the table and announced to everyone that one of the locals backing his opponent had instructed him to lose on purpose, to "dump that fat damn Yankee."

There was no way Spanky was going to dump. Certainly not after the fat damn Yankee had shown so much more confidence in his stroke than anyone else in the pool hall. Spanky went on to win the set, and Delicious leaped from his chair and engulfed the poor guy in a bear hug. The gap-toothed kid they called a dog made $7,500 that day. And he was fired up knowing he could hang at the table with anyone.

On and off for the next year, Delicious and Bartram roamed the country. But not unlike a baseball team out of playoff contention, in the languorous, anticlimactic days near the end of the season, Delicious sometimes felt as though he were just "playing out the string." He was already a celebrity in the pool demimonde. Now he was simply trying to hit up those last few spots before his hustling career expired. Which is not to say he and Bartram didn't have their share of adventures.

In Tennessee they visited a pool hall perched near the riverbank. Delicious ambled in wearing a tan fisherman's hat with an eight ball embroidered on the bill and a pair of cargo shorts, toting a rod and reel. Complaining that the fish weren't biting so he may as well try his luck at pool, Delicious asked if anyone wanted to play for a little money. A shortstop took the bait, so to speak. Within an hour, Delicious had won $2,500.

In Belvedere, South Carolina, across the Savannah River from Augusta, Georgia, Delicious and Bartram took on a pair of twentysomething brothers, Richey and Lynny Samonsky. Local legends, the Samonskys played at their father's poolroom, Lynny's, on a Diamond table with pockets shimmed so tight, it felt like you were trying to squeeze your ball through the neck of a Coke bottle.

Delicious and Bartram were playing the brothers in Scotch doubles for $32,000, each team having put up $16,000. As word of the action circulated on both sides of the river, more than a hundred sweaters ringed the rail. The roadmen started strong, helped by a sibling squabble. Richey was a lefty, Lynny was a righty, and they each complained that the other left him with lousy positions. "I thought they was gonna fight right there," says Lynny Senior. Finally the brothers calmed down and found a rhythm. About that time, Bartram's stroke went into hiding. After playing through the night, the Samonsky brothers ended up $24,000 wealthier.

Delicious was playing a room in Louisiana when he noticed a familiar face in the corner, a sandy-haired man with a menacing look and a jack-o'-lantern smile. It took a moment, but Delicious recognized him. It was Scotty Townsend, the copiously tattooed Cajun roadman who'd nearly flattened Delicious years before in Chelmsford, Massachusetts, when Delicious abruptly quit their set. Their eyes locked, and Townsend gave a subtle smile.

Delicious felt a surge of adrenaline and tried to concentrate on his set. When he looked over again, Townsend was gone. After Delicious pocketed his winnings, he and Bartram walked outside and saw Townsend leaning against a truck in the parking lot, drinking a beer. Delicious again felt his pulse quicken, sure that the Cajun was going to exact revenge for the Chelmsford incident. "Hey, Kid Delicious," Townsend called out. "How you been? Heard you been doing real good on the road. I'm happy for you. I was going to come over and say hi inside, but I didn't want to knock your action." They shook hands and spent half an hour exchanging spots, neither mentioning their previous encounter.

Bartram and Delicious drove through Normal, Illinois, and Santa Claus, Indiana, and Walla Walla, Washington. After winning eighty straight racks, at $50 per, against "Cheyenne" Pete Trujillo in a Wyoming hall — "It's true," Trujillo confirms, "that was some of the best pool I've ever seen someone play" — Delicious could proudly boast that he had won money in each of the lower forty-eight states.

Still, it was hard not to notice that as his legend grew, so did the frequency with which he was recognized. He was doing far less hustling than gambling. Sure, he was winning money, but he was playing on the square, making a game with an opponent who knew his identity and skill level all too well. Time and again, he called Greg Smith, the pool detective, asking to be steered to easy money, but 007 couldn't help. His response was always the same: "They know Kid Delicious ALL OVER THE DAMN country." Worse still, thanks to his notoriety, Delicious was knocking Bartram's action. Bartram was too nice to say anything, but Delicious knew the reality. Plenty of times Bartram was on the verge of playing for big money, but when opponents saw that he was with Kid Delicious, they pulled up.

Bartram and Delicious had a tip that there was a kid in Salt Lake City named Stuart who was only a B player but had a lot of gamble in him. They bounded for Eo's Billiards, a well-known, old-time room where the forgettable movie *Poolhall Junkies* was filmed. They were a few steps inside the door and a lanky blond kid shouted, "Holy shit! Kid Delicious!" It was Stuart, their mark.

Awestruck, he beseeched Delicious for an autograph: "You're, like, my hero!" He asked if he could "donate" $100, essentially paying for the right to pick up a few tricks from a superior player. Delicious accepted and played along, dispensing tips and telling stories. But he resented it: they had come a long way just to take a couple of lousy fifties from a breathless fan.

In fact, the only action Delicious got in Salt Lake came from a wealthy car salesman. The guy's game of choice was The Ghost. The rules of The Ghost are blissfully simple: one player breaks a nine-ball formation and then takes the cue ball in hand, usually setting it down near the one. If he runs the table or combos the nine, he wins. If he misses a ball, he loses. Call it pool solitaire. The car dealer, in other words, could win or lose without touching a cue.

Over innumerable hours, when he practiced pool by himself until needles of sunlight poked through the window, Delicious often played this game. In the absence of another player, it was a good simulation of a nine-ball match. Even on a bad night, he could win eight out of ten times. The catch was that this nine-foot table at Eo's was tricky, filled with dead rails and home to the tightest pockets this side of the Samonsky brothers' table in South Carolina.

Delicious agreed to play a ten-ahead set for $1,000. He was up a few racks, then down a few. But it was a hollow experience. Part of the charge of playing was the mano a mano, matching skills and mettle with another pool hound who thinks he can beat you, and you him. This was something totally different, like masturbation rather than sex. Delicious soon figured out the quirks of the table and went on a run to win the set. Feeling slightly dirty, he accepted the man's congratulations and the $1,000. But he had an unsettling feeling that this depressing set of The Ghost marked his last act as a true road player.

In most lines of work, the better you get, the more opportunities you get. In pool hustling, the opposite is true. Delicious was playing the best pool of his life. But from coast to coast his cover was blown, and now he wasn't going to advance any further. This was it: hustler's Valhalla.

He encouraged Bartram to join him in entering pro events. "You're a great player, Chris," Delicious said. "Don't you want to beat the best?"

But they wanted different things out of pool. For Bartram, pool was a job, not something that necessarily made his heart flutter. For him, playing professionally was a lousy business decision. Why enter tournaments where the winners make $5,000 when he could routinely make that in a single night of gambling and hustling on the road?

Sitting in the car driving back east, they spent the better part of two days arguing the merits of their positions. When they got to Bartram's hometown of Columbus, Ohio, 1,700 miles of interstate later, they hadn't reached agreement. Delicious thanked Bartram for being a terrific road partner and a better friend and dropped him off at his house. Already feeling tense and depressed, he headed home alone, contemplating what the hell he was going to do next.

15

RUNNING THE TABLE

I'm away from my desk right now. But leave your
name and number after the beep and I'll get back
to you. And remember: I'm on the move.

—Outgoing message, Kid Delicious' voice mail

B Y THE SPRING OF 2004, Kid Delicious was, in more ways
than one, squarely behind the eight ball. With his road action all but dried up, he could try to turn pro and hope
to make enough in tournament winnings, and in after-hours
matches played on the square, to cover his nut. A legion of once
successful hustlers have gone broke that way. Tournament pool
demands conservative play. Unlike hustling, there's no double or
nothing, no losing and then raising the bet in a rematch. Plus,
unless you win big, and win big consistently, the money in tournament play is negligible. And as they get increasingly desperate
for action, reformed roadmen often give up too much weight and
make games they can't possibly win.

The other alternative facing Delicious: he could hang up his
sticks and look for another line of work. Of all the guys who were
at Chicago Billiards with him, at least half of them had since
given up pool and found new careers, ranging from casino dealer
to mortgage broker. But after years of being his own boss, waking
when he pleased, dressing how he pleased, this option held little

appeal. Delicious concurred with the legendary three-cushion billiards hustler Danny McGoorty's observation: "A job is an invasion of privacy. Getting blasted out of bed by an alarm clock so you can go somewhere and do things you don't want to do, that's not my idea of living." And pool was still the best way he knew to stay one step ahead of his depression.

Delicious was stuck. Back home in New Jersey, he slept like a hibernating bear on morphine and let his voice mail fill with unreturned messages. Even Dave Basavich, who'd always been so supportive, gently floated the dreaded suggestion: "You have so much personality and charisma, Danny," he said, trying to sound encouraging. "You'd be great as a car salesman."

The thought of pacing a car lot, wearing a golf shirt, and trying to convince an accountant from Piscataway to buy a minivan only drove Delicious deeper into despair. As he confided to Carlos Santos at the time: "You know how people say it's do-or-die time? For me right now, it *is* do or die. If I don't *do* and figure out a way to keep playing pool for a living, I don't got a lot to live for."

As though Delicious needed yet another thing to darken his mood, his weight was now a runaway train, careening beyond three bills. He had a ready rationale for staying fat: were he to lose fifty or a hundred pounds, he would feel as if he were losing part of his essential self. Had Bristol Bob been on the scene, he would have told Delicious what cowardly thinking that was, how physical fitness was a form of self-respect. Every time Delicious ordered a jumbo wings platter or a double cheeseburger, he could hear Bristol's voice nagging him: *Think how much better you felt about yourself when you were skinny.*

He'd heard all the psychological explanations foisted upon anyone with a weight problem. The layer of fat symbolizes a fortress around his body, a protective layer to shield himself from the outside world. When he rummaged to the bottom of a bag of chips or fries, he was expressing a need to search for something missing in his life. One friend suggested that by putting on the hundred pounds — the rough equivalent of a woman's weight — Delicious was essentially creating a way to hug himself.

Delicious dismissed it all. "I like food. I like to eat food. I like to look at food," he said. "I wish I could be skinny, but it's not me. What's so bad about that?" As he saw things, his girth had always felt like it was part of his identity, part of his personality.

Still, he could outwit himself only up to a point. Part of him was keenly aware that his obesity was critically serious. Never mind the dim long-term prospects. More immediately, he knew that the heft was going to exact a price on his pool. Striking the ball accurately requires a player's eyes to be on the same plane as the cue. An overweight player has to strain to bend over, putting stress on his back. During his time with Chris Bartram, Delicious had used a bridge more often than his opponents did, and some- times his feet hurt after marathon sessions.

By the time he hit middle age, he was going to be in trouble. A life of back pain, easily strained muscles, shortness of breath — all of which, at a minimum, detract from a player's concentra- tion — awaited. Starting with the legendary Steve Mizerak, whose death in 2006, at age sixty-one, owed to his decades-long battle with obesity, pool has a large catalog of players who have eaten themselves out of the sport. (Ironically, in his book *Pocket Bil- liards Tips and Trick Shots*, Mizerak wrote: "Try to keep your weight down. Thinner players seem to have more endurance than their chubbier competitors.") In the winter of 2004, firmly in his mid-twenties, Delicious knew that unless he changed some habits soon, his body would make his career decisions for him.

That spring, in the throes of a low-grade but persistent de- pression, Delicious entered several events on the Joss Northeast Nine-Ball Tour, a regional circuit sponsored by a cue manufac- turer which threads its way through the Northeast. The events were open to both pros and amateurs — anyone, in fact, who was willing to pony up the entry fee. The purses were small, laugh- ably small to a hustler the likes of Kid Delicious, accustomed to winning $5,000 a set. The venues were often down-at-the-heels juke joints and roadhouses. The players usually outnumbered the sweaters by a significant margin. But Delicious knew that he had no better options. He threw his sticks in the trunk of the Tiburon and went back on the road.

At the Joss event in Albany, Delicious' reputation preceded

him. He fetched the highest price in the pre-tournament Calcutta and drew a small knot of fans whenever he played. Wilting under the pressure he was putting on himself, he disappointed spectacularly. In the double-elimination format, Delicious quickly lost to two rank amateurs and didn't finish in the top half of the forty-eight-man field. A player who had beaten Buddy Hall, Charlie Williams, Tony Ellin, Spanish Mike LeBron, and all the rest was getting his clock cleaned by a local plumber who picked up his cue on weekends. He hoped it was only a fluke.

But damn if the scenario didn't repeat itself at the Joss event the following week, outside Hartford. It wasn't just a crisis of confidence. Residing not far from his consciousness was the nagging thought: *If I can't get this to work, what exactly do I have to live for?* Concentrating less on the table than on his attempt to stave off a full-blown psychological breakdown, Delicious again lost to a pair of local ball-bangers.

He returned to New Jersey to practice around the clock and search desperately for his mojo. He had plenty of time to consider his fate and reckoned he couldn't quit pool like this. He'd had too many exhilarating times and rewarding moments to leave on such an unhappy note. He had to play at least one more event. Delicious thought of Bristol — W.W.B.D.? — and, channeling his old wingman's tenacity, he made a pact with himself: *I might not make it as a pro pool player, but I'll be damned if it's because I'm too nervous or scared. Other players are going to have to step up and beat me.*

The next stop on the Joss caravan was Snookers Café and Billiards, in an industrial pocket of downtown Providence. Snookers was one of the first rooms Delicious and Bristol had hit in the infancy of their partnership, and Delicious did a double take when he played his first match and scanned the faces on the rail. "Bristol Bob Begey!" he screeched. Home from Philly, visiting his folks in Connecticut, Bristol had decided to steal over to Providence and watch the tournament, maybe try to scrounge up some after-hours action.

Though he was still living in Philadelphia, Bristol had recently split with his girlfriend, Janelle. He had also stopped taking courses at Bucks County Community College and suspended his plans to become a teacher. Rationally, he knew it was nuts, but he wasn't ready to give up on pool. He had won some money games here and there, striking the ball flawlessly and playing with poise. The black art of hustling, once so off-putting, didn't bother him anymore. He got the old rush back. Somehow he *had* to get another fix and repatriate himself in the Republic of Pool.

Delicious' stroke was back in the groove too. After he won his first match handily, he and Bristol bear-hugged. The connection was instant, free of any awkwardness. Bristol filled in his old road partner on his life and explained that he still hadn't lost his burning urge to play pool.

Crazy as it sounded to an outsider, it all made perfect sense to Delicious. You find the one thing in the world that gives you the most pleasure, and you want to spend the rest of your life doing it. "I hear you, Bristol," Delicious said. "Follow your heart." He could just as easily have been talking to himself.

Bristol returned to Connecticut later that night. They had parted with a long hug and vowed to stay in better touch. Warmed by the visit, Delicious played his next match with a smile pasted on his face. Bristol drove back to his folks' happier than he'd been in weeks.

Meanwhile, Delicious was playing brilliantly, guiding the cue ball as though it had its own internal GPS. He faced little resistance the entire tournament, taking the final set 9–1. After he deposited the last nine ball, he playfully roared to the crowd. Everyone on the rail lapped it up.

The conventional wisdom is that pool is eighty percent mental, but perhaps that's a conservative estimate. Barely a week earlier, Delicious had been an insecure bundle of nerves, losing to one Joe Shortstop after another. Now dripping with confidence, he was playing flawless, authoritative pool. He added another $1,600 to his bankroll and never felt more invincible.

Having managed to blow only a small fraction of his winnings at Foxwoods Casino, in Connecticut, he treated himself to a few nights at a lavish hotel. A fan at the Providence event who worked security at a Hilton hotel near Boston had finagled Delicious a suite for $99 a night. Delicious luxuriated in his room, watching movies, taking long baths, and weakening the hinges on the mini-bar. For a few days, anyway, he felt like a rock star.

It was abundantly clear that the tour finale, held in Portland, Maine, was a tier or two above the other Joss events. More than seventy players, some from as far away as Hawaii, Alaska, and the Philippines, competed for a purse of $36,000. Many well-known pros (and scant few amateurs) joined the field. The host venue, Spot Shot Billiard Club, is a real players' room, with dozens of Brunswick Gold Crown tables covered with Simonis cloth. A joint that sits below street level and is filled with soul and charm — a real treasure if you're willing to venture a bit below the surface — Spot Shot is a nice metaphor for pool in general.

Were he in a less self-assured state of mind, Delicious might have cowered when he saw the draw sheet in Portland and contemplated the prospect of breaking balls alongside A-listers on the order of Earl Strickland, Keith McCready, and Grady "the Professor" Mathews. But he perceived this event as his personal cotillion, his entry into the society of professional pool.

He didn't just rip through the early rounds of the draw. With his belly drooping halfway to the floor and his distinctive voice echoing through the place with self-mocking jokes, he took on a cult following, drawing every bit as large a crowd as the bona fide stars. If he was never going to be able travel incognito and hustle action as an unknown again, at least he was entering the public domain on his own terms.

A railbird from New Hampshire was so taken by Delicious' talent and personality that he called the kid over after one of his matches and offered to be his backer-cum-agent. The proposition: as his agent, he would pay all of Delicious' travel expenses to future pro tournaments. In exchange, they would split the winnings fifty-fifty. He had plans to market Kid Delicious instructional videos and custom cues. In retrospect, Delicious could surely have negotiated more favorable terms, but he was so flattered by the vote of confidence, and so relieved for the chance to keep playing without sweating every meal and motel bill, that he quickly agreed.

Delicious' opponent in the semifinals was Rodney "the Rocket" Morris, a muscular, stocky Hawaiian whose father once worked as a bodyguard for Elvis Presley. A smooth, entertaining shotmaker, Morris, in keeping with his nickname, plays at a good clip, taking only a few seconds between shots. In 1996, Morris won the U.S. Open and was destined for big things, but shortly thereafter he was sent to a federal prison camp for four years on drug conspiracy charges. Like so many players, Morris is a genial and well-liked guy, which makes his past sins almost inconceivable.

Wearing his trademark Hawaiian shirt, he chatted easily with Delicious before their match. But after a few back-and-forth games he began to grumble about Delicious' slow play. It can be ruled a foul—and, at a minimum, it is a breach of etiquette—to speak directly to your opponent, but Morris repeatedly griped to the rail that Delicious was "messing up my rhythm." Inasmuch as Delicious was eager to join the fraternity of pro pool that week, he considered this part of the hazing ritual. Morris' status as a member in good standing entitled him to razz his opponent. Finally Delicious defused the tension. He faced the crowd and said, "Man, Rodney's messing up *my* rhythm with his fast play. Someone needs to tell him to sloooowwww down!"

With Morris leading 8–7 and fans standing three deep around the table, the Hawaiian took aim at the seven ball, more concerned with positioning than with making a relatively easy shot. Whether it was Morris' nerves or carelessness or the work of fate, the ball rattled around the edge of the pocket and defiantly refused to disappear.

The crowd groaned, Morris shook his head, and Delicious rose from his seat wearing an expansive grin. Playing at the same excruciatingly slow speed—sometimes taking three full minutes to shoot—he ran out the rack, broke the "hill-hill" game, and ran out the final rack as well. "*Yyyyyyeaahhhhhhh*," he bellowed, pumping his fist, before regaining his composure and shaking Morris' hand.

Given the pace of the tournament—seven rounds crammed into three days—Delicious scarcely had time to process what was happening. Here he was at a big-ticket event, loaded with the best pros around, about to square off in the finals against Earl Strickland, a five-time U.S. Open champion whose face — scowling, with intense blue eyes obscured by his trademark tinted shades — graces the sport's Mount Rushmore. What's more, Strickland had knifed his way through the losers' bracket, so Delicious needed to win only one of two sets to take the title.

Strickland is pool's answer to John McEnroe, a haunted, eccentric, love-him-or-hate-him temperamental genius who uses conflict and agitation as fuel. He has won more than one hundred nine-ball titles, and is a master of psychological warfare. Strickland jaws with opponents and demands reracks and, in his spicy Carolina twang, carries on a running gripe-athon with the rail. Some players carry an extra shaft and butt in their cases; Strickland carries a dozen, sometimes changing his shaft after every missed shot. A few players wear a glove; Strickland wears one on each hand, with holes cut through the fingertips. When he plays, his eyes remain wide open, as if he's somehow forgotten how to blink. One player likens Strickland's intimidating presence to that of a cop who's pulled you over on a deserted road.

Strickland's easily disturbed equilibrium and penchant for temper tantrums is leavened — as is McEnroe's, by the way — by a genuine love and reverence for his sport. Having grown up on a tobacco farm in North Carolina, Strickland still marvels at the opportunities pool has afforded him, and he has little patience for those who take the sport for granted. He is a dazzling shotmaker whose stroke resembles a sleek machine, all the parts working in harmony; he perceives it as a personal affront when other players neglect proper technique. He is physically fit, impeccably groomed, and always professionally dressed, usually in a golf shirt and slacks. Anything less would be a dishonor to pool.

He looked on with unconcealed disgust when he saw his opponent in the final. Weighing in at roughly 315 pounds, Delicious wore a black T-shirt under a rumpled, hideously unfashionable, untucked flannel shirt. His pants resembled a pup tent. He talked too much, laughed too much, sweated too much, and worst of all, he took forever and a day to hit his next shot. From the beginning, Strickland addressed him icily, and at one point grumbled, "No way that fat motherfucker got a shot against me." It was typical Strickland, trying his damnedest to unnerve his opponent.

As usual, Strickland also played breathtaking pool, firing off balls in a furious and violent yet quiet and dignified manner. Delicious didn't shrink from the challenge, performing his microsurgery and playing a few judicious safeties that left Strickland muttering to himself. At 8–8, Strickland offered a tasting menu of lavish skills to close out the set. "Good playing, Earl," Delicious said from across the room, clapping enthusiastically along with the rest of the crowd. Strickland looked briefly at him as if he were nuts, unsure if his opponent was pathetically naïve or just mocking him.

The first set had taken nearly three hours, and it was now eleven at night. The room was even more packed than when the finals had started. Most of the players who'd been eliminated stuck around to watch the match, an irresistible clash of styles and personalities. Just loudly enough to be heard, Strickland muttered, "I woulda won an hour ago if he didn't play so dang slow."

If this was another burst of psychological warfare, Delicious fired back: "Well, Earl, if I were a handsome, skinny guy like you, I could play faster." This drew an eruption of laughter from the gallery. "But, Earl, I can't help it. I'm a big, heavy guy. So deal with it." Strickland could only glower in response.

As if more pressure were needed, a local gas station magnate and pool enthusiast stood and announced that he would dip into his own pocket and add $2,000 to the purse. The winner would now claim $9,500. Asked by another railbird why he would voluntarily sweeten the pot like that, the magnate shrugged and said, "I just want to see the best match possible."

He got it. It was well past midnight and Strickland led the second, winner-take-all set 8–7. With designs of running out the final rack, Strickland broke with controlled fury but came up empty. A look of concentration carved on his face, Delicious stared at the table and stroked his goatee. Seeing no possibilities on the one ball, he pushed out. Given a choice of shooting or letting Delicious take another shot, Strickland chose the latter. Figuring he had nothing to lose, Delicious laced the cue ball with all sorts of draw and hit an exceptionally difficult kick shot. To the delight of the rapt crowd, the ball dropped. Now in control of the table, he played calm, collected pool and ran out.

He now broke for the final rack. Like Strickland in the previous game, he deposited a ball but had no shot on the one. So he pushed out. Chastened by what had happened moments earlier, Strickland attempted a safety. Had the cue ball stopped at its intended destination, Delicious would have been stuck. Instead, it rolled just an inch or two beyond and hadn't come to a stop before Strickland was grousing to himself.

As he rose from his seat, Delicious tried his best to suppress a smile. With a clear road map in his head, he drilled ball after ball. All the while, scenes of his personal pool landscape — his introduction at Elite Billiards, his boot-camp stint at Chicago Billiards in Connecticut, his adventures on the road — played like a documentary in his head. Blocking out the crowd, the potential payday, and his scowling opponent, Delicious ran out the rack.

No sooner had the nine dropped than he let out a guttural, uninhibited *"RRRRRRROOOOOOARRRRRRR"* that originated somewhere deep within him, exposing his tonsils to the gallery. Like a victorious boxer mounting the ring's turnbuckles, Delicious somehow jumped on the table without causing injury to either himself or the equipment and roared at the crowd in each of the four corners. Though the roar would later become Delicious' signature gesture, on this night it was spontaneous. It had all come pouring out. His joy with his play, particularly under such dramatic circumstances. His amazement at having beaten the great Earl Strickland. His victory — his temporary ceasefire, anyway — over his depression. His realization that, with his road-hustling days behind him, he still had a future in pool after all.

The fans went nuts. Strickland's girlfriend at the time, Diana Hoppe, was so overcome with emotion that she hugged Delicious, a gesture that didn't please her boyfriend. Alex Irvine, a well-known science-fiction novelist, happened to be writing an essay about the tournament for an alternative local newspaper. "Mostly what I remember was the way people talked about the Basavich-Strickland match," Irvine recalls. "It was like talking to someone who had been there for Kirk Gibson's Series-winning home run, or Franco Harris' Immaculate Reception. Their eyes kind of lit up, and this odd tone of reverence crept into their voices."

Larry Lisciotti, Delicious' mentor/tormentor at Chicago Billiards, had died a few weeks earlier. As Delicious accepted the winner's check, he grabbed the microphone and dedicated the win to Lisciotti. He then announced that the bartender should start a tab because he was buying drinks for the house. For hours, Kid Delicious, his new colleagues on the pro tour — sans Strickland — and his friends and disciples stood in Spot Shot Billiards drinking themselves stupid, toasting the hottest new player in pro pool.

With dawn yet to arrive, Delicious took a break from his party and stepped outside. He was filmed in sweat, and the cool breath of the New England night felt good. In the months to come, he would become a star on the professional pool tour, go on to win more big-time tournaments, and ascend briefly to the top spot in the UPA world rankings. He'd travel as far as Taiwan for a tournament. He would have his decision to turn pro further validated, as the poker boom siphoned off more and more road action. He would play on ESPN. *Sports Illustrated* would publish a lengthy feature on his adventures. A Hollywood studio would make overtures about producing a movie based on his life story. Depression still paid him periodic visits, though not with the same intensity as before.

But all that was in the future. Now he stood alone outside a vintage Maine pool hall and tried to take mental inventory of what he'd just accomplished. He smiled and giggled his silly giggle, silhouetted by a moon that looked for all the world like a giant cue ball in the sky.

EPILOGUE

IN THE SUMMER OF 2006, the sport of pool thought it had found its white knight. Flush with the cash he'd made from his controversial "natural cures" books and products, Kevin Trudeau was going to do for pool what Steve Jobs had done for Apple. With a rap that was smoother than freshly vacuumed felt, Trudeau launched the International Pool Tour (IPT), an eight-ball circuit that, the founder promised, would transform pool into "the next poker."

With a circuit attracting the best players from around the globe, international television rights holders and sponsors would line up. Then there were the prizes. Unfathomable to pool players accustomed to borrowing gas money, the top IPT winners would earn $500,000. A first-round loser who failed to pocket a single ball could make $5,000. Plus, Trudeau supposedly told players that those earning a "tour card" based on their 2006 results would make a minimum of $100,000 in 2007. In pool, this was akin to increasing the minimum wage by a factor of ten.

In retrospect, more than a little cynicism was in order. Pool had burned through plenty of tours in the past, none offering anywhere near this kind of prize money. And Trudeau's history was somewhat disconcerting. In addition to having served a prison term for felony larceny, Trudeau had often been in the crosshairs of the Federal Trade Commission and various consumer protection groups for making false claims. Some observers were concerned that Trudeau was using the pool tour as a platform for selling more books and products, noting that even the homepage for the IPT had a prominently featured link to naturalcures.com, his Web site.

Still, the initial events were successful, the checks cleared, and soon players were coming out of the woodwork to try to "get on the IPT." But if the poker boom sounded the death knell for hustling, the IPT was the final squirt of embalming fluid. Kid Delicious was among those selected for the tour. He played in his first event in Las Vegas in the summer of 2006. Despite shooting poorly, he left with $5,000 and was fired with optimism. "That settles it," he told me. "I'm going to play pool for the rest of my life."

It couldn't have come at a better time for him. His love for pool still burned, but playing opportunities, particularly against the best competition, were becoming increasingly scarce. He no longer hustled much, and the grind of tournament play—competing through the night in lonely backwaters so far from New Jersey that gas money could exceed prize money—had become wearying. Suddenly the IPT gave him a chance to play against top-shelf opponents at least once a month.

What's more, over the past few years he had rekindled his relationship with Danielle Graziano, the teenage girlfriend he had left because she was diverting his attention from pool. As if no time had passed, they felt an instant connection. She was recently divorced and still attracted to him. His physique, his personality quirks, his livelihood were all part of the appeal. He was still attracted to her and became a fatherly figure to her young son, Angelo. They reckoned that with the IPT money they could get married and buy a house in central New Jersey.

In keeping with the circadian rhythms of pool, the good times didn't last. At an event in Reno late in the summer of 2006, players flew to the venue on their own dime and paid for their own hotel rooms and meals. After the tournament, they were informed that the IPT was short of funds and could not give out the prize money. Trudeau, once so accessible and upbeat, was nowhere to be found. Over the Internet, the tour eventually informed players that the prizes would be paid in installments, eleven percent here, nine percent there. But future events were canceled, and as of this writing the IPT appears to be another name in the necrology of failed pro-pool tours.

Like many, Kid Delicious was left devastated. Part of it was, of course, financial. He'd figured that the IPT would provide some stability — and possibly much more if he could win one of those $500,000 checks. Suddenly having lost his livelihood, he was back on shaky footing, leaning on the generosity of friends and family, living with Danielle at her mother's house. But beyond that, he had again lost the intoxicating rush of competing at the pool table. One day in the fall of 2006, burdened by stress and still overweight, Kid Delicious, age twenty-eight, suffered what doctors believe was a heart attack. After visiting him in a New Jersey hospital a few days later, I realized that this was the one time in all our interactions that I didn't leave in better spirits than when I'd arrived.

Fortunately, he reverted to form within a few weeks, though the experience — he has never overcome his fear of doctors and hospitals — shook him to the core. He has vowed to lose weight, live healthier, and cut back on his excesses. Most of them, anyway. Okay, some of them. Tantalized by a Hollywood studio's acquisition of the "life rights" to his story, he holds out hope that *Kid Delicious: The Movie* will one day play at his local multiplex. Meanwhile, he and an enterprising friend and former road partner have created a Web site, pooljax.com, that sells Kid Delicious DVDs and cue case towels.

Doctors have told him to work on reducing stress. As he holds out hope that the IPT will regain its footing or that another pro tour will emerge in its place, he is easing himself back into competitive play. And while he still contends with his full-moon phases, he has found an outlet that combines his pool skills and his winsome personality. A few times a week he gives lessons in poolrooms and homes in New Jersey and New York. He's even given demonstrations at bar mitzvah parties. "Tell anyone who's interested to contact me at 1-877-348-0400 or at Delicious2@ aol.com."

● ● ●

As for Bristol Bob Begey, he and Kid Delicious remain bound by their experiences on the road. They speak frequently, though when Delicious neglects to return a phone call, Bristol will leave a string of increasingly irate messages. The old dynamic, in other words, remains intact. Bristol, too, has found a way to move on with his life without abandoning pool. Several years ago, he returned to Bristol, Connecticut, and has taken a variety of jobs. Both pool and painting, however, continued their magnetic pull. Working in an office or waiting on tables was simply a means of paying for table time and art supplies. In 2006, Bristol decided to combine his two passions and began painting pool murals and selling them online at bristolsportsart.com. In 2007, Bristol entered several small pool tournaments and claims that he's never shot better in his life. He's now considering a return to the road.

Beset by eye trouble, Greg Smith — 007, the lovable pool detective — is in semiretirement. He has "been winning real big at the racetrack," he says. He's also backing his eighteen-year-old son, Josh, an aspiring pool shark whom he has nicknamed "the Chicago Kid." "HE's GONNA BE DA best player in the world by the time he's twenty-five," Smith vows. Despite his best efforts, Smith can't stay away from the pool wire. I hadn't spoken with him in months, but then his unmistakable voice growled on my voice mail: "You wanna see real action? Get your ass to this small town outside OF NASHVILLE. Start driving and I'll GET YA DA NAME OF DA PLACE. They're gambling like FRIGGIN' CRAZY down there!"

Based largely on his reputation as a gambler, Little John Macias of Hattiesburg, Mississippi, was selected to play on the IPT. He bets high on the road, as always, and claims to have won $15,000 gambling at the 2007 Derby City Classic. And he confirms Greg Smith's tip that, in the winter of 2007, big action was passing through a juke joint outside Nashville.

• • •

Kid Delicious' on-again off-again mentor, Carlos Santos (a/k/a Carlito, a/k/a the Peruvian Prince), continues to embody the American Dream. Happily married, he lives in Old Bridge, New Jersey. In addition to his cockfighting business and billiard hall in Central America, he still owns Action Billiards in Plainfield, New Jersey, and works as an early-morning delivery driver for the Museum of Modern Art. "It doesn't leave me much time to play pool, but I'm happy."

While covering a tennis tournament in suburban Cincinnati, I stopped into a pool hall and found Bucky Bell, the victim of Delicious' first big score in Warsaw, Indiana. Age and fading eyesight have exacted a price on his stick, but Bucky makes for great company. He's a rollicking storyteller who can pull off the most dazzling card tricks you'll ever see.

In 2003, Cliff Macklin, the avuncular owner of Jack & Jill Cue Club in Glen Burnie, Maryland, underwent quintuple bypass surgery. As part of his treatment, he was prescribed Zoloft, a common antidepressant. As Macklin puts it, "That day changed my life." Free of his social anxiety disorder, he routinely shows up at his pool hall and continues to run Factory Discount Billiard Supply with his wife, Sandi Jo.

Like so many others, Chris Bartram was lured out of the weeds by the International Pool Tour. Once one of the country's stealthiest creatures, he can now be tracked down easily on the Internet. He has a harder time hustling, perhaps, but he still gets action, making games and, more often than not, winning them. Bartram won the Louie Roberts Action/Entertainment Award at the 2007 Derby City Classic.

Tanya Harig remains at her post behind the bar at Billiards at Broadway in Fargo, North Dakota. She plays pool when she gets off her shift.

· · ·

Doris and Dave Basavich continue live in suburban New Jersey. Doris holds down a civil service job, while Daddy Delicious plays tennis; his passion for eBay rivals his son's passion for pool. The Basaviches are still proud of Danny for following his heart. They worry about his health and think it's probably time for him to get a real job.

GLOSSARY OF POOL TERMS

Above the light The place — atop the light fixture hanging above a pool table — where small bets are held in escrow.

Ahead race A format in which a player tries to win by an agreed-upon margin of racks. For example, in a six-ahead race, a player prevails when he has won six more racks than his opponent.

Backer The person who bankrolls the hustler. Traditionally, if the backed player wins, he and his backer share the winnings fifty-fifty; if the backed player loses, the backer shoulders the entire loss. Lately, however, backers, especially those who were victims of dumping (see *dump*), have gotten creative, making less risky bets and sometimes requiring players to share a part of the loss.

Ball-in-hand The option of placing the cue ball anywhere on the table before shooting. A ball-in-hand is often awarded when an opposing player has committed a foul.

Banger, ball-banger An unskilled recreational player.

Barbox A small pool table, seven feet long, usually coin-operated and popular in the Midwest.

Calcutta An auction held before a pool tournament, not unlike a fantasy league draft. As a rule, the better the player, the higher the Calcutta price he fetches.

Cluster A number of object balls that are touching or bunched together.

Cut shot A shot that is not a center-to-center hit. The term is used to describe a shot that has more than a slight degree of angle.

Dead stroke When a pool player is in an "in the moment" state in which he is seemingly incapable of making errors.

Dog (verb) To miss an easy shot. (noun) A choker, a player who cannot perform under pressure.

Draw Backspin, typically achieved by hitting the lower half of the cue ball.

Dump To lose a game on purpose, which often occurs when two contending players make a deal beforehand to split the winnings.

English Spin, usually sidespin, applied when striking the cue ball.

Hanger A ball positioned on the lip of a pocket.

Heart A player's resolve to win.

Hill-hill A tie score in the decisive game of a set. In a race to ten, a 9–9 score is considered hill-hill.

Get the nuts To negotiate a favorable handicap in a money game.

Jam-up Outstanding. ("Don't bet with Alexander Verona. He's playing jam-up pool tonight.")

Object ball The ball that is struck by the cue ball.

Railbird A spectator at a pool hall. Many railbirds make side bets on the action. ("There was $500 above the light, but he also had $400 in side bets with the rail.")

Run out To make the required shots to win a set.

Safety A shot that is designed to miss and put the cue ball in a position that leaves the opponent with a difficult shot.

Set An agreed-upon number of games needed to win. ("They played a set to ten.")

Shark To intentionally distract a player.

Shortstop A capable local player without exceptional talent.

Speed Ability. A hustler rarely plays at full speed until he's in action.

Spot 1. A handicap ("I'll give the seven-eight-nine and the breaks as a spot"). 2. A tip about where to find action ("Gabby gave me a great spot in South Philly").

Stakehorse See *backer.*

Weight Handicap. A superior player often gives up weight in order to make a game.

ACKNOWLEDGMENTS

The cue ball is white. Thus began and ended my knowledge of all matters pool when, in the fall of 2004, I began reporting a *Sports Illustrated* story about a mysterious pool hustler with the irresistible nickname Kid Delicious. In the ensuing two years, I was swept up by the undertow of the "green felt ocean," completely seduced by pool and its relentlessly rich subculture.

My immersion would have been impossible without the extraordinary generosity of the Republic of Pool. By reputation, hustlers are, of course, nefarious characters, as opaque as an eight ball. This was at odds with my experience. To a man, the players I contacted could scarcely have been more helpful, candid, and accountable.

My most obvious debt of gratitude is to Danny Basavich and Bob Begey (Kid Delicious and Bristol), whom I quickly came to view less as subjects than as friends. For all their differences, they share a fundamental decency and generosity of spirit. What I would have given to have been in the disheveled back seat of the Tiburon during their road odyssey. In many respects, this book is as much theirs as it is mine.

A word here about methodology. When I began this project, I recalled an early passage from John Steinbeck's *East of Eden:* "I must depend on hearsay, on old photographs, on stories told, and on memories which are hazy and mixed with fable." In the course of my writing for *Sports Illustrated,* most events are easily verified. There are box scores and write-ups and hundreds of witnesses to even the most forgettable games. Not so pool hustling. The local papers don't cover the money set on the back table of Shooters; there is no statistical bureau to confirm that, yes, Cheyenne Pete really did bust the Sandman out of three large that night in Butte.

More often than not, I first sought the recollections of Bristol and Delicious. I then attempted to confirm or flesh out details with other sources, be they opponents, stakehorses, or railbirds. I can't promise that every account will go unchallenged — "That third set in Hattiesburg was for $2,000, not $1,500!" — but I can assure that, whenever possible, I sought out independent verification, aware that this book could not simply be an exercise in dictation. While men who make their living hustling and conniving are not necessarily ideal sources, the overwhelming majority of the time, the accounts offered by Delicious and Bristol were fully corroborated, down to the minutiae.

In any event, the citizens of Pool Nation don't get to see their names in print often enough. With that in mind, a special thanks to Gary Abood, Eddie Abraham, Jamie Baraks, Chris Bartram, Doris and Dave Basavich, Barry Behrman, Bucky Bell, Harry Bennenhaley, Carl Bolm, Jesse Bowman, Tom Dennehy, Toby Dick, James "Duff" Doran, Pete Fusco, Janelle Gootee, Danielle Graziano (and Cheeks), Tanya Harig, Jay Helfert, Rory Hendrickson, Greg "Spanky" Hogue, Diana Hoppe, Jeremy Jones, Mason King, Bob Kobus Sr., Bobby Law, Mike Lebron, Jeanette Lee, John Macias, Cliff Macklin, Jennie Malloy, Brian McGrath, Ralph Procopio, Andy Quinn, Alex Ragle, Lynny Samonsky, Carlos Santos, Greg Smith, Jimi Smith, Ryan Soucy, Dale Sweet, George Texiera, Ty Wilson, Ron Wiseman, and Alex Zimmerman.

Thanks to a corps of readers — "Jam-Up" Jack McCallum, Bob "Death" Roe, Sam "Skip" Silverstein, Jerry Forsyth, Jeff "Gramps" Spielberger, and "Bad" Bill Syken — who were generous with their time and red ink, marking up various drafts. This project would never have gotten off the ground without the diligence of my agent and literary stakehorse, Scott Waxman. Chris Hunt's typically expert editing of the original *Sports Illustrated* story played no small role in kick-starting this project. Susan Canavan at Houghton Mifflin embodied all a writer could ever ask for in an editor. Thanks too to her assistant, Will Vincent, and to Larry Cooper, the Efren Reyes of manuscript editing. As always, Terry McDonell and the other chieftains at *Sports Illustrated* could not have been more encouraging and accommodating during the writing of the book.

And finally a loving tip of the fedora to Ellie, my road partner.